The Writing Path 2

The Writing Path 2

Poetry and Prose from Writers' Conferences

Edited by

Michael Pettit

Ψ University of Iowa Press
Iowa City

University of Iowa Press,
Iowa City 52242
Copyright © 1996 by Michael Pettit
All rights reserved
Printed in the United States of America

Design by Karen Copp

Printed on acid-free paper

ISBN 0-87745-552-X cloth
ISBN 0-87745-548-1 paper

01 00 99 98 97 96 C 5 4 3 2 1
01 00 99 98 97 96 P 5 4 3 2 1

For my students

Nor is there singing school but studying
Monuments of its own magnificence . . .
      —W. B. YEATS, "Sailing to Byzantium"

Contents

Michael Pettit   **The Writing Path**   xi

Gail Galloway Adams & E. Bruce Hoch   1

Gail Galloway Adams   Hunger   2

E. Bruce Hoch   The Cleaning Woman   8

Ron Carlson & Greg Changnon   13

Ron Carlson   A Note on the Type   14

Greg Changnon   We Don't Have Suits   24

Kelly Cherry & Dennis Ward Stiles   39

Kelly Cherry   Alzheimer's   40

My Mother's Stroke   41

How We Are Taken   42

The Almost-Baby   43

Dennis Ward Stiles   Butchering   45

Shoe Salesman Tries on an Hour in Church   47

My Island   48

Notes on a Poet at Work   49

Stephen Dunn & Maureen Noelle McLane   50

Stephen Dunn   At the School for the Deaf   51

Empathy   53

Power   55

Road Stop   56

The Sensualist's Fast   58

Maureen Noelle   The Secret History of Rock-n-Roll   59

McLane   Dorothys   61

The Doubter   64

Linda Gregg & Gray Jacobik 67

Linda Gregg   On the Other Side of Love 68

Hephaestus Alone 69

The Calves Not Chosen 70

The Center of Intent 71

Gray Jacobik   Sappho's Voice 72

The Chinese Chestnut Breeze 73

Sandwoman 74

Skirts 75

Pam Houston & Roy Parvin 76

Pam Houston   Eight Days in the Brooks Range
with April and the Boys 77

Roy Parvin   May 85

Philip Levine & Charles H. Webb 97

Philip Levine   Holy Son and Mother of the Projects 98

My Given Name 99

The Letters 100

The Seven Doors 102

Good Monday 104

The Dead 106

Charles H. Webb   Marilyn's Machine 108

The Dead Run 109

Health 110

Flying Fish in the Jet Stream 111

Buyer's Remorse 113

Four-Wheeling 114

Michael Pettit & Julie Kamrowski 116

Michael Pettit   A Dog's in Heat 117

Leonard Road 118

Matins 120

One Drum 122

Lost Gloves 123

Julie Kamrowski   Magnolia 125

That June 126

Reservoir 127

Canals 128
Nora 129
Heathen Bed 130

Francine Prose & Michael Byers 131
Francine Prose A Coincidence at the Vet's 132
Michael Byers In Spain, One Thousand and Three 137

Bob Shacochis & Tom Paine 164
Bob Shacochis Going Back 165
Tom Paine Will You Say Something, Monsieur Eliot? 185

Kim R. Stafford & Florence Williams 197
Kim R. Stafford The Good Son 198
Florence Williams Mesa Flight 776 201

Gerald Stern & Henry M. Seiden 203
Gerald Stern Self-Portrait in His Sixties 204
Above Fourteenth 205
This Time 208
Someone to Watch over Me 209
Henry M. Seiden The Story as I Understand It Is 210
Looking for Lola 212
Theology 213
Tinnitus 214
Kumquats 215

**Joan Wickersham &
Deborah Kelly Kloepfer** 216
Joan Wickersham The Off-Season 217
Deborah Kelly Kloepfer Exchange 234

Terry Tempest Williams & Leslie Ryan 245
Terry Tempest Williams The Erotics of Place 246
Leslie Ryan The Other Side of Fire 250

Al Young & Monica Wesolowska 266
Al Young Distances 267

Airborne 268
A Lizard Considers the Season 269
A Toast to Charles Bukowski 271
Monica Wesolowska   Mira 272

Acknowledgments 283

The Writing Path

Michael Pettit

Behind my house in western Massachusetts are woods—maple and ash, birch and pine—where I walk my thoughts, or walk to lose them in the act of looking. In May I see trillium and wild geranium, then fiddleheads, swamp pinks, mountain laurel. I walk and look, look and think, phrases coming to me, like birds suddenly on a branch, spilling out their stories as song. I walk back, distracted, to my study, repeating what I've heard.

Though at first I blazed trees for my children, the blazes now have weathered and grown dim, and who needs them? By now the track is beaten bare, and to a certain point we know the way. We know the rocky knob beyond the big rock, the little stream that goes dry in summer, the old stone walls grown up in touch-me-nots. We know the way, to a certain point. Beyond that we are on our own, wandering, more deeply distracted or more necessarily attentive to our surroundings as we stray. Who knows what we'll find, or what might find us. If the discoveries seem worthwhile, we'll be back.

We take urban journeys too, and find our way or lose it in small towns, in libraries, on the beach. Wherever, we follow and break trails. Language necessarily *moves*, moves by way of us, moves with us, moves through us, changing and changing us.

Good teachers of writing, and there are many, know that their job is to prepare students to work alone, more or less. Good teachers never seek to keep the same students at their sides. There's no need. Students keep coming, women and men keep following the call of language, their own stories itching to get out. Good students keep coming, and leaving. They come at different times of their lives, from scattered places, to study with the human beings who wrote the books they admired back in Tupelo or New York City. They spend a week or two taking in all they can before heading back, distracted, to their studies. Good teachers and good students occasionally have the good fortune to find one another; writers' conferences and festivals are designed to make those chance connections possible;

The Writing Path exists to convey the discoveries that seasoned and new writers make.

"*Caminate no hay camino, / Se hace camino al andar.*" So wrote the great Spanish poet Antonio Machado. "Walker, there is no road, / The road is made by walking." Theodore Roethke—an exceptional teacher and poet—writes, "I learn by going where I have to go." And Flannery O'Connor, an acerbic critic of short-cut fiction, observes in "Writing Short Stories": "The only way, I think, to learn to write short stories is to write them, and then to try to discover what you have done.... The teacher can help the student by looking at his individual work and trying to help him decide if he has written a complete story." What they say clearly and eloquently is that finally we are on our own, which is a very difficult condition. As writers, as teachers and students of language, we attempt an impossible transcendence in our stories, poems, and essays. That too is our condition, the attempt, as E. M. Forster notes in *Aspects of the Novel*: "We cannot understand each other, except in a rough-and-ready way; we cannot reveal ourselves, even when we want to; what we call intimacy is only a makeshift; perfect knowledge is an illusion.... Fiction is truer than history, because it goes beyond the evidence, and each of us knows from his own experience that there is something beyond the evidence, and even if the novelist has not got it correctly, well—he has tried." Beyond the evidence, breaking trail, the established and new writers in *The Writing Path 2* carry on.

The Writing Path 2

Gail Galloway Adams & E. Bruce Hoch

Wildacres Writers' Workshop

Shortly after Stanley Elkin's death, I was rereading an interview where he said two things which seemed perfect for Bruce Hoch's stories. "Fiction provides a stage where language can stand," Elkin said in defense of his elaborate style; in the lush language and oppositions of experience that are in Bruce Hoch's fiction—those dual and contradictory images and doppelgänger reflections—I find a similar delight. They also illustrate Elkin's second statement: "It's not just the yoking of disparate objects, it's the *rightness* of the yoking." Bruce Hoch's writing has this rightness.

"The Cleaning Woman" has all the qualities of fiction that I read and love: intelligence, wit, obvious love of language, and a warm and generous spirit presented in an unmistakable voice. One question I ask beginning fiction writers is what they remember about the story; almost always that will be a compelling image. Hoch's "The Cleaning Woman" gives us a story of improbable love and its loss, then fixes that moment in an image so fresh, so sad, so vivid, that no one I know who's read this story ever forgets it.—**Gail Galloway Adams**

Gail Galloway Adams won the Flannery O'Connor Award for *The Purchase of Order*, and her fiction was selected for the Texas Institute of Literature Award in the Short Story. She teaches at West Virginia University.

E. Bruce Hoch is currently finishing his M.A. in creative writing at the University of Florida, where he also teaches expository writing. His story "The Graphologist" was published in the North Carolina O'Henry Collection.

Hunger

■ ■ ■ ■ ■ ■ ■

Carole Jordan hovered over the edge of a group of girls clustered on the steps of Henck Hall. Because she was so good at disguising it, she didn't look that thin. Naturally lean, she had a build that in a man would be called rangy: long limbs, hands that spanned two octaves, shoulders squared in perfect posture, and she was that little bit bowlegged that's appealing, somewhat sexy even. Except everything that showed on Carole was too taut or else shrouded under layered sweaters, bulked over with heavy argyle knee socks.

It was a Wednesday afternoon in October, soon after midterms, and Carole stood listening intently to a classmate describe an exam.

"And every single essay question was totally unfair." This indignant girl whose name Carole thought might be Sandra or Sydney shook her head. Fluffy hair stood straight out from her scalp like a frieze of nylon tulle; it bounced emphatically, all of a piece. "He makes me so sick. Doesn't Pike make you sick?"

Was that question directed at me? Carole tried to shrug, tried to say yes. Why can't I just say yes, or no, or something? Why do I just stand here holding my books and bobbing my head like some peasant from the Dark Ages?

"He's got a reputation for being really hard." A plump blond in purple glasses answered Carole's question. Is she helping me out? Carole thought. "I've never heard of anyone who ever got an A," the blond added.

"A—shit! How about a C!" The group was drifting away from the central complainer, whose cheeks were patchy with flush, and Carole wondered why she still stood there. Why can't I just smile, say good-bye, back down the stairs, and go? Am I so desperate? she asked herself. Am I? The campus clock in Delman chimed the half hour and a tiny metronome of pain pulled behind Carole's right eye. She didn't even feel the tic anymore, not really. She only knew it was back because her vision blurred slightly each time.

"Tension," the ophthalmologist had diagnosed in August. "It'll pass.

Try deep breathing. You might try running. Or take the contact lens out if it bothers you." Dr. Reilly's face was so close Carole saw the pores in his nose. EEEs on the chart behind him jiggled up and down until the whole row of letters looked like the fences she'd practiced jumping her pony Buttermilk over. "No," she'd told him then, "it doesn't bother me much," and the lie made the gear under her eyelid shift into high.

"Well, I've got to go now," she murmured as she sidled down the wide stone steps.

"What did you get?" the Sandra girl demanded, her voice loud and abrasive. "You're always taking so many notes."

"I bet she's mean," Carole thought, suddenly panicked. "I bet she can really be nasty." The girl's face suddenly looked cruel surrounded by that stiff mane.

"Got to go," Carole said and hurried away, waving a brief good-bye to the last two on the stairs. The day was brisk and wind scuttled leaves across the flagstone walks as she walked past Clayton Hall; past Eustus she picked up her pace. It would be almost four by the time she got home. Four four four four began to beat a steady singsong in her head. She had to stop once when no one was around and say to herself: Be still, be still. She breathed in and out in and out; it was what the doctor ordered to get that rhythm out of her head. Wind blew through the campus pines and teased Carole's hair from its side barrettes. She stood, a pitifully thin girl with downcast eyes, lips moving in what might be a silent prayer and only a close and compassionate gaze would have seen the pull release at the edge of her right eye, like a wink practicing all by itself.

She pushed into her small apartment thankful to be home among the familiar odors of Ivory and Johnson's Baby Powder and Oodles of Noodles; there was a faint aerosol fragrance of Carpet Fresh; hers alone and no one to share it with, quiet and peace. She double-locked, then chained the door. Seven minutes to four and walking to the bedroom, she wished for a cat. Lolly back home had been her cat for so long, but when Jana had developed allergies, Lolly had to go. After, Jana still sneezed at everything, everything made her eyes swell shut, her throat shut down.

Carole changed clothes, and each layer removed revealed how cleverly she concealed her wasting away. Bra cups pleated in were barely filled, nipples dark blurs on her chest, and her stomach was concave under practical cotton panties slung low. She never looked at her body anymore, those bones insistent under her skin; sometimes it hurt when she sat on the porcelain floor of the tub. She shivered. She was always cold. Lolly used to snuggle right under her chin, butting up with the top of her head and purring. Or sometimes that cat had sprawled in front of Daddy, who'd dig his bare toes into the tabby's belly, kneading and stroking. They'd all laughed at Lolly's ecstasy, the way the cat stretched long and sensuous, then spring coiled around his instep to gently bite his toes.

"She loves you, Daddy," Carole had said delightedly. "See how she loves you."

"Always need your harem girl, right, Dan?" That was her mother, hanging on the doorjamb, an eyebrow lifted, but laughing.

Almost four now. Carole bundled up in gray sweats and knobby tweed socks with Curious George red toes, padded into the small kitchen to put on the kettle.

"Eat something," she ordered herself, "eat starch, eat fats, eat sweets." She stood by the little kettle not covering the electric ring completely and watched the circle first glow rust, then blue orange. Her hands were so cold she wavered them above the kettle awaiting the faint steam that would spew forth. She imagined her fingers splitting open like hot dogs in steamers, swelling fat then bursting along the seams. And if my fingers split open, she thought, I wouldn't be able to answer the phone. No one could blame me.

4:15. Carole sat hands wrapped around a mug of Constant Comment and gingerly sipped the tea. It has orange peels in it, she told herself, that's food. The phone rang. Exquisite relief and grief. Would it ever stop? Could it ever?

"Hello, Mother," she said and held the receiver inches from her ear. She heard her mother's voice roll out furious and aggrieved. Her list of complaints was never ending, her bitterness unabated; every day a new discovery, every day a new humiliation.

"Ten months, Carole," she said, "and we still don't have the final tally. Ten months and the bank still hasn't cleared it up yet. You know what I think . . ."

Yes yes I do, Carole thought and rubbed her knees anxiously; under her palms they felt like cups of bone. Yes yes I do, she wanted to say, wanted to scream, "Let it alone." Tea rose, bitter gorge in her throat. No please she prayed as she felt her stomach knot. Please don't let me be sick.

"That bastard that prick." Her mother was angry, screaming. Carole couldn't tell if she was furious or crying, but it was always the same and what could you say? He was dead. Wasn't that bad enough? Who could you say that to? That my father's dead. Could she have said that to that mean girl today? Said who cares about any exam. My father is dead. But Carole guessed death wasn't enough, not the way that Daddy was dead. He was not only dead but betrayed: his life and theirs—Carole and Jana, and Mother—especially Mother. Carole held the phone farther away and her mother's voice spilled out into the kitchen in an invisible mist: every day this poison at four.

"You be there at four o'clock. Do you hear me?" her mother demanded, weeping, sobbing, sounding almost insane. "I need to know that you're there. That you're OK. Promise me that? Do you hear me?"

"Yes yes," Carole had assured her. She thought now every day at four o'clock of that privileged custom of tea. Of their trip to London three years ago, of Daddy and Banbury cakes with raisins that crumbled and left crumbs on his beard and her own comic shudders at clotted cream, viscous in a flowered bowl.

"Oh no, don't make me eat that. I couldn't," she'd wailed, and Daddy had laughed and slurped down a huge spoonful. Later climbing high in the rafters of a theater, all those wooden stairs. "This is the Royal Theater," her mother whispered. "It's been here for ages." Sitting between Mother and Daddy in the top on what seemed like planks and seeing down below the stage as all enchantment and green glen and the actors' voices so clear and pure, but Carole couldn't understand all that they said. She'd looked at her father in wonder, at the tears dripping off his chin and he making no effort to hide them. And remembered her mother's face in the semidark, eyes glossy, her voice almost smug as she said, "Your father's a sensitive man, tenderhearted. You're a lucky girl, Carole." Then added, "He'll understand."

Now there was all this endless scrabbling over Daddy's money all squirreled away and such trouble to get it, but really it's all over his death, which was unexpected and dire and not only his, but a young woman's who was with him. She'd had her head in his lap and he'd run the car off the road. The three days before they'd shared a master suite at the Chestnut Ridge Bed and Breakfast; the inn's receipts were in a leather portfolio he used for business trips. They'd thought he was in Portland; he'd called them each night.

"That girl, oh that girl," her mother had cried. A girl who was everything she was not: blond and short and buxom and young, oh so young— just Carole's age—ignorant, unlearned. Carole thought maybe she'd seen the girl once, sliding files in a drawer. Home from college and taking Friday off, Carole had gone to the office to surprise Daddy.

"What are you doing here, chicken?" he said as Carole perched on the edge of the desk.

"For money! What else?" They'd both laughed because he knew that she loved him. Didn't he? Had she even noticed that girl? Her name was Misty, a name they'd made fun of when she was first hired.

"When she has a bad day you can call her Hazy," Carole's mother joked, and they'd all started adding things to the idea like Dusty and Smoggy. Daddy had laughed too.

"Oh, what good is it?" her mother had shouted soon after he was buried, soon after the obituaries appeared side by side—in black and white— her father and that girl. Somehow it seemed more awful in print. But Carole knew that her father and that girl had shared something; Carole knew that they'd had some kind of life and then death—together.

"Oh, what good is it to ever believe in love?" That's what her mother said over and over and she tore all his photographs into little pieces and carefully scissored him out of the groups. Carole rescued some pictures and hid them between book covers. Her mother had flung all his clothes to the floor and kicked at his shirts and his suits, stomping on pinstripes and blazers, ripping the sleeves off his shirts. One day Carole saw her mother sitting in the mud room holding Daddy's dirty golf shoes in her lap; she was crying, but when she saw Carole looking she whammed the shoes against the tile and the cleats made black dents that were still there.

Jana, two years younger than Carole, seemed to share none of their grief. Maybe she knew, Carole thought, watching her sister's implacable matte powdered face. Jana spent all her time in her bedroom, and when she emerged thundering drumbeats seeped from her earphones.

"I don't want to talk about it," she said flatly the one time Carole stood weeping at her bedroom door. "What good does it do?" She'd closed the door firmly in her sister's face.

"Oh please," Carole had begged. "Let me go." She yearned to go back to college, not to the dorm, but to a place of her own, to be alone, away from all this: this grief and this house where the air was charged by hysterics and fever and tears and the faint odor of menstrual blood from periods that seemed without end. Tension and stress the doctor said or women cycle together when they live in close groups. Each night in separate bedrooms the three of them curled around heating pads moaning and crying; unbearable.

"So go so go you want to go go!" her mother screamed. "You think I need you?" She faced Carole, her image, her twin, both tall and elegant, both dark with faces of a Greek chorus: women with liquid black eyes.

"Look at you." Her mother's voice trembled as she whirled Carole around. In the foyer's oval mirror Carole stood reflected: tall and sturdy, a strong girl with a summer tan still holding to her skin, the color of honey and her pupils bright as though she'd swallowed belladonna, and her mouth—Carole's mouth was her father's—wry and full and too carefully sculptured.

"So full of yourself. You make me sick." Her mother almost sounded like she was gagging. That's what she said, but it was only grief talking. It was only sorrow that said, "Get out of my sight." Her mother collapsed on the floor, blue satin robe spread out around her like a small pool of grief.

On the phone her mother cried softly, she apologized at the end of each talk for not having control, she talked about her support group, the progress with the therapist; sometimes she asked questions, but Carole knew she did not want, never wanted to hear the real answers; she couldn't handle them. Carole knew that.

"Fine yes fine. I'm doing really well. Got an A on a midterm from a really hard professor." That Sandra's face flashed into her mind; she was glaring at Carole. "They say no one's ever got an A from Pike before. And I am eating right." Tea taste was strong in her mouth. "I know you worry, Mother, I know." Now this, get through this. "Yes, I love you too," she said, "and hugs and kisses to Jana."

She did not put the phone down when her mother hung up but let it hum its one clear note in the air until it turned insistent. Outside the kitchen window she could see the vacant lot where sometimes people played games. Four guys were tossing a ball back and forth. "Here, pass it here," one guy on the outside kept shouting, "here." She didn't know any of them, but one reminded her of a boy in her econ class. He sat two rows in front and she'd noticed his handwriting first, letters so perfectly formed, the *a*'s like tiny pyramids. His hair was dirty blond and cut high around his ears and there was a dark plushy mole right above his back collar.

She stood near the window and held to the sill, her legs trembling with faintness, cold, tired. How lovely, she suddenly thought, it would be to kiss that boy, to lean over and gently rest her head on his shoulder, feel her cheek against his flannel collar. Could anyone ever do that? She rested her forehead against the window and felt a steady rush of air; the pane grew cold against her skin and her mind swarmed with her mother's anguish and questions: How could it happen? Doesn't love matter? Who wants to live?

The Cleaning Woman

■■■■■■■■■■■■■■■■■

Her father, Theresa Craighead told Milos Studebaker one sweltering May night, read Kierkegaard and Schopenhauer to her in his underwear in their kitchen when she was eleven and gangly. She made Colombian coffee for him and poured it over cracked ice into chilled glass mugs. Slouched on a barstool, his toes gripping the edge of the countertop, her father read aloud to her of angst and fear and trembling and the precariousness of existence. She was twenty-five now, fair, tall, voluptuous, and beautiful.

He told her that his own father had always secretly wanted to be a stand-up comic. His father made Henny Youngman seem cerebral. Milos Studebaker was short, paunchy, and combed his hair over on the top to hide his baldness. Taciturn, he had long ago given up on love, yet stared at her wide-eyed over half-reading glasses which had become necessary if he was to read any print smaller than

AMERICA LANDS MAN ON MOON

Reluctantly, he had been skipped ahead in the fourth grade: she held back, embarrassedly, in the second. He confided to her that hearing music on the world's subtlest sound systems enabled him to believe in God. She urged him to speak only in her right ear, as she had lost the ability to hear anything out of her left.

Two days later, early on a morning in spring, he took her to his new home. It was unfinished, the first house he had ever bought. They lay on their stomachs in the upstairs loft facing the forest. Below, on the paint-smeared and splintered wood floor, lay abandoned drop cloths. Iron tubes of scaffolding were propped against holes in walls where sliding glass doors would go. The magnolias shuddered heavily in the breeze.

She sat up, speaking exuberantly, her face gleaming. Her arms flailed and the bodice of her silk shirt fell forward and he saw the profusion of her breasts. Her linen skirt rode up on her thighs, revealing the touching whiteness of her underwear. He lay still, trying not to breathe lest he blow away the grace that had transfigured his new home.

"Your house will never be more beautiful than this," she said. He felt certain she was right.

For six years he had worked in cramped cubicles, writing in fountain pen, a doctoral dissertation asserting the loss of linguistic credibility since Newton and the consequent and oppressive ascendance of mathematics.

She hoped one day to enter graduate school but was too frightened to sit for her preliminary examinations.

Offering herself, she read Joyce to him:

Yes, first I gave him the bit of seedcake out of my mouth,
Yes, my God after that long kiss I near lost my breath—
Yes, he said I was a flower of the mountain.
And then he asked would I say yes, to say yes, my mountain flower.
Yes. And his heart was going like mad and yes, I said, yes.
I will, yes.

Afraid to believe her, he read Eliot:

I grow old . . . I grow old . . .
I shall wear the bottoms of my trousers rolled.
Shall I part my hair behind? Do I dare to eat a peach?
I shall wear white flannel trousers, and walk upon the beach.

They could not have been more different: He, forty-seven, arthritic, wary as a tortoise. She licked her fingertips, pressed back his hair, said, "Much better." Her mother had late in life taken her vows as a nun. His sister had become a year ago a fundamentalist Jewish proselyte.

It was inevitable then that Milos Studebaker and Theresa Craighead told each other, almost immediately, and at the very same time, "I love you."

For three months they went everywhere together. At museums, she cautioned him to leave off touching the Great God Siva with his own mortal fingers. They ate black beans and rice, amused at the waiter, who kept asking her if she would be having the same as her father. It went so well they made a pact no matter what they would never go on Oprah.

From magazines, she cut out pictures of famous couples too tall and too short for one another, too old and young, too patrician and plain, too duckling and swan. She mailed them to him. "We'll write our own script," she wrote.

In public they could not keep from touching each other. He spoke to her in fitful bursts, enthusiastic as an auctioneer, wanting to tell her everything. They went to tobacconists' shops and, slipping clandestinely into chilly humidors, kissed with friendly, searching mouths, stopping to buy hand-rolled cigars from Guatemala, from Honduras.

Outside, they wandered hand in hand, lit up their stogies, and rushed to buy lamé sheets, perfumed oils, scented candles for the heart of the night.

They lay in his bed and talked till dawn. She wept for her father, who now collected plaster replicas of camels and placed them all around his front lawn to please his second wife. She cried and called her father "The Incredible Shrinking Man." He suffered from a calcium deficiency and grew shorter every year.

They slept clumped against one another in her fold-out sofa which left them stiff and tilted when they woke. They drove to each other on the Interstate, meeting halfway and opening each other's clothes even as they were saying hello.

They reveled in the joyous good fortune which produced in Milos an elation so unaccustomed that the Fourth of July phone call from Theresa came almost as he had been steadfastly waiting for it. She needed time to think, she said in a voice Milos did not know.

He began staying at home, calling her only when he could no longer bear not to. She answered with a tone of bewildered obligation. There had been one morning when he had slipped out the front door before she woke. He had uncoiled the garden hose and begun watering. She tapped on the vertical windows in the wall overlooking the yard and waved to him. She was naked; she went and baby-powdered herself and pressed against the panes and blew him a kiss.

He looked out his windows at his yard and his garden. And when he stared at the young river birch and the red elm and the sweet gum trees he had planted and watered faithfully every day, at his impatiens set in the ground in parallel lines around his sloping walkway, the amaryllis with its fragile protuberant fronds, all of this he saw through a glass window upon which remained the powdered outlines of Theresa. He saw what there was of his life through the white tracery of her body. Her rib cage was still visible, its thin bifurcating line vertically cleaving her torso in two. If he peered intently enough at the glass, there was even the minute depression of her belly button; in life, a tiny perfect declivity; on his window, an oval limned with white powder.

Her image, incorporeal, became an apparition that plagued him. In place of the warm, full breasts once proffered to him so eagerly, there remained only a shallow frieze made with Theresa's body serving both as camera and film.

He would take it down shortly with cotton cloths and Windex. He would obliterate the ghostly image with sponges and pools of white vinegar. He would efface it with rolled-up sections of Sunday *New York Times* dipped in kerosene. With acetone and mineral spirits he would strip it from the glass.

It was just talcum pressed into glass where she had flattened herself against the pane for him. Baby powder could be dislodged, perhaps as easily as by breathing on it with breath heated in one's mouth by holding it there for as long as one could. Nonetheless, it was the last he would ever see of Theresa's breasts or her wrists, or her waist, and as he walked past the window with her body smudged on it, he decided to clean it later. When he went to bed, he reminded himself to take care of it the next morning. But in the morning he would remember that it was in the afternoon with the sun streaming through the window that the image was most visible, and he would go up and put a small cane chair near it and peer through Theresa's body till dusk.

For a long time, then, he did not do anything about the image in the glass.

Sometimes in bed, in the middle of the night, he would wake thinking of her, shaking. He would turn on the security lights and in his underwear go outside and look up at the white phantasm.

One day, Milos realized he could never clean it. So he put an ad in the classified section of the paper for someone to help around the house and soon he had hired a desiccated Filipino woman named Estrella who was four feet four inches tall. She told him, without his asking, that she was an expert in reflexology. He would feel better, she insisted, only after he let her take hold of his feet. She suggested they boil the bark of a papaya tree and drink the broth with salted peanuts.

Milos went upstairs and sat in the cane chair for one last time listening to Estrella shout up to him her many skills. "I can convert Kelvin to Fahrenheit, write for you haiku, there is nothing I cannot flambé." And she spoke, too, of deeply satisfied customers. "Dr. Lavender's wife loves my work. Call the DeFuniaks; I have their number right here."

Finally he rose and calling down to her from the loft in a voice as brittle and shrill as a floe breaking roughly away from an iceberg, Milos asked Estrella,

"Do you do windows?"

Ron Carlson &
Greg Changnon

Napa Valley Writers' Conference

Greg Changnon's "We Don't Have Suits" is a quiet, affecting story of a man standing disoriented and scared at the edge of his world—in this case next to a motel pool near the hospital where his wife lies gravely ill. The story does not resort to melodrama or lapse into the deadpan, but with sure steady prose it offers us a moment in this complicated, heartfelt territory. It feels simply real. I read the story this summer at the Napa Valley Writers' Conference and it stayed with me long after the sessions.—**Ron Carlson**

Ron Carlson's most recent book is a collection of stories, *Plan B for the Middle Class*. His fiction has appeared in the *New Yorker*, *Harper's*, *Story*, and many other journals. He lives in Tempe, Arizona, where he directs the Creative Writing Program at Arizona State University.

Greg Changnon lives in San Francisco and is currently a student in the Creative Writing Program at San Francisco State University.

A Note on the Type

No alphabet comes along full grown. A period of development is required for the individual letters to bloom and then another period for them to adjust to their place in the entire set, and sometimes this period can be a few weeks or it can be a lifetime. No quality font maker ever sat down and wrote out *A* to *Z* just like that. It doesn't happen. Getting Ray Bold right required five months, these last five months, an intense creative period for me which has included my ten-week escape from the state facilities at Windchime, Nevada, and my return here one week ago. Though I have always continued sharpening my letters while incarcerated, most of the real development of Ray Bold occurred while I was on the outside, actively eluding the authorities. There is a kind of energy in the out-of-doors, moving primarily along the sides of things, always hungry, sleeping thinly in hard places, that awakens in me the primal desire toward print.

And though Ray Bold is my best typeface and the culmination of my work in the field, I should explain it is also my last—for the reasons this note on the type will illuminate. I started this whole thing in the first place because I had been given some time at the Fort Nippers Juvenile Facility in Colorado—two months for reckless endangerment, which is what they call Grand Theft Auto when you first start in at it, and I was rooming with Little Ricky Grudnaut, who had only just commenced his life as an arsonist by burning down all four barns in the nearby town of Ulna in a single night the previous February. Juvenile facilities, as you can imagine, are prime locations for meeting famous criminals early in their careers, and Little Ricky went on, as everyone now knows, to burn down eleven Chicken Gigundo franchise outlets before he was apprehended on fire himself in Napkin, Oklahoma, and asked to be extinguished.

But impulsive and poultry-phobic as he may have become later, Little Ricky Grudnaut gave me some valuable advice so many years ago. I'd moped around our cell for a week—it was really a kind of dorm room—staring at this and that, and he looked up from the tattoo he was etching in his forearm with an old car key. It was Satan's head, he told me, and it was pretty red, but it only looked like some big face with real bad hair—and he said, "Look, Ray, get something to do or you'll lose it. Make something up." He threw me then my first instrument, a green golf pencil he'd had hidden in his shoe.

It was there in Fort Nippers, fresh from the brutality of my own household, that I began the doodling that would evolve into these many alphabets which I've used to measure each of my unauthorized sorties from state-sponsored facilities. Little Ricky Grudnaut saw my first *R* that day and was encouraging. "It ain't the devil," he said, "but it's a start."

I have decided to accept the offer of reduced charges for full disclosure of how and where I sustained my escape. I had been sharing a cell with Bobby Lee Swinghammer, the boxer and public enemy who had battered so many officials during his divorce proceedings last year in Carson City. Bobby Lee was not happy to have a lowly car thief in his cell and he had even less patience with my alphabets. I tried to explain to him that I wasn't simply a car thief, that I was now, in the words of the court, "a habitual criminal" (though my only crime had been to steal cars, which I had been doing for years and years), and I tried to show him what I was working on with Ray Bold. Bobby Lee Swinghammer's comment was that it looked "piss plain," and it irked him so badly that he then showed me in the next few weeks some of his own lettercraft. These were primarily the initials *B* and *L* and *S* that he had worked on while on the telephone with his attorney. And they are perfect examples of what is wrong with any font that comes to life in prison.

The design is a result of too much time. I've seen them in every facility in which I have resided, these letters too cute to read, I mean flat-out baroque. Serifs on the *T*'s that weigh ten pounds; Bobby Lee had beaked serifs on his *S*'s that were big as shoes. His *B* was three-dimensional, ten feet deep, a *B* you could move into, four rooms and a bath on the first floor alone. I mean he had all afternoon while his lawyer said, "We'll see," a dozen different ways, why not do some gingerbread, some decoration? I kept my remarks to a minimum. But I've seen a lot of this, graffiti so ornate you couldn't find the letters in the words. And what all of that is about is one thing and it's *having time*. I respect it and I understand it—a lot of my colleagues have got plenty of time, and now I've got some again too, but it's a style that is just not for me.

I became a car thief because it seemed a quick and efficient way to get away from my father's fists, and I became a font maker because I was caught. After my very first arrest—I'd taken a red Firebird from in front of a Seven-Eleven—in fact in my first alphabet, made with a golf pencil, I tried my hand at serification. I was thirteen and I didn't know any better. These were pretty letters. I mean, they had a kind of beauty. I filigreed the *C*'s and *G*'s and the *Q* until they looked like they were choking on lace. But what? They stood there these letters so tricked up you wouldn't take them out of the house, too much makeup, and you knew they weren't any good. For me, that is. You put a shadow line along the stem of an *R* and then beak the tail, it's too heavy to move.

The initials that Bobby Lee Swinghammer had been carving into the back of his hand with a Motel 6 ball point pen looked like monuments. You could visit them, but they were going absolutely nowhere.

And that's what I wanted in this last one, Ray Bold, a font that says "movement." I mean, I was taking it with me and I was going to use it, essentially, on the run. Bobby Lee was right, it is plain but it can travel light.

I want to make it clear right here, though Bobby Lee and I had our differences and he did on occasion pummel me about the head and upper trunk (not as hard as he could have, god knows), he is not the reason I escaped from Windchime. I have escaped, as the documents point out, eleven times from various facilities throughout this part of the West, and it was never because of any individual cellmate, though Bobby Lee was one of the most animated I've encountered. I like him as a person and I'm pleased that his appeal is being heard and that soon he will be resuming his life as an athlete.

I walked out of Windchime because I had the chance. I found that lab-coat folded over the handrail on our stairs. Then, dressed as a medical technician, with my hair parted right down the middle, I walked out of there one afternoon, carrying a clipboard I'd made myself in shop, and which is I'll admit right here the single most powerful accessory to any costume. You carry a clipboard, they won't mess with you.

Anyway, that windy spring day I had no idea of the direction this new alphabet would take. I knew I would begin writing; everybody knew that. I always do it. I've been doing it for more than twenty years. When my father backhanded me for the last time I fled the place, but not before making my *RaY* on his sedan with the edge of a nickel. It wasn't great, and I don't care to write with money as a rule, but it was me, my instinct for lettercraft at the very start.

I also knew I'd be spending plenty of time in the wilderness, the high desert there around Windchime and the forests as they reach into Idaho and the world beyond. I know now that, yes, landscape did have a clear effect on the development of Ray Bold, the broad clean vistas of Nevada, the residual chill those first few April nights, and the sharp chunk of flint I selected to inscribe my name on a stock tank near Popknock. That first *RaY* showed many clues about the alphabet to come: the *R* (and the *R* is very dear to me, of course) made in a single stroke (the stem bolder than the tail); the small case *a*, unclosed; and the capital *Y*, which resembles an *X*. These earmarks of early Ray Bold would be repeated again and again in my travels—the single stroke, the open letter, the imprecise armature. To me they all say one thing: energy.

I made that *RaY* just about nightfall the second night, and I was fairly sure the shepherd might have seen me cross open ground from a rocky bluff to the tank, and so, writing there in the near dark on the heavily oxidized old steel tank while I knelt on the sharp stones and breathed hard from the run (I'd had little exercise at Windchime), I was scared and happy at once, which as anyone knows are the perfect conditions under which to write your name. *RaY*. It was a beginning.

People have asked me about the type. "Why do it?" they say. "You want to be famous?" It is a question so wrongheaded that it kind of hurts. Because what I do, I do for myself. Most of the time you're out there in some dumpster behind the Royal Food in Triplet or you're sitting in a culvert in Marvin or in a boxcar on a siding in old Delphi (all places I've been) and what you make, you better make for yourself. There aren't a whole lot of people going to come along and appreciate the understated loop on your *g* or the precision of any of your descenders. I mean, that's the way I figured it. When I fell into that dumpster in Triplet I was scratched and bleeding from hurrying with a barbed wire fence, and I sat there on the old produce looking at the metal side of that bin, and then after I'd pried a tenpenny nail from a wooden melon crate I made my *RaY*, the best I knew how, knowing only I would see it. And in poor light. I made it for myself. It existed for a moment and then I heard the dogs and I was on the run again.

There was once a week later when I took that gray LeBaron in Marvin and it ran out of gas almost immediately, midtown, right opposite the Blue Ribbon Hardware, and I could see the town cop cruising up behind, and I took off on foot. And I can run when there's a reason, but as I run I always think, as I was thinking that day: where would I make my *RaY*. The two are linked with me: to run is to write. That day after about half a mile, I crawled into a canal duct, a square cement tube with about four inches of water running through the bottom. And with a round rock as big as a grapefruit sitting in that cold irrigation water, I did it there: *RaY*. It wasn't for the critics and it wasn't for the press. They wouldn't be along this way. It was for me. And it was as pure a *RaY* as I've ever done. I couldn't find that place today with a compass.

At times like that when you're in the heat of creation, making your mark, you don't think about hanging a hairline serif on the *Y*. It seems pretty plainly what it is: an indulgence. Form should fit function, the man said, and I'm with him.

After Marvin, that night in the water, I got sick and slept two or three days in hayfields near there. As everyone knows I moved from there to that Tuffshed I lived in near Shutout for a week getting my strength back. The reports had me eating *dogfood*, and I'll just say to that I ate some dogfood, dry food, I think it was Yumpup, but there were also lots of nuts and berries in the vicinity and I enjoyed them as well.

Everyone also knows about the three families I met and traveled with briefly. The German couple's story just appeared in *Der Spielplotz* and so most of Germany and Austria are familiar with me and my typeface. I hope that their tale doesn't prevent other Europeans from visiting Yellowstone and talking with Americans at the photo vistas. I'm still amused that they thought I was a university professor (because I talked a little about my work), but on a three-state, five-month run from the law you're bound to be misunderstood. The two American families seemed to have no difficulty believing they'd fallen into the hands of an escaped felon, and though I did interrupt their vacations, I thought we all had a fine time, and I returned all of their equipment except the one blue windbreaker in good condition.

Though I have decided to tell my story, I don't see how it is going to help them catch the next guy. Because those last five weeks were not typical in the least. Fortunately, by the time I arrived in Sanction, Idaho, Ray Bold was mostly complete, for I lost interest in it for a while.

Walking through that town one evening, I took a blue Country Squire stationwagon, the largest car I ever stole, from the gravel lot of the Farmers' Exchange. About a quarter mile later I discovered Mrs. Kathleen McKay in the back of the vehicle among her gear. When you find a woman in the car you're stealing, there is a good chance the law will view that as kidnapping, so when Mrs. McKay called out, "Now who is driving me home?" I answered, truthfully, "Just me, Ray." And at the fourway, when she said left, I turned left.

Now it is an odd thing to meet a widow in that way, and the month that followed, five weeks really, were odd too, and I'm just getting the handle on it now. Mrs. McKay's main interests were in painting pictures with oil paints and in fixing up the farm. Her place was 105 acres five miles out of Sanction and the house was very fine, being block and two stories with a steep metal snow roof. Her husband had farmed the little place, she said, but not very well. He had been a Mormon from a fine string of them, but he was a drinker and they'd had no children, and so the church, she said, had not been too sorry to let them go.

She told me all this while making my bed in the little outbuilding by the barn, and when she finished, she said, "Now I'm glad you're here, Ray. And I hope tomorrow you could help me repair the culvert."

I had thought it would be painting the barn, which was a grand building, faded but not peeling, or mowing the acres and acres of weeds which I could see were full of rabbits. But no, it was replacing the culvert in the road to the house. It was generally collapsed along its length and rusted through in two big places. It was a hard crossing for any vehicle. Looking at it, I didn't really know where to start. I'd hid in plenty of culverts, mostly larger than this one, which was a thirty-inch corrugated steel tube, but I'd never replaced one. The first thing, I started her old tractor, an International, and chained up to the ruined culvert and ripped it out of the ground like I don't know what. I mean, it was a satisfying start, and I'll just tell you right out, I was involved.

I trenched the throughway with a shovel, good work that took two days, and then I laid her shiny new culvert in there pretty as a piece of jewelry. I set it solid and then buried the thing and packed the road again so that there wasn't a hump, there wasn't a bump, there wasn't a ripple as you crossed. I spent an extra day dredging the ditch, but that was gilding the lily, and I was just showing off.

And you know what: she paid me with a pie. I'm not joking. I parked the tractor and hung up the shovel and on the way back to my room, she met me in the dooryard like some picture out of *The Farmer's Almanac*, which there were plenty of lying around, and she handed me an apple pie in a glass dish. It was warm and swollen up so the seams on the crosshatch pie crust were steaming.

Well, I don't know, but this was a little different period for old Ray. I already had this good feather bed in the old tack room and the smell of leather and the summer evenings and now I had had six days of good work where I had been the boss and I had a glass pie dish in my hands in the open air of Idaho. What I'm saying here is that I was affected. All of this had affected me.

To tell the truth, kindness was a new thing. My father was a crude man who never hesitated to push a child to the ground. As a cop in the town of Brown River he was not amused to have a son who was a thief. And my mother had more than she could handle with five kids and preferred to travel with the Red Cross from flood to fire across the plains. And so, all these years, I've been a loner and happy at it I thought, until Mrs. McKay showed me her apple pie. Such a surprise, that tenderness. I had heard of such things before, but I honestly didn't think I was the type.

I ate the pie and that affected me, two warm pieces, and then I ate a piece cool in the morning for breakfast along with Mrs. McKay's coffee sitting over her checked tablecloth in the main house as another day came up to get the world and I was affected further. I'm not making excuses, these are facts. When I stood up to go out and commence the mowing, Mrs. McKay said it could wait a couple of days. How'd she say it? Like this: "Ray, I believe that could wait a day or two."

And that was that. It was three days when I came out of that house again; it didn't really make any difference to those weeds. I moved into the main house. I can barely talk about it except to say these were decent days to me. I rode a tractor through the sunny fields of Idaho, mowing, slowing from time to time to let the rabbits run ahead of the blades. And in the evenings there was washing up and hot meals and Mrs. McKay. The whole time, I mean every minute of every day of all five weeks, I never made a *RaY*. And this is a place with all that barnwood and a metal silo. I didn't scratch a letter big or small and there were plenty of good places. Do you hear me? I'd lost the desire.

But in the meantime I was a farmer, I guess, or a hired hand, something. I did take an interest in Mrs. McKay's paintings, which were portraits, I suppose, portraits of farmers in shirtsleeves and overalls, that kind of thing. They were good paintings in my opinion, I mean, you could tell what they were, and she had some twenty of the things on her sunporch, where she painted. She didn't paint any of the farmer's wives or animals or like that, but I could see her orange tractor in the back of three or four of the pictures. I like that, the real touches. A tractor way out behind some guy in a painting, say only three inches tall, adds a lot to it for me, especially when it is a tractor I know pretty well.

Mrs. McKay showed some of these portraits at the fair each year and had ribbons in her book. At night on that screenporch listening to the crickets and hearing the moths bump against the screens, I'd be sitting side by side with her looking at the scrapbook. I'd be tired and she would smell nice. I see now that I was in a kind of spell, as I said, I was affected. Times I sensed I was far gone, but could do nothing about it. One night, for example, she turned to me in the bed and asked, "What is it you were in jail for, Ray? Were you a car thief?"

I wasn't even surprised by this and I answered with the truth, which is the way I've always answered questions, "Yes," I said. "I took a lot of cars. And I was caught for it."

"Why did you?"

"I took the first one to run away. I was young, a boy, and liked having it, and as soon as I could I took another. And it became a habit for me. I've taken a lot of cars I didn't especially want or need. It's been my life in a way, right until the other week when I took your car, though I would have been just as pleased to walk or hitchhike." I had already told her that first day that I had been headed for Yellowstone National Park, though I didn't tell her I was planning on making *RaY*s all over the damn place.

After a while that night in the bed she just said, "I see." And she said it sweetly, sleepily, and I took it for what it was.

Well, this dream doesn't last long. Five weeks is just a minute, really, and things began to shift in the final days. For one thing I came to understand that I was the person Mrs. McKay was painting now by the fact of the cut fields in the background. The face wasn't right, but maybe that's OK, because my face isn't right. In real life it's a little thin, off center. She'd corrected that, which is her privilege as an artist, and further she'd put a dreamy look on the guy's face which I suppose is a real nod toward accuracy.

"Are these your other men?" I asked her one night after supper. We'd spoken frankly from the outset and there was no need to change now, even though I had uncomfortable feelings about her artwork: it affected me now by making me sad. And I knew what was going on though I could not help myself. I could not go out in the yard and steal her car again and pick up my plans where I'd dropped them. I'll say it because I know it was true, I was beyond affected, I was in love with Mrs. McKay. I could tell because I was just full of hard wonder, a feeling I understood was jealousy. I mean there were almost two dozen paintings out there on the porch.

But my question hit a wrong note. Mrs. McKay looked at me while she figured out what I was asking and then her face kind of folded, and she went up to bed. I didn't think as it was happening to say I was sorry, though I was sorry in a second, sorrier really for that remark than for any of the two hundred forty or so vehicles I had taken, the inconvenience and damage that had often accompanied their disappearance. What followed was my worst night, I'd say. I'm a car thief and I am not used to hurting people's feelings. If I hurt their feelings, I'm not usually there to be part of it. And I cared for Mrs. McKay in a way that was strange to me, too. I sat there until sunrise, when I printed a little apology on a piece of paper, squaring the letters in a way that felt quite odd, but they were legible, which is what I was after: "I'm sorry for being a fool. Please forgive me. Love, Ray." I made the Ray in cursive, something I've done only three or four times in my whole life. Then I went out to paint the barn.

It was midmorning when I turned from where I stood high on that ladder painting the barn and saw the sheriff's two vehicles where they were parked below me. I hadn't heard them because cars didn't make any whump-whump crossing that new culvert. When I saw those two Fords, I thought it would come back to me like a lost dog—the need to run and run, and make a *RaY* around the first hard corner. But it didn't. I looked down and saw the sheriff. There were two kids in the other car, county deputies, and I descended the ladder and didn't spill a drop of that paint. The sheriff greeted me by name and I greeted him back. The men allowed me to seal the gallon of barn red and to put my tools away. One of the kids helped me with the ladder. None of them drew their sidearms and I appreciated that.

It was as they were cuffing me that Mrs. McKay came out. She came right up and took my arm and the men stepped back for a moment. I will always remember her face there, so serious and pure. She said, "They were friends, Ray. Other men who have helped me keep this place together. I never gave any other man an apple pie, not even Mr. McKay." I loved her for saying that. She didn't have to. You have a woman make that kind of statement in broad daylight in front of the county officials and it's a bracing experience; it certainly braced me. I smiled there as happy as I'd been in this life. As the deputy helped me into the car I realized that for the first time ever I was leaving home. I'd never really had one before.

"Save that paint," I said to Mrs. McKay. "I'll be back and finish this job." I saw her face and it has sustained me.

They had found me because I'd mowed. Think about it, you drive County Road 216 twice a week for a few years and then one day a hundred acres of milkweed, goldenrod, and what have you are trimmed like a city park. You'd make a phone call, which is what the sheriff had done. That's what change is, a clue.

So, here I am in Windchime once again. I work at this second series of Ray Bold an hour or two a day. I can feel it evolving, that is, the font is a little more vertical than it was when I was on the outside and I'm thickening the stems. And I'm thinking it would look good with a spur serif—there's time. It doesn't have all the energy of Ray Bold I, but it's an alphabet with staying power, and it has a different purpose: it has to keep me busy for fifteen months, when I'll be going home to paint a barn and mow the fields. My days as a font maker are numbered.

My new cellmate, Victor Lee Peterson, the semifamous archer and survivalist who extorted all that money from Harrah's in Reno recently and then put arrows in the radiators of so many state vehicles during his botched escape on horseback, has no time for my work. He leafs through the notebooks and shakes his head. He's spent three weeks now etching a target, five concentric circles on the wall, and I'll say this, he's got a steady hand and he's got a good understanding of symmetry. But a target? He says the same thing about my letters. "The ABCs?" he said when he first saw my work. I smile at him. I kind of like him. He's an anarchist, but I think I can get through. As I said today: "Victor. You've got to treat it right. It's just the alphabet but sometimes it's all we've got."

We Don't Have Suits

■■■■■■■■■■■■■■■■■■

I forgot to pack Connor's swimsuit. The motel we've checked into—the Hilltop Motor Lodge—is shaped like a horseshoe with a swimming pool in the center. Every room has a view of that glistening square of blue-green water. To make things worse, Connor insists on sitting right by the pool, his jeans rolled up, his feet dangling in the water. We're expected at the University of Iowa oncology clinic by two, and I'm certain he'll sit out there all morning. I know that at the hospital Connor will tell his mother that I forgot his trunks.

It was my wife's nurse who suggested this motel rather than the expensive campus hotel that's next door to the clinic. Here, at the Lodge, twelve miles outside Iowa City, rooms are forty-nine dollars a night and because it's not run by the university, guests don't have to put up with vain, sullen college students ruling the front desk. But then there's this damned heated pool.

I take Connor to the motel gift shop. The front desk clerk also handles the souvenirs; she's a woman with a flattened gray bun and a frazzled grimace on her cracked lips. A name tag—"Welcome, My Name Is . . ."—is pinned to her wrinkled blouse, but the space for her name is left empty. She presides over postcards, sunglasses, and stacks of the *National Enquirer*. This is flat farm country so the gift shop also sells fluffy stuffed pigs that squeak when you squeeze them and haystack refrigerator magnets. But no swimsuits.

Connor rises up to his toes, his hands on the counter, and says to the woman, "Can I have something so I can swim in the pool?"

The woman looks around her store and sticks a pencil in her bun. "All I can do is look in the lost and found. That's all I can do." She disappears in her storeroom, and I really wonder if she'll ever come back.

Connor turns to me with a lopsided smile. Everything about this kid gets to me in the strangest way: his shaggy blond hair, his large, bony elbows, the lovely, floppy ears he inherited from his mother. Sometimes, I can't even look at him. For the rest of his life—and he's just turned eight—he's going to remind me of her.

"Dad?" Connor, on tiptoes, reaches over the glass counter and spins the rack that holds the postcards. "How come this place is called Hilltop? I don't see any hills around here."

"Good question." Great question, I think. I don't have a clue.

"You don't know?" He stares at me with a curious look.

If I had spent more time with Connor, if I hadn't spent most of my adult life working as legal counsel for the Illinois State Lottery, I would have had more experience conjuring up quick answers to the questions sons ask. For most of Connor's life, I've been at my wide, mahogany desk, my name, Charles J. Aspern, Esq., glued to a metal plate, each letter painted on a ping pong ball like the ones we blow around in a cage for the Lotto Spin. For the past twelve years, I've sat there in that stiff, ergonomic chair my wife, Nancy, bought after the first time she came to the office and saw the old wooden chair I had been using and ignoring. I've sat in that chair through Connor's eight years, litigating prize pay-out schedules and staring at the ancient oil painting of spoiled Victorian children that hangs on one wall. Sometimes I'm afraid I know these pale, thin, two-dimensional kids, dressed in ruffles and holding nineteenth-century hoops, better than I know my own son.

When in doubt, I always refer Connor to the wisdom of others. "Why don't you ask the happy lady about it when she comes back?"

Connor shakes his head and clenches his teeth in mock horror. The gesture is familiar. Before she got sick and left for the clinic, my wife, Nancy, would fill me in on the day as we got ready for bed. In her Mr. Planters the Peanut Man nightshirt, Nancy stood on the bed and went through her favorite Connor expressions, pantomiming his exaggerated grimaces, his exuberant laugh, his hunchbacked way of holding himself. One evening, Connor watched from the doorway, then hopped up on the bed to join her. They bounced around, frowning, scowling, guffawing like a silent movie slapstick team. I stood away from their stage and nursed the raw feeling of exclusion.

When Connor came into our lives, I was nervous, unprepared, wary that each of my mistakes would be fatal. I used to think hard work was ironing out the legal ramifications of the Quick Pick Six, the Scratch Jackpot, and the Millionaire Match. Nancy told me to watch her with Connor and pay attention to the details. To see how she held him, how she rubbed the skin between his eyes to relax him, how she stuck her pinkie in his tiny mouth to keep him from fussing. Instead of learning, I simply watched and wondered how in the world this small, helpless stranger got to be my son.

I remember late-night feedings when Connor was an infant, stumbling around in the dark for a bottle of milk when Nancy was too tired to get up. Half asleep, stuck in a fog of fatigue, I would hold Connor just like Nancy did. As the baby nuzzled the plastic tip, I rested my eyes and imagined ways to get the earth's babies to sleep through world hunger. The clunk of the plastic bottle on the wood nursery floor was my signal to place Connor back in the crib and feel my way back to bed. In the morning, I was never sure if I had indeed woken up and tended to my son or if I had only dreamt it.

The motel woman shuffles back from the storeroom, holding up a small purple bikini dangling from a hanger. "This is it . . . this is all I have." The woman covers up her mouth and looks at us as if she will be fired for this.

"Connor, you think it might be your size?" I joke.

He stares at me, his right shoulder tilting forward, closing off his body to me. My son must think I don't know the difference between a boy's and a girl's suit. "Dad," he says with a seriousness that is unfamiliar, "what is wrong with you?" Slowly, he flashes me an impish grin. "I hate purple." He lopes away from the counter, back toward me.

"Connor, listen." I drop my hands on his shoulders, holding him still. "There's a color TV in the room. And it's got cable. You like cable?"

"Mom says no cable until I'm thirteen."

"All right. No cable then."

Connor turns away from me. "Hey, lady, can I swim in my undies?" As the woman squeezes her eyes shut, I wonder about my son's obsession with the pool. Perhaps he is the one that doesn't want to be alone with me.

The woman grabs a tissue from behind the counter, holds it to her nose, then crumples it into a ball. "I'm actually very sorry, but to swim, you have to have a suit."

A phone rings from somewhere behind the woman. She turns toward it quickly, then spins back to us. "I've got to get that," she says, pointing over her shoulder.

"Well, you let us know when you get a new shipment of bathing trunks." But the woman is gone.

We walk, side by side, back to the pool area. My hand falls off Connor's shoulder as he moves in front of me. I take the concrete stairs up to the

26

second level where our room is, but Connor remains below, staring at the empty water, hopping from the ground to the first step and back again.

"Before we go see Mom, you can take me to a store somewhere."

The idea of a shopping center, of aisles and aisles of kids and moms, chills me. Whenever I went to the mall with my wife and child, I ignored the floors and floors of snazzy boutiques, the waterfall in the concourse polluted with pennies, the elevated stage which, at different times of the year, offered a skinny Santa Claus or a droopy-eared seven-foot Easter bunny or an Oktoberfest quartet dressed in lederhosen and wrestling with accordions. I could only stare ahead of me as Nancy, in her pink sweat suit and sturdy tennis shoes, navigated us through the crowds. Whenever Connor or I was distracted by the Sun Glass Hut or the "Your Face on a T-shirt" stand or the waxy platters of Chinese food on display in the food court, Nancy would grab our arms and steer us away from impulse buys and toward the things we came for. She could decipher the mall directory in seconds. I just stared at it, searching for the red "You Are Here" dot.

"Connor, I'm not so sure stores around here sell suits."

"I saw one that might. That Lucky Mart place. You weren't looking."

"We're from Illinois. We're not allowed to shop in Iowa." Perfect reply. I might still be an amateur to parental subterfuge but I'm learning quickly.

"Bull." Connor stops moving, hands on hips. "Try again."

"I don't know your size."

"Boy's medium."

"I don't have cash."

"Charge it."

"Your mother doesn't want you to swim."

Connor stares at me, deciding whether to believe me or not. I see his eyes rimming with tears. He's thinking of his mother. And I'm jealous of a motel pool. The sharp morning sunlight makes the water shimmer like a chandelier. I'd sell my soul to have it drained.

"She said that?"

"No, she didn't. And I'm sorry I said it. I just don't think we have much time to go shopping."

"It's OK. Sometimes, I know I don't think it through." He sits down on the first step of the stairway with his back facing me. The hot summer wind rakes his hair to one side, and I notice the pale, flaky skin of his scalp, lined with tiny dark veins. I know that he has learned that phrase "think it through" from Nancy.

"Listen, Connor. Why don't we take a pair of your jeans and cut off the legs?"

He turns to look up at me, his eyes narrowing, his long sun-bleached lashes bunching together. I think back to what I've said, wondering if I've once again said something inappropriate. "Are you sure that would be alright with Mom? We should find out."

"Fine, but let me ask her myself, OK?" Last night, after we drove the five hours from Chicago, we stopped at the hospital, but Nancy was unable to talk with us. She watched Connor, her eyes following him around as he explored the room, but she did not have the energy to speak. My wife's nurse told me that we have to be careful about her energy. We have to save her energy. In order to calm myself as I sit behind Connor on the steps, I say this to myself over and over. Save the energy. Save the energy.

"I'll tell you what," my son says to me. "I'm sticking around down here. You can go upstairs and watch me from the railing there."

Following orders, I climb up to the second level and stand in front of the doorway to our motel room. Connor walks along a crack in the concrete to the side of the pool. I watch him closely. I have to watch him closely; whenever we're apart, I worry about something horrible happening. Last week, wanting to protect him from anything that would remind him that his mother is sick, I parked Connor by a yellow rocking horse outside of a medical supply store in Chicago. I needed to see what items I could buy at the store for when Nancy came home but I didn't want Connor inside, walking down aisles of oxygen tanks and aluminum walkers and thin, portable beds. I put a quarter into the pony's coin slot and it started to jiggle, more side to side than up and down. "These make me throw up," Connor said, standing behind the thing and watching it shake. Frustrated, I told him I'd be back in five minutes. When I returned empty-handed, the horse was frozen midleap, its front hooves tucked under its porcelain chest. Connor was now all the way to the curb, talking to a beefy police officer who sat in the driver's seat of an idling squad car. "Your son here says he's pretty bored," the officer said, staring at me over the top of his wrap-around sunglasses. "He's that age," I replied, grabbing for the back of his neck. The policeman tilted one thick arm and looked at a metal wristwatch the size of a desk clock. "Twenty minutes bored, according to me." We stared at each other, the cop licking the ends of his mustache and me shuffling on the curb, holding on to my son, afraid that I'd broken some kind of regulation. "Well, sir," I finally said, "that pony there is broken. It doesn't run long enough to keep kids interested." I turned and guided Connor away from the police officer and back to our car, waiting for the siren to start any second.

From up here on the second floor of the Hilltop, with one eye on my son, I can see into some of the other motel rooms. A woman in a brown uniform in a room on the first floor stands over a little girl, braiding her hair. A man in the next room is hunched over a suitcase that rests on the double bed. Inside the case are large vacuum hoses. Directly across from me, two small children in pajamas drop lit matches off the second-floor walkway. This place reminds me of the motels in black and white thrillers where fugitives have sex with lonely waitresses while horns wail on the sound track, but I don't remember ever seeing any kids around in those movies.

A boy has joined my son at the pool area, wrapped in a towel. He's about Connor's age but with crazy red hair and freckles. He removes the towel and slips into the water. Connor, in his street clothes, sits down on a lounge chair and watches the boy dog paddle from one side of the pool to the other. An older man with thick limbs and a tomato-red bathing suit pulled up onto a beer belly walks out to the edge. He stands for a moment, then jumps high into the air and grabs his knees, shouting "CANNON-BALL!" He lands seat-first in the water with a sharp, painful slap. After coming up spitting out water, the red-haired boy paddles out to him and grabs his shoulders. They swim together, the man floating on his back, the child balancing on his father's swollen stomach. Connor moves closer to the water as the man stands on the bottom of the pool, snatches up his son, and throws him. The boy dives into the water and resurfaces, giggling.

I wonder if anybody else is watching this. The vacuum salesman is now standing at his window, holding a drink in his hand. He sees me staring at him. He twirls the ice cubes in his glass and scowls at me. He must be wondering why I'm not down there with my son at the pool, why I'm not letting him swim.

"We . . . don't . . . have . . . suits," I mouth silently, shrugging my shoulders, but the man reaches out and pulls the curtain closed.

Down below, the father has swum over to Connor's side of the pool. The little boy hangs off his father's shoulders and flipper kicks behind him. The man is saying something to Connor. I lean over the railing and try to catch the words. He's saying something about somersaults. My son moves closer to him.

"Yes? Hello?" I call out over the iron railing.

"Hi there," the man calls up to me. "Is he yours?"

I nod my head, wishing this man would not speak so loud in public.

The man puts his hands around his mouth and shouts, "He says he has no bathing suit." I look around to see who else might be listening to this. The two children in pajamas stare at me, waiting for my answer.

In order to keep the man quiet, I quickly take the stairs down to the pool area. Connor sits down and leans over to touch the water. Before I get to him, the man pulls his son off his back and sets him up on dry land.

"Hi, Jim Katz." He stands in the pool and sticks out a hand. "Like the musical."

"Charlie Aspern," I reply, shaking his hand. "Like the headache pill." His palm feels warm and soggy; he won't let go. He pulls me once sharply toward the water.

Chuckling, Jim then helps me regain my balance. "My boy Brad here brought an extra pair of swim trunks."

Connor, biting his top lip, looks up at me, his eyes huge.

"If you want, Connor, go ahead and borrow the suit."

Connor jumps up while Brad grabs a room key from a nearby picnic table. When Brad runs toward the stairs on the opposite side of the motel, Connor follows. They instantly fall into excited conversation. Already they're best friends.

Jim Katz pushes himself up onto the deck and I can see that his trunks are really a pair of boxer shorts printed with naked Cupids, poised to shoot. Even after he has climbed out of the pool, the water is still protesting. It slogs from side to side, overflowing onto the concrete. From my spot on the deck, the pool looks bottomless.

"Hey, you swim, Charlie?"

I stand still, not saying a word, as Jim pulls over two lounge chairs. The truth is I can't even remember the last time I went swimming. Probably on my honeymoon at the Hyatt in Sydney, where Nancy taught me to lift her up out of the water, holding her hips while she balanced her hands on my shoulders. We dove through a tunnel to an underwater bar where we sipped foamy drinks while little waves lapped at our hips. "No," I say to Jim, "I can swim, I just, you know . . . it's for the kids."

Jim shoves one of the loungers behind my legs. "Go ahead, get comfortable. You can be the lifeguard." He wipes off his arms, the water dripping onto the deck, making strange patterns. "I saw you at the hospital last night. With your son. You'd just gotten in."

"At the hospital?"

"My wife's a couple doors down the hall." He leans back onto his lounge chair. "Things are tough for us. It's ovarian."

I turn my head quickly away from him. I'm amazed at how this Katz fellow can throw something like "ovarian cancer" out like a first pitch on opening day. I think of the words I have recently considered taboo: "breast" and "liver" and "inoperable." I could never say these words to a stranger. I couldn't even find the courage to say them to Connor. Nancy had to do it.

"How about you?" Jim asks.

"Me?"

"What're the doctors telling you?"

I concentrate hard, trying to mentally force the boys out of Jim's motel room. We need to shift the focus back to the children. But Jim is waiting for an answer. I have to say something. "Day by . . . ," but I stop before such a horrendous banality can cross my lips. Jim looks at me with wide, concerned eyes. He must think I can't complete a sentence without breaking down. I quickly spit out " . . . by day. Yep, day by day."

Jim corrects the fit of his boxer shorts and leans back. "Well, God can screw you in mysterious ways."

Connor and Brad run back to the pool. My son wears a dark green suit that hangs down to his knees. He holds his clothes in a bundle at his side. I suspect that he has carefully rolled up the clothes so that his underpants are perfectly placed inside and out of sight, the way I used to hide my own underwear when I was in summer camp on the shores of Lake Michigan. But when he gets near, he tosses me the clothes and his underwear flies out, the little swatch of gray cotton landing at my feet. I snatch it up and tuck it between my knees with the other clothes.

After the kids dive in, Jim starts up again. "I thought we had it beat a couple times, Charlie, but cancer is sneaky. Lenore used to be an outpatient. In and out for chemo, then life pretty much back to normal. Then, she got this heavy depression, things got real bad, and they sent her here."

"Lucky you brought two suits," I reply, motioning to the two boys now spinning flips in the water. What are the chances, I think, that Connor and I would end up in the same motel as this Jim Katz and his son? A million to one? Six million to one? What are the odds that Jim and I would both be here at the Hilltop while our wives lie together on the same floor of the University of Iowa hospital? The same as the Scratch Jackpot, the Millionaire Match?

"From the looks of your skin," Jim says, "I say you use Factor 15. Is that right? I'm gonna live dangerously this summer and drop down to a 7." He shows me his tube of lotion and points to the number 7 on the label. "Hey, you checked out that movie theater over in Stallton? Eight screens."

"Holy cow."

"You think that's a lot?"

"That's pretty much . . . yeah, for Iowa."

"That's nothing, Charlie. Absolutely nothing."

"I guess it's not."

"You know, I think Brad's doing real well with everything," Jim says. "He's keeping his chin up."

"Kids have a way," I reply. I'm afraid that this is the extent of my coping skills: imagining myself a player in a television soap opera.

Jim starts talking about Dilaudid, Tylenol 3, and morphine sulfite. I can't listen to this. I nod as he speaks, unsure of how all his words fit together. I concentrate on Connor, memorizing what he can do in the water. Next year, I'll put him on a swim team and I'll have to know what to tell the coach.

Connor's hair is still damp when we get to the hospital. The air-conditioning hums here, covering the sound of heart machines and respirators, raspy coughs and emergency beeps. Nancy's nurse points Connor to the children's playroom, then asks me to sit down with her to go over the things we'll need for terminal home care. I wonder if I should have let Connor go play by himself out of my sight, but I figure hospitals are safe; no police officers here with thick sunglasses and too much time on their hands.

"Don't worry, Mr. Aspern," the nurse says. "We have a care-giver there. He'll be just down the hall." Connor goes off without hesitation, and the nurse shows me into her cubicle. I check the required items on her xeroxed sheet: an inclined, portable bed; folding medical table; IV stand; oxygen tanks. I repeat the list in my head, trying to memorize what we'll need. Bed, table, tanks, stand. Bed, table, tanks, stand.

After the meeting, I go get Connor but he isn't in the playroom. I quickly think of a movie I once saw on late-night television after coming home late from the office. It must have been from the seventies, back when movies had messages. A woman was distracted on the street and didn't see her child disappear into a dark car with tinted windows. The woman ran up and down the street, collapsing in tears, then paid thousands of dollars to a private investigator with whom she promptly fell in love. Connor, like the boy in the movie, is forever gone. I will spend all my money looking for him and marry the child-care provider who is smiling at me now from the inside of a plastic log cabin in the center of the playroom. From somewhere above us, a stereo system plays squeaky nonsense songs. My son, bored with all this, must have gone to Nancy's room.

When I pass the hospital gift shop on the way to oncology, I see Connor wandering the aisles of the store, poking through the plastic flowers and thumbing through racks of fashion magazines. He turns to me when I step to his side but then quickly returns to his walk through the merchandise. I follow him to a rack of pajamas and robes that hang from a metal pole like loose, limp skins. We pass a pile of stuffed farm animals stacked up into a pyramid and a display of greeting cards. Connor looks at several, front and back, and then hands me one. "Look at this," he says.

Below the words "We Are With You" is the silhouette of a family holding hands in front of a sunset. I dig in my pocket for change.

Connor turns away from the display. "I think that card is so lame. It's the dumbest one of all these." Before we leave for Nancy's room, I tuck the card behind a row of others.

I make sure Connor's hair is completely dry before we go into Nancy's room. I let Connor go in first and after a few moments, I push open the door. Nancy is rubbing the length of Connor's thin, soft arm. She whispers to him. When they are through, Connor walks over to look out the window, his back to the room. When I make my way to the bedside, Nancy sinks back into the bed and says she put two swim suits in the bottom drawer of Connor's bureau. She tells me if things are getting too rough for me, I can always call her parents in Florida. They will be coming at the end of the month but Nancy says I can bring them up sooner if I need a break from all this.

"Save your energy," I reply. Nancy puts her fingers on my open palm and makes tiny circles on my skin. I want to tell her about the purple bikini at the motel and ask if she remembers that crazy pool in Sydney. I want to confess that sometimes I know I should say something wise to Connor but the words never come to me. That I'm concerned about not being able to figure out what our son is thinking. But all I can manage is "Save your energy." I repeat these words to her as she closes her eyes, her fingers moving slower around my hand.

On the way back to the motel, driving on the empty interstate, I notice there are no road signs, only acres and acres of cornfields. It's dusk, but my rearview mirror never captures any headlights. Connor is slouched in the passenger seat next to me, his feet up on the dashboard. Again, I want to say something perfect but nothing, absolutely nothing feels right to me. Connor wiggles his toes in his damp socks to some secret rhythm. He looks completely comfortable sitting next to me as I drive, like he's been right there every day of his life. Yet to me, he feels like a stranger.

Finally, he says, "I think Mom needs a new nightgown. I saw an OK one at that store in the hospital."

"Tomorrow," I say, wondering why I didn't think of it, and how in the world my eight year old thought of it instead.

At night, a huge flood lamp illuminates the pool in a dull yellow glow. Moths swarm around the bulb, sucking up the light. From my spot on the lounge chair, I can see the boys underwater, twisting in a cloud of bubbles and paddling their way up to the surface. A hot evening breeze blows over us from the surrounding farms. The smell of manure wafts through the air, mingling with the acrid odor of chlorine.

"Well, Charlie," Jim says, "the night's our oyster." He rustles through a paper bag at his feet. "I'm celebrating tonight. Lenore's CA 125 is moving up. Inching up to normal. How about a beer?"

Jim looks behind us toward the front desk area. The passageway is dark, devoid of management. A bug machine bolted to the concrete wall outside of the lobby glows blue and pops every fifth second or so. Jim pulls out two beer cans from the brown bag. He pops open the tabs on both cans and gives me one. "The boys are great together, huh? Just takes a friendly face to make the medicine go down."

A large semi rumbles by the motel on the interstate. The boys fly into the pool, and water spills over the sides. It's funny to think that I would never have spent time with someone like Jim if it wasn't for our sons. Or our wives. I remember Nancy talking about the other parents at Connor's grade school. The clown school graduate married to the undertaker, the mini-dress mother, the stay-at-home dad with the yarn always trailing from his shoe, all unexpectedly becoming her confidantes. Each from a different galaxy yet connected through children. Now I know what she means.

Jim taps his fingers on his beer can. "By the way, Charlie, what's your trade?"

"I'm a lawyer for the lottery. In Illinois."

"The lottery? Hey, exciting."

"Not really. I'm on a leave of absence for a while. Who knows if I'll go back."

"Try manufacturing industrial glue. Let's switch for a month and then get back to me." Jim chuckles and pushes dents into the sides of his can. "So what's wrong with it?"

"The whole idea of instant millionaires bothers me."

"I sniff envy."

"A third of our winners go bankrupt within three years."

"A good man could eat a hell of a lot of lobster in three years."

"I just don't think lives are meant to be changed so drastically."

Jim takes a swig from his beer can, then wipes his lips. "Yeah, but when they do, you gotta just start loving the lobster."

Behind us, the bug machine zaps an entire swarm of bugs, the electric pops sounding like shots from a tommy gun. The last time I ate lobster was back before Connor was born.

The boys make their way down the edge of the pool, hand over hand, moving closer, splashing water up to our feet.

Jim turns to me. "Let's chicken fight."

"Chicken fight?"

"The boys get on our shoulders. First team down buys more beer."

"I can't. No suit."

"Improvise, Charlie. You wear boxers or briefs?"

"Oh, Jesus. You're going to make me get in, aren't you?"

Connor treads water directly below us. "Come on, Dad."

Slapping the surface of the pool, the boys start chanting.

"Chicken fight!"

"Chicken fight!"

"Chicken fight!"

Before anyone can come out of their motel room and pound on the railings, shouting along with the kids, I strip off my shirt and step out of my pants. Imagining my white Jockey shorts glowing in the dark, I quickly lower myself into the pool. The water swallows up my legs, making my skin tingle. It rises to my stomach, my chest, stealing my breath and squeezing it dry. I hold my hands up. I don't want to get completely wet.

Connor swims to me and climbs onto my back. He pushes down on my head, trying to dunk me in the water. Jim watches me from the deck as I hold my son. His crooked smile makes me think he's planned all this; he looks pleased with his results. He takes a deep breath and performs another one of his cannonballs.

Jim explains the rules: the fathers cannot kick or trip each other; the boys are the only ones who can touch; the first family underwater loses. Brad scurries onto his father's shoulders. With our inexperience as a team, Connor and I appear to be no match for the Katz family. Despite his signature dog paddle, little Brad has proven himself to be quite a swimmer. Jim has powerful legs and a padded belly and his determination has been stoked by cheap beer. With Brad on top of Jim's thick shoulders, they tower over us.

Connor kicks his heels on my chest. He drops his hands on the top of my head, brushing the hair out of my eyes. He bends over to rub my shoulders and arms. I feel the rush of his breath in my ear, the play of his cold fingers on my chest. He touches me like he's been holding me every day of his life.

"Dad, get out of the deep end." Stumbling with Connor's added weight, I move up the slope of the pool closer to where Jim stands. He looks ready for the kill, gripping Brad's legs and staring us down.

"Ready?" asks Brad. I think, He's a carrot-topped pip-squeak. Connor can take him. And his dad sells glue. Let's get 'em.

"Any last words, Charlie?" Jim licks his lips, shifting back and forth, his feet getting a better feel for the bottom of the pool.

"Is it too late for poker?" I grab Connor's calves and try to match Jim's tough stare. The water swirls around our chests.

The Katz duo lunges at us and I lean away. Connor shouts as we tip back. "No, go forward. Forward." My back wrenching from the effort, I pull Connor up and stumble toward the competitors, stubbing my toe on the bumpy concrete bottom.

"Grab on to him, killer," Jim growls, laughing. Like a two-tiered giant, Jim and Brad wobble to one side. They're falling over. At the last second, I see it's a fake-out. Brad twists around and grabs my son's arms, jerking them one way then the other. Everyone is yelling. Water splashes into my face.

I hear Connor's voice cut through the slosh of the waves. "Don't fall, Dad. Hold on tighter." His legs clamp onto my sides and I can feel them pulling me off my feet. Brad yanks Connor down toward the pool.

"Almost, killer, almost."

"Stand up, Dad, stand up."

No longer sure which direction to go, which instructions to follow, I take a sudden gulp of air and squeeze my eyes shut. If I stand with my muscles as tight as possible, we can hold out and win this game. I'm convinced the chicken fight is a test. If I can keep on my feet, holding Connor above the surface, maybe I will be able to care for him by myself and I won't have to send him off to Nancy's parents down in Lake Okeechobee.

Water splashes into my ears, drowning out the shouts, the grunts, the laughter. The backs of Connor's thighs press against my shoulders, and I can sense his racing pulse. My heart is pounding to the same beat. My fingers are digging into his thin ankles, and I feel the blood throbbing in his flesh.

"We got 'em," Jim screams. I open my eyes and see him still standing but thrashing now in the water, Brad above, his teeth clenched.

Yelling "no, no, no," Connor tumbles to the left, his legs still wrapped around me. I try to keep standing but it is impossible. I feel the material of my Jockey shorts—yes, inappropriate swim attire—pull against my crotch. My feet lose their grip on the bottom, and Connor and I crash into the water.

Bubbles rush around my head. The sound of them, a muffled, angry roar, is disorienting. Through the fuzzy blue water, I see the shimmering image of my son as he squirms to right himself. His mouth moves, but underwater, I can only hear the urgent, garbled timbre of his voice. He pushes off from the bottom, his body slicing through the water, and I can see him break the surface.

I drop to the bottom of the pool, blowing out the air that kept me dangling just below the surface. I don't want to face the leering, victorious face of Jim Katz. My disappointed son. I don't want to spend another night alone with my son in a strange hotel room. Another day at the hospital. I feel weak and stupid, so scared of what's to come. A current brushes my stomach, turning me sideways. I feel the hair rising off my head. Free of gravity, pushed by the tiny current in a swimming pool, my skin tingles, the pounding in my heart slows. I close my eyes and let myself drift in darkness.

Then someone grabs me under my armpits. It's Connor, his cheeks round with air, his legs kicking furiously, trying to pull me up. I am too heavy for him, even down here. He pulls his arms back and stares at me, his eyes wide and round, struggling to see through the blue shade of water. He sticks up both thumbs from two small fists and points them up, toward air, then bends his knees and pushes to the surface, showing me how it's done.

When I come up, Connor is waiting for me, his chin bobbing just above water. "Don't joke," he warns me. His legs, still kicking, beat against my thighs. He pushes me once backwards, toward the side of the pool.

Gasping to catch my breath, I take hold of the side. I rest my forehead on the edge and spit out pool water.

Connor swims over to me. "Dad, what happened? Are you mad or something?" My lungs burn from lack of air, my legs ache from defeat, and my eyes sting from chlorine and tears.

"Don't worry," my son says, tilting his head so that he can look straight into my face. "We'll just ask for a rematch." While I quickly think of strategies for the second round of chicken, Connor places his warm hand on my back and makes tiny circles on my skin. I have a vision—quick and cinematic—of a fuzzy science-fiction thriller; the world, spinning in reverse, is ruled by children.

Kelly Cherry &
Dennis Ward Stiles

Charleston Writers' Conference

Poems by Dennis Ward Stiles stopped me in my tracks. I saw that there was nothing I could teach him. I could be a reader, I thought, but that was going to be to *my* benefit, not particularly his. Unless I could bring his work to the attention of other readers, who surely would love about it what I loved about it: intelligence of a life lived in a large world; words so shaped and polished that they are like pebbles in a fast-running stream; the immediacy and drama of personality; a smart heart, wise to paradox, generously accepting of the truth.

Denny Stiles grew up on a dairy farm, flew rescue missions for the U.S. Air Force, and served as a military diplomat in Egypt and Austria. But to be the superlative poet he is, he must always have been, at the same time, a poet at work, studying "the leaping silence" and "the flakes of ash so still / in the cold fireplace."—**Kelly Cherry**

Kelly Cherry is the author of several books of poetry, fiction, and non-fiction, including *My Life and Dr. Joyce Brothers, Time Out of Mind*, and *Writing the World*. She is the recipient of a grant from the NEA, as well as the Poetry Award from the Fellowship of Southern Writers, and her work has appeared in *Esquire, Southern Review*, and *Georgia Review*.

Dennis Ward Stiles served in the U.S. Air Force for thirty years before retiring to Charleston, North Carolina, to write full time. His poetry has appeared in the *Northwest Review, Poetry Northwest, Southwest Review*, and other journals.

Alzheimer's

■ ■ ■ ■ ■ ■ ■ ■ ■ ■ ■

He stands at the door, a crazy old man
Back from the hospital, his mind rattling
Like the suitcase, swinging from his hand,
That contains shaving cream, a piggy bank,
A book he sometimes pretends to read,
His clothes. On the brick wall beside him
Roses and columbine slug it out for space, claw the mortar.
The sun is shining, as it does late in the afternoon
In England, after rain.
Sun hardens the house, reifies it,
Strikes the iron grillwork like a smithy
And sparks fly off, burning in the bushes—
The rosebushes—
While the white wood trim defines solidity in space.
This is his house. He remembers it as his,
Remembers the walkway he built between the front room
And the garage, the rhododendron he planted in back,
The car he used to drive. He remembers himself,
A younger man, in a tweed hat, a man who loved
Music. There is no time for that now. No time for music,
The peculiar screeching of strings, the luxurious
Fiddling with emotion.
Other things have become more urgent.
Other matters are now of greater import, have more
Consequence, must be attended to. The first
Thing he must do, now that he is home, is decide who
This woman is, this old, white-haired woman
Standing here in the doorway,
Welcoming him in.

My Mother's Stroke

■ ■ ■ ■ ■ ■ ■ ■ ■ ■ ■ ■ ■ ■ ■ ■

Your right eye goes blank,
Can't see even the dark.
The dog barks, and you hear
No bark.

Messages your brain sends
Down your left side, derailed,
Never get where they're going,
And the slow slide

Of your whole brain
Is like that of that train
To Southend—
Went straight off at the bend, didn't it,

And into the lake.
But you can still make
The odd, small gesture,
That thought-out investiture

Of movement with sense,
And in your mind, you dance
Under the lake. The puff-fish, the pancake,
Even the devilfish trailing his whispery wake

Nod and bow
As you waltz underwater.
The music bubbles to the surface and me,
Your wondering, admiring, loving, listening daughter.

How We Are Taken

■ ■ ■ ■ ■ ■ ■ ■ ■ ■ ■ ■ ■ ■ ■ ■ ■

*Lines written while thinking of my recently
deceased parents and what they are missing*

How deeply we are taken by the world
And all its glories—how it draws us in,
Until we are surrounded by the pearled
Light of day, the cool transparent resin
Of a clear sky across which the virtuoso
Sun (this image reminds me of my father)
Has swiftly drawn its fine Italian bow,
Espressivo. And breathe—and smell—the rather
Romantic, yet classical air. And feel it too—
This world's beauty present to all our senses,
Surprising them, like guests who jump out at you
From behind chairs and couches, or like sentences
That draw you in and take you where you never
Expected to go and wish you could live forever.

The Almost-Baby

■■■■■■■■■■■■■■■■

It was almost a baby,
Inadvertent tissue
Unexpected
At this late date,

A mere mouse
Of a baby.
We set no bait gates—
They were unnecessary.

The baby dropped down the flue
Of my body, dead
As a sparrow.
I love you more than bone loves marrow.

I love you more than God loves sorrow.
Tomorrow
I'll eat toast and think
About you, the way

You slept on top of me,
Your lips at my breast,
Me smiling, glad and knowing
That my cup was overflowing.

I love you more than
The almost-baby,
More than my populous blood, the well-schooled fish
Egging each other on

In their ovarian currents,
Diving for air.
I love you more than life
Or death, my dear.

Butchering

■ ■ ■ ■ ■ ■ ■ ■ ■ ■

This is a song of amazement

first the delicate dance of execution
the end of the rifle easing around
its tiny track
my father's arm locked up like a stunted wing
the hog wary and finally bored

and down
before the sound of the shot
with a simple hole the size of a fly
staring out of its forehead

then the brutal speed of blooding
the hog going blind on its knees
the hurry of knives under the skin
the whittled armor of fat

the sloppy rhythm of block and tackle
a slit up the belly
a mammoth tumble of guts
into the ransacked snow

the saw searching down the spine
the handful of bonedust
an uneven balance of halves
a heavy pail of heart and liver

and steam from the water
steam from the blood
steam from my father's hands

the hog's last grunt in the air
like a seed
you wish you could plant

Shoe Salesman Tries on an Hour in Church

In the beginning are choir girls
stained red by the light. I think of the songs
they sing on Saturday night.

The minister has a careful voice.
I listen until I can unlatch
the bones in my middle ear.

When the ushers pass the plate
I drop my handful of coins
where they will hit the paper.

I have never
had any money
or serious intentions.

Some days I pray
over a woman's foot
believing in incense and bones.

After the service I wink
at the organist in the mirror.
She is angel enough, and I
am like my father, not meant to sit still.

Outside I dodge hellos.
My weight feels fresh in new loafers.
There are sidewalks leading everywhere.

My Island

■ ■ ■ ■ ■ ■ ■ ■ ■

No one asks questions.
The god of this island
is a total loss
and he knows it.
He makes everything
as easy as he can.

We keep to warm currents.

My wife floats by
with apple on her breath
with blossoms blooming
and wilting in the same hand.

My father comes up
smiling with his anger
looped around his wrist.
He draws me
a map in the sand.

My mother brings gifts
which she opens herself
and throws away.

Even the sharks are given
to tears. Turtles sing.
Butterflies do the arithmetic.

I am devout
and devoted. I fish
for poems, throw out a line
with the hook in my tongue.

Notes on a Poet at Work

He studies the silence in bathtubs
the smaller silence in cups
the mute shadow in thimbles

the silence in knees
on a bus
the crooked silence in hanging coats

the silence in smooth water

the leaping silence
that beams from his flashlight

the flakes of ash so still
in the cold fireplace.

He studies dawn's great stealth
before he is quite awake
not yet ready
for any echo of what he has learned.

Stephen Dunn &
Maureen Noelle McLane

Bennington Writing Workshops

My dream as a workshop teacher is to be so taken over by a poem that I'm not compelled to read like a critic. Maybe that's simply any reader's dream. The fact is, of course, that the critic in me is usually activated immediately—with, say, the first imprecision, the first clunky rhythm. What I dream of is for a Maureen McLane to come along, to be carried through a poem from start to finish by her kind of authority. She has what is unteachable, a voice, which is to say she allows us to hear in the way she wants us to hear how the poem discloses itself. In "The Secret History of Rock-n-Roll," for example, there's no moment that doesn't signal its tone.

These are poems, we can say, with an attitude. We can hear her *thinking* in them—countering, playing off of, refining—and a large part of their pleasure exists in how unpredictable that thinking is. But as much as they think out loud they also suggest some informing grievance behind them, something that's pushing them toward their surprising clarities. Needless to say, I felt lucky to encounter her and her poems at Bennington this past summer. Her work is both talented and substantial.—**Stephen Dunn**

Stephen Dunn's collection of poems, *Local Time*, was selected for the National Poetry Series. He is the author of nine books of poetry, including his most recent *New and Selected Poems: 1974–1994*. He teaches at Richard Stockton College in Pomona, New Jersey.

Maureen Noelle McLane is a Ph.D. candidate in English literature at the University of Chicago and an editor on the Poetry Board of the *Chicago Review*. Her essays and reviews have appeared in the *Chicago Review* and *Erato*.

At the School for the Deaf

■ ■

After three days watching their slangy, fast-
   fingered exuberant talk,
then their slow, crude placement of words

on paper, I wanted only to reach the girl
   who'd do nothing
I asked. One morning she gave in,

wrote "Silence has a rough, crazy weather"
   and shoved the paper at me,
this hearing person she didn't trust.

Oh I loved her for her resistance
   and her great small truth,
and she knew it, kicked the nearest chair

when I looked her way, turned her face
   into stone.
She must have known how soon

I'd retreat into my other, easier world
   and—in weather like hers—
what compliance she couldn't afford.

There've been others smart enough
   not to let themselves
be loved by me, but I can't remember

wanting so hard what I couldn't get;
   one more line, I'd sign,
one more word. She wouldn't lift her hand.

Her classmates flashed fingers at her.
   She flashed back
expletives anyone could understand.

Empathy

■■■■■■■■

Once in a small rented room, awaiting
a night call from a distant time zone,
I understood how one might feel
bereft enough, say, to get a tattoo.

Some mermaid on my biceps. Company
forever. Flex, and she'd dance.
The phone never rang, except for those
phantom rings, which I almost answered.

I was in D.C., on leave from the army.
It was a woman, of course, who didn't call.
Or, as we said back then, a girl.
It's anybody's story.

But I think for me it was the beginning
of empathy, not a large empathy
like the deeply selfless have,
more like a leaning, like being able

to imagine a life for a spider, a maker's
life, or just some aliveness
in its wide abdomen and delicate spinnerets
so you take it outside in two paper cups

instead of stepping on it.
The next day she called, and it was final.
I remember going to the zoo
and staring a long time

at the rhinoceros, its enormous weight
and mass, its strange appearance
of tranquillity.
And then the big indignant cats.

Then I went back to Fort Jackson.
I had a calendar taped inside my locker,
and I'd circle days for which I
had no plans, not even hopes—

big circles, so someone might ask.
It was between wars, and only the sergeants
and a few rawboned farm boys
took learning how to kill seriously.

We had to traverse the horizontal ladder,
rung after rung, to pass
into mess hall. Always the weak-handed,
the weak-armed, couldn't make it.

I looked for those who didn't laugh
at those of us who fell.
In the barracks, after drills,
the quiet fellowship of the fallen.

Power

■ ■ ■ ■ ■ ■ ■

It comes to this; dwarf-throwing contests,
dwarfs for centuries given away
as gifts, and the dwarf-jokes

at which we laugh in our big, proper bodies.
And people so fat they can't
scratch their toes, so fat

you have to cut away whole sides of their homes
to get them to the morgue.
Don't we snicker, even as the paramedics work?

And imagine the small political base
of a fat dwarf. Nothing to stop us
from slapping our knees, rolling on the floor.

Let's apologize to all of them, Roberta said
at the spirited dinner table. But by then
we could hardly contain ourselves.

Road Stop

■ ■ ■ ■ ■ ■ ■ ■ ■

Not all laundromats are sad.
Back in the Village, the one I frequented
was a place to read and watch what women
turn on the delicate cycle for.
I was younger then and wanted to live
in a city, and count myself among
the fashionably poor. Now these women
at the Wash 'N Dry, fingering their coins
in this terrible brightness, just seem tired.
Maybe all the women back on Bank Street
were tired; I wouldn't have noticed.
Maybe all women everywhere are tired
and even their loveliest, flimsy things
sometimes feel like burdens to take off—
late at night, say, in the wrong mood,
and someone waiting with a smile.
Today these machines look like
the secured masks of deep sea divers,
and what whirls in them is controlled
confusion, which each of us understands.
I mix my whites and darks together,
as I always do, and a young woman
with a child and a *Live Free or Die*
T-shirt says No, that's bad.
I tell her I'm interested in speed.
I don't say I've a house
with a washing and drying room, or
my clothes are old enough not to bleed.
Nor do I say I haven't been
to a laundromat in twenty years.
This could be a bus station

the way the solitary faces stare, but she
has a child to scold, no time to stare.
I'm far from home. There's no telling
how I look to those who look so hard
or what, to them, my laundry reveals.
Here's a clean man, they could be thinking.
He must have done something wrong.

The Sensualist's Fast

■ ■ ■ ■ ■ ■ ■ ■ ■ ■ ■ ■ ■ ■ ■ ■ ■

I feel light enough to rise
and the pain satisfies a part of me
that likes clean arguments,
the shortest distance
between sensation and idea.

Three days now, and I understand
the sumptuousness of denial.

Purists, don't count me among you.
This has just been another thing
for the body to know and take in,

a cool, dry wind
for a hidden flame.

The Secret History of Rock-n-Roll

So what's your favorite band? inquires the girl who'll never be
my own best friend, and I rouse myself to blurt out *Beach Boys*,
proving I will be forever out of touch. And: Are you gay?
Well I suppose I'm happy enough. I knew I'd answered
wrong. The whisperings and smothered laughs confirmed it.
My favorite band? I couldn't really say. My parents liked
the Beach Boys, that was all. I had no taste. I had no
likings. It took everything to stay afloat in the mysterious sea
of the classroom, everything not to sink into my own inchoate self.
Inchoate? I did not use such words, I had few words, I tried out
new ones here and there, at dinner, said *vehement*, said it
wrong and made my father laugh as he would later when I stuffed
my bra with Kleenex. Did he laugh or did he sneer? I think
it was a laugh; I took it as a sneer, forever suspicious, forever
martyred, bearing always ahead of myself the plate where I would place
my head whenever it came off, so sure it would. Don't bite
my head off, my sister said when mother snapped. All of us afraid
of others' mouths, the teeth, the words, but most of all the secret
coiling things at the throat's back, waiting for the time, the exposed
neck, to strike.
                    But is it generational, the history
of rock-n-roll, or anti-generational, or? My mother should have done
the Twist, she should have loved the Beatles, but mother plays
Glenn Miller and she worships Guy Lombardo. My mother born
too late, she says, for her time. Her regret is boundless, has a swing,
obeys its own conductor. That song takes me back to . . . what?
To what you never had? To what was always lost?
                                        The early childhood
drift, the later haze when all I loved and fiercely was my sister
and she had to bear it, how I made her sing, made her call
refrains when I bathed her, some deeply moving ballad

by the Eagles or Carole King; I wanted no one to touch her
but me, eight years old, touch her perfect toddler's body
which I towel-dried only after: *Sing that song, sing
it*, and she would to stop the goosebumps bursting all along
her pinkish dripping skin. I rocked her in the towel when she complied.
She recalls this too, recalls it wryly as she will, enters it
in the list of sufferings she was made to undergo and got through
more or less.

        We don't much talk, but when we do we talk
about her music, hiphop now, alternative before. She sleeps
with headphones on, she says it calms her, says she can't relax
to silence or to anything but this. But what about the words,
I ask, the words—don't they upset you? I don't care
about the words, she says; words come later—first
the sound.

        The canopy over the bed, the stuffed
animals, the posters on the bedroom wall, and the gangbanging
motherfuckers blaring from the boombox: all arise in her,
she holds it all, holds herself apart from me, from mother,
from all the women who would make her listen.

Dorothys

■ ■ ■ ■ ■ ■ ■ ■ ■

1. DOROTHY WORDSWORTH

She knew she'd have to kill someone; most days
she managed not to. The small animals
piled up torn and dead in the very back
of her mind. One day she would see a bird,
stone it, pick it up, lay it on his bed,
or better still: hang it round his neck.
A wedding gift from one who never came.
O the albatross, the albatross:
she could never get it off her mind.
Dorothy took to her bed, the wedding
passed; she ever after called the new wife
"darling sister." She keeps the apple core
her William left and fingers it at night;
she's the antiquarian of all
he left behind. Her insides rot, her flesh
distends, and as the years go by she falls
farther from herself and him. One day the core
gives out. Fat and gone she stays in bed
for years until she dies, a grotesque burden
on the ones who say they love her best.

2. DORA'S CASE

She has found it terribly difficult,
this business of living with them all.
Each morning Mother rustles through the hall,
trailing fingers on the wood for dust:
she beats the ones who leave the dirt behind.
Mother is ever so clean, so precise.
And then there is Father, miraculous

man; and then the close friends, the very dear
friends, who summer with them yearly by the sea.
This autumn she hurls herself before a train
and lives, stupefied by her own desire;
Mother and Father distinctly displeased
send her to the learned physician, strange
neurologist who will pick the bleak locks
of her mind. She dreams, they talk, she dreams,
he guesses she's in love with all of them.
Oh it's too too true, Dora wants to fuck
them all, the friend, his wife, Father, Mother,
but especially the captivating
doctor. Greedy greedy child, wanting all
to go her way, and most trying in denying
this is so. She keeps her heart encased
in Mother's jewelry box; she opens
it most nights to check that it's still there.
In dreams the flames are burning up the box.

3. DOROTHY NEVER LEFT HOME
She saw the pigs rutting and never got
over it, the grunt and strain and squealing
thrust. One would think a farm girl would have known.
Sometimes to scare herself she walks atop
the pig-pen fence; if she's not careful she
could fall into the muck. Today she skims
her magazines, fingering herself on her bed
until she spasms absent-mindedly. Below
the creaking bedsprings lies the mutt who yaps
at everyone but her. She thinks the farm
may turn to dust; she hopes it will and stops
herself. Her hand lies still and cold. She scans
the ads and bios, flips the pages splayed
across her bed. The stars call from the wall.
She posts another up there, makes a wish.
In the kitchen aunt and uncle hum.
She throws her moonbeam face into the glass;
the mirror throws it back, remote and flat.

Somewhere, somewhere else the stars are smiling.
A storm brews, a witch's pot; what knocks
her out is knowing there's no way to leave
and no one ever crashes into Kansas.

The Doubter

■ ■ ■ ■ ■ ■ ■ ■ ■ ■ ■

He doesn't know
what she wants
so he asks
what she wants.

She says I want
this, maybe;
next week she says
something else.

No, I want that
definitely.
He doesn't know
if it's true.

He asks how
she feels. He wonders
how he feels
to her, nights.

She says oh
you know, good.
Very good!
Terrific.

Still he doubts.
He smothers it
almost; it thrives.
Another night

he asks again.
How is it?
Are you happy?
She smiles, blinks.

He cares too much
for words. She wants
to be left alone
with him

in silence.
But he can't be
sure. He hopes.
He decides

he will decide
what he knows
for sure. He knows
how she feels

pulsing against him.
He knows he knows
how he feels.
Couldn't he assume

she feels the same?
Isn't she like him?
Is it possible
he could know?

Why ask?
Why speak?
He needs to rest.
She turns to the wall.

Take a walk
he tells himself.
He takes himself
for a walk.

Beneath his feet
the ground is sure.
The inhuman ground
lays itself out.

Linda Gregg &
Gray Jacobik

Rhode Island Poetry Workshop

One of the most interesting things about the poems of Gray Jacobik is the abundance of their spirit. There is a sensuousness of language married to unabashed passion and the richness of her mind. It is a pleasant surprise in this time when so much poetry seems conceptual and distanced. Jacobik's poems echo D. H. Lawrence on the one side and Colette on the other: the striving in Lawrence for mindless absoluteness through sexuality, and the effortless (always intelligent) merging with the body's consciousness. In poems like "Skirts" and "Sandwoman," Jacobik captures female awareness in its physical magnitude and celebrates the larger, often ecstatic, victory beyond that.—**Linda Gregg**

Linda Gregg has published four books of poetry, most recently *Chosen by the Lion*. She has been a Guggenheim Fellow and has taught at Syracuse University, the University of Iowa, and the University of Houston. Her work has appeared in the *Atlantic, Antaeus*, and the *Nation*.

Gray Jacobik is an associate professor of literature and serves as poet-in-residence at Eastern Connecticut State University. She has work forthcoming in the *Georgia Review, Ploughshares*, and *Prairie Schooner*. In 1993 she received an NEA fellowship.

On the Other Side of Love

■■■■■■■■■■■■■■■■■■■■■■

There is the sound of creekwater under
the trees in a transparent darkness
called shade. Deer trails wander up
the mountain in the raw light and wind.
The sky is a blank blue, and above that what?
And above that? The valleys are visible
for a long way, then the ocean.
What stands? Which stand?
We die and harry on our way to it,
ready for union with something.
God or death, only the hunger stays.
The path goes down to an empty house
full of day, of gods gone, of ghosts,
the momentary reality of deer,
and a hawk hovering in the steepness.

Hephaestus Alone

■ ■ ■ ■ ■ ■ ■ ■ ■ ■ ■ ■ ■ ■ ■

The fine sounds of nature come through
the open windows night and day, hurting me.
The moon and sun, all that is elemental
keep the pain alive. My heart is like a boat
that sets forth alone on the ocean and goes
far out from me, as Aphrodite proceeds
on her pleasure journeys. I pour the gold
down the runnels into great mysteries
under the sand. When I pull it up by the feet
and knock off the scale, it is a god.
What is it she finds with those men
that equals this dark birthing? I make
each immortal manifest while the deities
remain invisible in their pretty gardens
of grass and violets, of daffodils and jasmine.
Even my wife lives like that. Going on yachts,
speaking to the captains in the familiar.
Let them have it, the noons and rain and joy.
I make a world here out of frog songs
and packed earth. Look, I have made even
my wife so she contains the green-fleshed
melons of Lindos, thalo blue of the sea,
and one ripe peach at five in the morning
when the sun woke me. You see, I know
all that. How the whitewash on the houses
of Paros is made from the marble dust
of statues. I fashioned her by the rules,
with love, made her with rage and disillusion.

The Calves Not Chosen

■■■■■■■■■■■■■■■■■■■

The mind goes *caw, caw, caw, caw*,
dark and fast. The orphan heart
cries out, "Save me. Purchase me
as the sun makes the fruit ripe.
I am one with them and cannot feed
on winter dawns." The black birds
are wrangling in the fields
and have no kindness, all sinew
and stick bones. Both male and female.
Their eyes are careless of cold and rain,
of both day and night. They love nothing
and are murderous with each other.
All things of the world are bowing
or being taken away. Only a few calves
will be chosen, the rest sold for meat.
The sound of the wind grows bigger
than the tree it's in, lessens only
to increase. *Haw, haw* the crows call,
awake or asleep, in white, in black.

The Center of Intent

■■■■■■■■■■■■■■■■■

Is there a lesson in the way this new silence lasts?
Is it like the river's genius for making the water
the same shape constantly as it pours between these
two boulders? This silence has the power to wreck,
but cannot eat away the foulness in the chasm
of the flesh, the perishing between the beginning
and the end of love. Where is the fineness of God?
Why is he away? Is He all or none, as different
from us as the ocean from the stars? Is there
some reason why the bird is always hungry and the body
never gone? Is there some explanation for the odor
of the sea grass here? Do the hot hills understand
the story of the heart? Why must we bow down,
yield to the flowering? Maybe love is the Lord's trap.
Maybe He sees us as the tree leaning over the stream.
Perhaps He can't experience the difference between
our pain, our loneliness, and the heron flying
through the special silence at evening.

Sappho's Voice

■ ■ ■ ■ ■ ■ ■ ■ ■ ■ ■ ■ ■

I love the traffic of percussives in her voice,
her susurrations, her fricatives, the wave slaps
and ululations that run counterpoint, polyphonous

syllables that lift to words that run to sentences
so dazzling in intonation, one thinks of angels
with silver tablets on their silver laps composing

under olive trees in the Mediterranean
of the soul's true home. Well, she is a perfect
creature, a *criatura*, formed for poetry's sake,

so one ought to expect her voice to spill
across her lips as fluidly as water slips across
a lip of fountain stone or drips from the tips

of olive leaves after summer storms. I would
lick each drop, each word as it slips, filling
my spirit with the sound of her good sense.

Can grace turn on a voice, the way a body turns,
grace and the body in a kind of auditory spin,
or spinning flight that makes sound waves its sky?

Her voice leaps with light turned back upon itself,
light turning to sound then back to light;
now desire, now the mind's surrender to desire.

The Chinese Chestnut Breeze

The fragrance weaves through the painter's studio,
surrounds the bright-white canvas on her easel.
Perhaps she's a nihilist, or an existentialist,

bound to project an unrivaled view. No lines.
No colors. No shapes except the chaste format:
An oblong so long it shows the full extension

of her history. Perhaps she has painted the light
we pass into when we meet pure extinction.
In she walks. Observes and waits. She turns on

Handel's water music. Black cat flexes then sleeps
on the windowsill, framed by the many-tasseled
green canopy awash in wind. Some say the smell

is pleasing-sweet; some are sickened by it, the tree
blooming in spiral clusters that flop open in jumbled
arrays. Too much. Too sexual. Provoked by Handel,

the painter's caged starling sings. At last, the dichotomies
have aligned themselves in sensuous display:
light and dark; sound and silence; sweetness, sickness.

Sandwoman

■■■■■■■■■■■

The woman lay firm in the damp berm of the beach;
she flowed into it and was contiguous with it,
was, in fact, formed of it. The sky chinked through
its hours, its gradations of sky-hues, the azures,
ceruleans, deeper blues, and the golds and roses
of evening. Sky was all she could see, all she
opened her legs to, all her breasts and belly strove
to touch. The sum of her changes were color
and cloud until the lips of the sea reached her,
those lascivious lips bruised by the moon.
Seaform threw its lace shawl over her shoulders
and fans shrouded her face. Slowly, slowly,
in licks and then sometimes in spills, the sea
overcame her, her wavy hair running down the beach,
right breast and then left breast crumbling like turrets.
Waves gathered back the seaweed of her pubis
then licked at her sex until she dissolved the way,
so tasted, all women dissolve. She had given her
heart to the blinding smack of noonday light
and to the soft coruscations of the lamb-back clouds
that traversed her body through the late afternoon,
so she was only a shadow by night. Still the one who
shaped her with hands, and the other who shaped her
with mind, saw how the whole of the erotic
had contoured her limbs, sculpted her face,
teased wide the splay of her legs, and each knew
that love and the body are like sand, open and
vulnerable and enduring until the tide shifts.

Skirts

■ ■ ■ ■ ■ ■

Women spin and dance in skirts, sleep and wake
in them sometimes, ascend and descend stairs.
Some have walked into the sea in skirts,
which is like tossing a skirt over a man's head,
or pressing his face against the tent of one.
Some woman—maybe wearing a velvet skirt—
has embraced another woman, so that one skirt brushes
against another. Women wash and wring and hang
skirts up to dry, spray them, iron them, hem them,
slip them over slips, over tights. Once, I confess,
I owned six black ones: rayon, wool, gabardine,
linen, cotton, silk. The wind can blow the bulk of a skirt
between a woman's legs, or wrap her in a twist,
or billow underneath so skirls of wind touch faintly,
delightfully. Some women hear skirts murmuring or
sighing, or conversing with the flesh they cover.
But most skirts drape in silence, the silence of slow
snow falling, or the hushed liquid glide of a woman's
body through a sunlit pool, the sweet descent
to sleep, or passion, or passion's nemesis, ennui.
A woman's spirit lengthens or widens in a skirt,
magnified by cloth and cut and her stride through
the quickened space. If instead a woman wears
a tight skirt, she feels containment and its
amplification—reduction's power to suggest.
Right now my favorite is a crimpy cinnabar silk
I twist into wrinkles to dry. I wear it walking in
the evenings. I vanish as its folds enfold the sky.

Pam Houston &
Roy Parvin

Napa Valley Writers' Conference

Roy Parvin writes like an angel. His stories are deep and dark, rich with metaphor, shot through with grizzly humor, playful, intense, strange. His prose is rhythmic and dense, intoxicating but never inaccessible . . . there's little to say except that he hears the music, always in his head. And he loves words, loves the way they jangle together, loves the obscure detail, the minorly tragic, the moment when the small ugly thing turns, for only an instant, strong and beautiful, loves the edges and courts them, relentlessly in every line.

Roy is full to overflowing with the one part of the writing process that cannot be taught to anyone: he is driven by the cadence he hears in his head, he is a slave to that music, he loves words, loves story like other men love cars and women, and the result of that passion is stories that are always fresh, always surprising, deeply satisfying, and almost too beautiful to bear.—**Pam Houston**

Pam Houston's two books are *Cowboys Are My Weakness* (stories) and *Women on Hunting: Essays, Fiction, and Poetry*. Her work has appeared in *The Best American Short Stories 1990* and in *Mademoiselle*, the *Cimarron Review*, and *Quarterly West*.

Roy Parvin lives in a remote wilderness cabin in the California Trinity Alps and has published work in *Turnstile*. "May" is part of his collection of stories, "The Loneliest Road in America."

Eight Days in the Brooks Range
with April and the Boys

■■■■■■■■■■■■■■■■■■■

It is 7:00 A.M. on Easter Sunday when we take off in a nine-seater airplane on a charter flight out of Fairbanks, Alaska, and our pilot, Fred, turns the nose to the north. North to the Brooks Range, north to the valley of the Sagavanirktok River, north to an airstrip two hundred miles above the Arctic Circle, a place still waist deep in winter, the place we will sleep and eat and explore by dogsled for the next eight days.

It is a sparkling blue morning, and we fly low, first over the mighty Yukon River, then the smaller Koyukuk, then up into and among the peaks of the Brooks Range, in view of the Gates of the Arctic, and over the Chandalar Shelf. Still to the north is Atigun Pass, our corridor to the other side of the Brooks Range, and the frozen treeless netherworld of Alaska's North Slope.

I am traveling with my friends Roy and Janet, the two people most responsible for pulling me through a San Francisco winter fraught with too much loneliness and too much rain, with death threats and lawsuits and an accompanying faithlessness I've never known the likes of before.

Wild places have always healed me. But the prescription I've written again and again—adrenaline-producing adventure combined with the dramatics of landscape—has an acid test in store for itself this time. It is Easter Sunday and I want a resurrection. I want to rise out of the mire of the most difficult winter of my life in this, my thirty-third year, and sail over the Arctic tundra on wings like a clearheaded angel.

"Nice place to be on Easter Sunday," Fred says, just at the moment it seems to me that our wing tips will brush the snow from the rock walls on either side of Atigun Pass, and I agree. I see the shadow our plane makes against a massive cornice, smaller than a speck of dust.

"Not much of a pass, really, is it?" he says, as the landscape opens below us and the snowy plain slopes northward toward the frozen Arctic Sea. We can see a flat patch of snow that passes for an airstrip, and beside it two miniature pickup trucks, their engines making tiny exhaust clouds in the

−11° morning, one of them piled high with the boxes that make up a Husky Hotel.

"It makes you think people aren't meant to be up here," Fred says, "when the land makes them look that small."

As we step from the plane the temperature hits us like a jolt of adrenaline, freezes the insides of our noses and eyes. We meet first Brandon, our outfitter, who is wolfish and handsome. He's telling wilderness stories before the hellos are finished, full of a kind of energy that says "this man was born to spend his life outdoors."

Bill Mackey, the dog handler, offers only a shy hello. He is himself more sled dog than man and bears the countenance of someone from another place, another century. He is quiet and kind with eyes that don't miss anything, that reveal an innate goodness, a knowledge of what it means to live well. His brother Dave and his father, Dick, are both Iditarod champions, and Bill places high in the years he chooses to run. He tends to each of the thirty-six dogs that will carry us as if this were the Iditarod. Seventy-two eyes stay fixed on him constantly as if at any moment he will start distributing T-bones. The dogs wag their tales in unison when he so much as looks in their direction, and they stand as tall as they can when he walks past them, hoping his hand might drop to their shoulder for a pat along the way.

While Brandon and Bill get the sleds ready, the rest of us fumble through our packs with rapidly freezing fingers and in moments we are more correctly layered than we have ever been in our lives. On top I wear a Capilene undershirt, a long-sleeved pile T-shirt, a pile pullover, then another, a down vest, a Gortex anorak, and finally a parka with a huge fur-rimmed hood. On the bottom it's Capilene, pile, pile, pile, and Gortex. On my hands are silk liners, wool gloves, then down-and-leather mittens. On my head a neck gaiter, a balaclava, a face mask, and a bomber hat with flaps that close under my chin. My pack is almost empty and the volume of the outfit I'm wearing is exceeded only by its value. I am leaning on a pickup truck two hundred miles above the Arctic Circle, and I've never been more expensively dressed in my life.

Brandon asks us if we've come with full water bottles and when we say no the look on his face gives us all a little lesson in respect for the place we find ourselves. We have tried to outsmart the cold by bringing pencils instead of pens and plenty of extra camera batteries. But something as simple as unfrozen water has never entered our minds.

"It's okay," Brandon says. "We'll make water first thing tonight in camp, after we get the tents set up and the stove going."

Bill's got the dogs divided into teams now and harnessed, and they are pulling hard at the sleds, which are tied to the trucks' bumpers with quick-release straps and anchored to the snow with big metal hooks. In a few moments we will leave the trucks behind and commit ourselves to eight days in a place where it's a big project to make a drink of water. The cold is already creeping into my fingers and toes.

Bill is showing me how my brake works and where to put my feet and hands on the sled.

"April, Blue, Paint, Blackie, Silo," he says, pointing to one dog at a time. "If you lose their attention it's a good thing to call them by their names."

"Lose their attention?" I say.

"April is in your lead position. She's got a lot of village blood in her, a lot of Eskimo dog. It makes her very smart and a little hardheaded. If we pass caribou she may decide to kind of peel off." He makes an arc with his hand. "You might have to remind her . . ."

These are more words than Bill has spoken all day.

"Ready?" he says, and before I've nodded he's pulled the quick release and we're sailing along as if suddenly weightless. The sled, loaded to the gills with sleeping bags, camp gear, and dog food, skitters across the snow as if it's filled with feathers. I learn fast how to shift my weight like a water skier, how to lean into the corners and brace for the bumps, how to use the brake to keep from running over Blackie and Silo on the long downhills.

The dogs are running hard, pulling at their harnesses, tails wagging in time to each step. Every now and then April throws a glance over her shoulder at me, checking me out, and I try to maneuver the sled in a way that meets with her approval. When I have enough confidence to look behind me I see Janet and her dogs racing toward me, the same icy and surprised smile on her face that I know is on mine.

Surrounding us now there are only varying degrees of whiteness: the blue-white sky, the pure white tundra, the distant snow-deep mountain peaks, somehow whiter still. When I was a child flying in airplanes I wanted nothing more than to climb out the window and jump into all that fluffy whiteness. The only thing that would have made it better, had I the power to imagine it, would have been to be pulled through that wonderland by a pack of smart and happy dogs.

"Stand on your brake hard!" comes Bill's voice from the front of the line, and I'm snapped back to the present just in time to see his sled disappear over the lip of a canyon. In seconds we are flying, straight down the side of a hill as long and as steep as anything I'd care to ski. It's all I can do to keep my sled behind the dogs, to stay upright myself at that speed, as the sled twists and leaps over bumps and drifts. Then the ground levels out and I dare to look up and I see we've entered a massive canyon decorated with the looping ribbon of a frozen river, punctuated with side canyons, narrow and dramatic, crowned to the south by a ring of deeply serrated peaks.

We stop at the bottom of the hill, breathless, amazed at ourselves for not falling, amazed even more by what's around us: infinity softened by sun. A cold wind blows upstream from the Arctic Ocean and cuts like a switchblade through all our layers.

"We'll make camp as soon as we hit the river," Bill says. And the dogs leap to attention at the sound of his voice.

Our tents are called Arctic ovens. They are big and well insulated, and they come equipped with tiny stoves. Since there are no trees on the North Slope we have brought enough Duraflame logs to burn one per evening. We follow Brandon's instructions to saw our log into three pieces, to burn one third at 9:30, one third at midnight, and the final third at 6:00 A.M. Though they smell a little toxic, the logs are like miracles. We can sit in the tent in only two layers instead of five.

The next morning we leave our camp at the river and take the empty sleds across the Sagavanirktok Plain toward Atigun Gorge. The lightened sleds skid across the snow more easily than ever, and I am at my dogs' mercy, my brake having almost no effect at all. As mushers, we are improving, and Bill gets less careful about the terrain he chooses. By the time we've been under way for an hour we're bouncing over buried tundra tussocks and climbing and descending riverbanks and we've all face planted at least one time.

We learn fast the single most important rule of dog sledding: Don't ever let go of the sled. The challenge is to remember this as we are falling, to make a dive for the runner with some part of our over-clothed bodies, to let ourselves be dragged, the snow filling our parkas, our cameras bumping along underneath us, till we can get a leg back around to the runner, or claw with our arms up the back of our sleds.

Once inside Atigun Gorge the wind stills and the going gets easier. A small herd of caribou come down the hillside to greet us, curious. When they get our scent they spring straight into the air and bound away.

"If we're lucky we'll see Dall sheep in this canyon," Bill says, and it's not five minutes until I do see them: eleven rams, no more than pinpoints on the horizon but unmistakable. It is better than winning the Publishers Clearing House Sweepstakes, being the one to spot those sheep, and I keep my eyes on the hillsides the whole rest of the day.

We see twenty-five sheep in all, and a set of wolverine tracks, and a whole flock of ptarmigan taking flight at once, still in their winter whites, only a touch of brown in the tip of their tails. We climb high enough to get a glimpse of the Pipeline, snaking its surreal way across the horizon on its path to the oil fields in Prudhoe Bay.

We're almost back down to the mouth of the canyon when something makes me look up and I see who Brandon calls "the big guy in the brown suit" on the horizon. A full-grown grizz, all 8 feet and 750 pounds of him, keeping up with us at an easy lope just one layer of canyon formation above. Adrenaline surges through me and I shout to Bill, wave my arms to Janet, lose my sled, and drop my camera, wind up stuck waist deep in snow and stranded, but still getting to watch him run across the top of the scree. The blond tips of his dark coat gleam in the sunlight, and the rhythm of his lope makes a mantra in my head: life is good, life is good. We watch him climb to the next higher layer of canyon, then up and over an ice flow and beyond the canyon rim.

Already, I am thinking of these dogs as mine. April is my brilliant child, bossy, confounding, a little aloof. Blue is the melancholy one, the poet, with eyes the color of glacier water in June. Silo is my bruiser, always picking fights with Blackie, who is the invisible one, wholly dedicated to the task of turning dog power into mileage mushed. And Paint . . . Paint is my special child, a product of accidental inbreeding. He's sweet and lovable and dumb as a box of rocks. Mornings, when we are about to take off, he barks so hard he flips himself over, tangling his harness so badly that we are always the last sled to leave.

On the third day, it's warmer, and the river ice has an inch or more of water on top that sloshes between the feet of the dogs. The ice groans and creaks under the weight of the sled and April slows a little, feeling her way across ground she's not sure is solid. Paint misunderstands and keeps barreling into her, behavior she corrects with a couple of nips to his ears.

Up until now the rivers have been frozen white and crystalline, but today for the first time we see a hint of blue below the surface. At one place the water has pushed the ice up, welled itself into an igloo shape, fifteen feet high and gleaming, and I wonder about our nearness to it, and watch it for a sign.

"Spring's a comin'," is all Bill says when we go by.

When we turn back for camp below a peak they call Cloud we make a figure eight with the sleds that is truly a thing of beauty: the bright colors of our Gortex, the crisscrossing of the sleds, the thin line of dogs reaching homeward against all that vast bright white.

Then April finds a caribou carcass and dives for it, the rest of the team close in tow. They get so tangled I have to unhook Blue before I can move them, and Blue, an escape artist, wriggles free of my hands. I dive for him successfully but wind up face down in the caribou carcass. Paint thinks this is a wonderful game and dives hard on top of me, Silo close on his heels. We are all so tangled, my dogs and I, that Brandon has to rescue us. I can hear Roy's happy laughter behind me. From the top of a nearby hill Bill waits and watches, graceful, even when his sled is still. In the cock of his head there is more than amusement; even at this distance he sees everything essential his dogs are giving to me. In minutes we're back up and traveling. April grins at me over her shoulder. I want this trip never to end.

In the evenings we sit in the cook tent and tell stories. Brandon's got beautiful forearms and crazy eyes and tells a better story than anyone I have ever known, though both Roy and I take turns trying to give him a run for his money. I've got the range, and Roy's got the ruthlessness, but Brandon's got a cast of Alaskan bushmen, better sound effects than Universal Studios, and a penchant for turning a day hike into a life-threatening event. The only thing that interrupts the stories is the barking during Bill's nightly feeding, and we wait to take up the talking until we've heard the after-dinner chorus—thirty-six little voices, howling their thanks.

On day four we break camp and travel farther upvalley, through a place where the whole Sagavanirktok River squeezes through a slot canyon, above which lies a whole new landscape of steeper canyon walls and higher peaks. We spend hours moving on ice which today is wetter still and covered with thin sheets of crust that shatter under the dogs' feet into shapes like petals, the sleds weaving the softest trail imaginable in their wake.

I am grateful for the way this landscape demands my whole attention, how it forces me at every moment out of my head and into it, how once I'm in it, it's impossible for me to feel alone.

The day gets warmer and warmer until we shed our parkas completely and change our hats for headbands. The ground starts to smell like spring-time and the ice gets bluer still. By the time we get to camp I am down to only three layers, and after we set the tent up we lie on the ice in front of it and take in the most spectacular 360-degree view of our adventure-filled lives. We could be at Club Med, the sun on our faces is so warm.

We spend the next two days exploring the high valleys of the Sagava-nirktok, watching herd after herd of caribou move north for the summer, watching the snow melt, watching the river turn blue as Blue's eyes.

"If we don't get out now we're here for the summer," Bill says the next morning, and he turns out to be right. On our trip back down the valley water stands eight inches deep on top of ice so thin it crackles. April slows, almost to a stop sometimes, and the muscles in my legs tense for the fall. Where there were fifty ice heaves on the way upriver, there are now five hundred, and the snow on the south face of even the highest peaks is all but gone. When we get to the slot canyon water is thundering down the surface of the ice and around the boulders, and I maneuver the sled be-tween them like a raft on a river, April and the boys in belly deep and swimming for home.

When we get back to our first base camp the river is broken free and running strong behind the tent site. This will be the first night we don't need to melt snow for drinking water; it will be the first night we eat dinner outside. When I take April's harness off she lets me rub her belly until the sun has dried it, and she falls sound asleep under my hand. I look up to find Bill watching, that same good dog look in his eye.

Brandon has saved his coup d'état story for this, our last night together: the time his wife shot him through the neck with a .22 on their honey-moon. We watch the late spring sun roll not toward the horizon but along it; for several nights now it hasn't gotten truly dark. The dropping tem-perature sends us toward bed, but then the northern lights come out and we run in place to keep warm while we watch them, their liquid green translucence made even more ghostly by twilight as they dance across the sky.

When the light show is over Bill takes me aside. "If you ever decide you want your own dog team," he says, "you come see me about it," and I nod and shake his hand.

It is a brief exchange, one good dog to another, but possibility washes through me like good medicine, and I go to sleep dreaming of six little Aprils of my own.

The next morning there is nothing to do but pack up the tents and begin the long mush up and out of the canyon. We climb the canyon wall slowly, our sleds suddenly cumbersome and heavy, and we run along behind the dogs to help them with the load. What had been an all-white landscape on Easter Sunday is suddenly fraught with color, the brown tundra, the black mountain tops, the snake of river now almost sapphire in the sun. But when we reach the canyon rim we find plenty of snow still standing, and the minute the ground levels the dogs begin again to fly.

In this moment I feel only two things: the cold wind in my face and my own deep happiness. I am moving from light into light on a surface purer than air and kinder than water. I am thankful for the holy shimmer of these backlit peaks and top-heavy cornices and for the way the wind howls around them. For the crack of the ice under padded dog paws and the water that bubbles below. For the feathered emerald ghost dance of the northern lights in the forever twilight of an Alaskan evening. For the way April offers first one leg, then the other to the morning's harness and my hand. And I know today that I have found my miracle: to fly across the earth in this heaven called the Brooks Range, on the wings of five little angels, furry, and wise.

May

■ ■ ■ ■ ■

May had gone all draggle-tailed working the drift. Swinging an eight-pound pickax seven hours on end will do that. It didn't matter the mercury was edging toward the skinny side of 40°, it being early November. Hard-scrabbling would get the sweat running like sap.

"Getting close, Gruff," she said. "I can feel it. That vein's going to rise like—what'd you always call it?—a varicose vein." Nobody else was in there with her. In her head, hell yes, Gruff was there. But stooping in this crosscut of the abandoned Jubilee Mine, it was only May, a pickax, a rusty wheelbarrow, the rest of her hand tools.

She'd been that way, rickety-headed, for some time, over two years the best she could make out, maybe more. Whatever she could excavate from inside her head, she'd done already, and mostly what she found was more gray than gold, the walls too thick to penetrate any farther.

She knew there was the man and the little girl, her husband and daughter she took them to be. Sometimes the picture came in clearer, like she had fiddled with a set of rabbit ears, but they never got any more real than dreams, shadows.

They were about as good to her now as pyrite anyway if they weren't some other trick of her mind. If they actually were real—that was another life. She could remember as far back as two and a half years ago, the day she stepped out of the swollen river, the rapids running crazy, she covered in blood and mucus like a newborn, but no more. Two weeks later was when she became May.

"You know what I could do with right now? Some AN-FO cartridges, Gruff," she said, though she knew she was just saying that. May didn't want the Forest Service to get wind of her being in the old Jubilee because she had no claim to it. A charge would just as likely set them off as loosen the hard rock overburden. No, her pickax and hand tools would do just fine, thanks.

She knew soon, in a few weeks probably, the rock would get too hard to work with any kind of tool—jackhammer, stoper, drifter, what have you. And she'd have to close out for the season.

By then, the hills around Boulder Creek would be thick with bear hunters, their packs of hellhounds running until they treed a bear or dropped, the hunters acting no better usually worse, greasy from skinning hides and lit up from drink, full of noisy animal lust at the Goldfield campground, reliving the kill in the cold nights outside their tents until they themselves dropped.

May swung the pickax, smoothed the wall face, swung again. Deep inside the adit, a nostril in the rise of decomposed granite, she could feel night coming on. "It's just a matter of time, Gruff," she said. "I've sent out my twenty letters. That vein's going to rise."

And she thought about what that faint glimmer in the wall, catching, bouncing the light from her lantern, would look like. Three more swings of the pickax and she laid it down, shoveled the waste rock into the wheelbarrow, resealed the adit with the board, and walked the two hundred yards to her blue two-man tent at Goldfield.

May had latched on with Gruff north of here, two weeks after picking herself up out of the river, after being vomited into the shallows and hitching rides south from the Cascades through Oregon and into Klamath, her ears still ringing with the sucking sounds of the rapids, the yelling of the water.

She was wandering 96 looking like a lost calf when Murphy's Dodge drove by, stopped, and backed up. What a sight she was! Still undone from slamming through the oxbows, she had one shoe on, the other foot, her right, filthy and bloody and bare; her pants were torn every which way; her shirt raggedy to just this side of decency, the purple bruises on her upper arm starting to yellow.

Murphy leaned out the cab and said, "You look like you were rode hard and put away wet."

Palmer elbowed him, stopping Murphy's smile before it grew any, Palmer being the Christian one of the lot. "What's your name?" Palmer said.

She worked on this while the Dodge shook there roadside in neutral, thinking as far back as she could. She heard the river's voice, was locked once again in its frigid womb, and shivered the way the stoper did if you didn't grip down real firm on its handles. The man and the girl washed through her head briefly but sank. And after all that, she had no answer.

"Where you coming from?" Palmer asked gently, interrupting her vision of spray, rocks, and sky.

North, she pointed.

"You want a job?"

She nodded slowly.

"Here." Palmer passed a pair of coveralls out the window to her. "Climb in back."

She first saw Gruff then, sitting in the pickup bed with the caps and cartridges, air cylinder, hand tools, jackhammer, the rest of their sorry equipment. Even with him sitting back on his haunches, he was an enormous sight—a body that was more a small hill than a body, a face lined like puzzle bark. They didn't say anything on the ride to Lucky Boy. Later when she passed him carting out tailings, he said, "Careful. Mind that jackleg, girlie," and she did.

Back at the truck at day's end, Gruff squinted at her, pinching his face up. He looked over toward the claim, then Murphy and Palmer fooling with the air cylinder. "God damn, you believe it's May already," he said to nobody in particular and returned to trying to make what he could of her, taking her in with eyes that looked like water. "So what's your name, honey?"

She thought again. "It's May," she said, deciding finally.

"Mine's Griffin." His voice was full of rasps and nails and she thought of him as Gruff after that.

May bunked in Gruff's shack at Horse Creek while they worked Lucky Boy because he said she could and because she had no other place to stay. Over the summer she turned as hard as the rock walls lining the tunnel, the fat from who she was before disappearing, sloughing off seemingly every day like the loosened overburden she carted out of the stope. And in time she fully became May.

It was tolerable living with Gruff. The shack was small but the beds were separate and he wasn't interested in coupling. Once in the beginning he tried to take her from behind but it wasn't with much spirit and she didn't think he worked right, had no steel in him, and he never tried again.

Most nights after they shook the rock dust from themselves and cleaned up, they sat out front the shack on the planks he called his deck.

He told her a little about himself, that there was trouble in his past, some jail for boosting construction tools at a job he was working, problems with liquor. At night when he talked in the dark he looked more bear than man, sounded it, too, his voice growling.

May understood how a mind could flood, how it could run wild. She knew about darkness though she didn't tell him about the river. And what was there to tell? He knew everything about her since she became May and whatever happened before, she couldn't account for anyway. The man, the little girl, it was like trying to hug water; you just come away with an armful of nothing.

She did have something from that other life, though. An address book. It was still sticking out of her back pocket after she was pounded downhill through the miles of white, pressing heavy on her achy hip when she found herself on her knees in the shallows. May handled it like it was some precious alluvial deposit except the names inside meant nothing to her, as if written in a language she didn't understand.

Some nights Gruff went to his meeting in Hamburg. That's what he called it, his meeting. The state had taken away his license so he thumbed rides there or Palmer drove him on occasion out of the goodness of his heart and he talked about the bottle with a number of other people at the church. Gruff didn't hardly mention the meetings with her. He'd come back to the shack with the shine dulled in his eyes, smelling of cigarette smoke.

One night in late summer after they'd found a thin vein at Lucky Boy that afternoon, he told May about gold. A fire crackled in the oil drum across the yard and she could hear the propane lamp gasping inside.

His voice snagged in his throat, the grind of rusty machinery. "Gold— it's not just a mineral, it's a meaning," he explained to her. The fire spat out sparks. "Always has been. The Egyptians, the Greeks, the Romans—gold always meant the same thing, didn't need no translation. It goes back forever, lifetimes way before ours."

May considered her address book, how the names inside reached back to a life before this one, and understood what he said.

"You take away the el and it's God." She could see moonlight gleaming in his eyes. "That means it's all tied together. The earth, the trees, the wind, the river—they can tell you things."

"I know," she said, remembering how the river called her name before it was May.

They listened to Horse Creek falling over rocks. "You listen to the trees and wind and river and if you listen hard enough, you can tell where the gold is." Gruff scratched a spent match back and forth against his leg. "That and a good map," he laughed.

As was her habit, May scouted the cars and their license plates occupying the campsites at Goldfield on her walk back from the Jubilee. It was early November, a year and a half since the chain letter came, since that last night with Gruff.

There weren't but two cars tonight because of the lateness of the season. Only the hearty or bear hunters came this close to winter. Both cars had California plates.

During the spring and summer, that had been a different story. Come weekend, the six other campsites would fill with families or couples or solitary campers, the cars and trailers carrying plates from all over the U.S., some with the towns right there in raised lettering on the plates, towns and counties she never heard of before. The people were friendly, eager to find out about these hills, the hiking trails, the good fishing spots, eager also to share with her where they hailed from.

One summer night she talked to a family from Plano, Texas. "We got the best high school football team in the state," the little boy said, "probably the country," his accent stretching the words as if it were a bungee cord.

May spent a good while by their fire and heard about their boating out on Lake Lavon, how god-awful hot the summers got. They invited her to sit down with them at the picnic table to eat dinner, but she politely declined.

"I was wondering if you could do me a favor once you get back to Plano."

The family looked at her with puzzlement, the boy, his head cocked over a bit to the side the way a dog does when given a command it doesn't understand.

"I was hoping you'd mail this letter for me. I like having my letters go out with postmarks from all over."

Their faces relaxed again around the campfire and they assured her they would, sitting a bit prouder now that Plano would be part of her life. They talked more about Boulder Creek and she told them of a nice rill by the bridge beyond the campground, wide enough for fly casting, and May pulled the letter from her back pocket to give them before leaving.

The letter was going to Frakes, Kentucky, sent to a name she didn't know from the address book. This was the way she sent out all twenty letters during the spring and summer. She randomly picked a name from the book, addressed the letter in her blocky writing, and in would go the chain letter, she waiting to meet the people around the campfire in the evenings, looking for the license plates that sounded far off. Plano, Texas; Bossier City, Louisiana; Kingston, New York; Reston, Virginia; San Diego, California; North Platte, Nebraska; Keene, New Hampshire—twenty of them in all.

But now, early November, there were just the two cars with the California plates, both parked in adjacent sites, campers huddled around the fire ring. She was stiff from working with only the hand tools in the drift and she swung her arms windmill fashion to loosen up the sockets, shaking out her day's work in the Jubilee. The people looked up when they heard her come by but she didn't stop; her twenty letters had gone out, all the links were connected, the chain cast out. On the way back to her campsite she listened to the trees and wind and the river, listened for the gold.

Boulder Creek was running heavier now, the rains coming up high in the mountains, the trees moving more in the wind, freed from their burden of leaves. She listened and thought she heard something familiar but couldn't say, not exactly, what that was.

When Gruff fell off the wagon a year and a half before it was with a tremendous clatter. Everything was fine through closeout of Lucky Boy. After that, he turned darker with the season.

Gruff and May worked some small construction jobs, clearing and burning brush if weather permitted, to keep busy until spring and stocked in food. But in the Klamath the people mostly hunkered down for the duration like the black bears did or migrated somewhere else like warblers.

The snow piled up around Gruff's shack, the world closing in around them. Everything stopped; if Horse Creek didn't move the way it did, it would have frozen up and stopped, too. May could see Gruff wanted to keep himself moving. At first, he tried going to more meetings in Hamburg, but the traffic wasn't what it was during the summer on 96, and even then it was a trickle, so thumbing was next to impossible. Also he didn't feel quite right asking Palmer for a lift, no matter how good a Christian Palmer was, because they wouldn't be working together again until spring.

It was boredom that finally got him and strung him up. And Gruff and May eventually stopped talking the way they did out on the planks during the summer nights.

Gruff took to walking—to his meetings, to the store for any such thing, to the VFW Hall to see if any jobs were posted, installing a woodstove, cutting wood, what have you, walking to just about anywhere his legs would carry him. His beard grew out and he looked more like a bear, a restless one that'd been woken up early from a winter's sleep.

Just before the thaw in March, he got in his cups again, going on a three-day binge at the cabin, boozing on grain alcohol. He was a sloppy drunk at first, not mean, pissing himself, burbling the liquor out of him the way a baby spits up.

On the second day of the binge, he talked to May about gold again. "I know where the gold is." His voice was rougher yet from drink.

"A few more weeks we'll be working with Palmer and Murph again," she said, thinking that was what he was talking about, hoping this ugliness would pass with the season.

He swatted his hand a couple of times at that notion and some of the liquor came back up and out onto his shirt and he cursed to himself. "No, no. Not Lucky Boy. The *gold*," he said, his pupils narrowing in the red that surrounded them. He got up and fell, tried again and fell again, stumbled on rubber legs to the wall, and pried away one of the pine boards. He brought back a sheaf of papers.

"Gold," he said, thumping the papers with his thick hand.

She thought it was what Murph and Palmer looked at. Maps.

Gruff made a sound with his mouth, an exhaling full of derision. "This here's real gold, girlie."

And she came around to look.

"It's from the old Liberty Mine Company," he said. "They worked all over these parts until the war. Then the boys went off to Europe and the Pacific. They was digging trenches instead of drifts." He started waving his arms, wanting to say more, but the drink overtook him and all he could manage was putting the old maps back and making his way to his bunk before spilling some more of his liquor out his mouth and falling asleep.

On the third day of the binge, Gruff mostly slept, waking up to sip some more, then knock out again. The following day he cleared, but he wasn't the same after. From then on, he looked at May with suspicion, unsure whether he'd shared with her his secret or not, not remembering. It grew worse. He'd come home from one of his walks and look like he was ready to shoot her, sizing her up with squinty eyes that threw off heat like fire.

The next week he got to tippling again and, coming back from a walk, lousy drunk, he started to accuse her of stealing his gold, but his tongue was too thick, the words strangled in his mouth, and all he could make was animal sounds and he swatted her around the shack like she was no more than cloth and stuffing. When his arms grew punch heavy, he fell back onto the bunk, missed it, and thudded to the floor.

And May looked like she did the day she walked out of the river. After he collapsed she wrapped herself in blankets and didn't return for the whole night. It hurt to walk but going back inside would only hurt more and she walked. Horse Creek was running like an unbroken roan, brown and over its banks, the waters surging in the shadow of spring. She heard the sucking sounds, the yelling of the water again. But this time, seeing the fall line of the river, she knew it was Gruff being swept away and she didn't want to be carried with him.

She returned to the shack in the morning, opening the door more than timidly. His face was creased but he was sober and when he saw what he had done to her, the bruises and welts and cuts, his expression nearly folded in on itself. And again like the night before his words were strangled, but this time it was from shame, not drink.

"Go to a meeting," she said gently.

Gruff nodded and picked himself up.

"Please," May said through her swollen lips, "go to one of your meetings." And he did.

While Gruff was at his meeting in Hamburg the mail came and in the delivery was the chain letter. Reading it the best she could, the words it said ran through her like electrical current. It told of a man in New Hampshire who didn't believe in the power of the words and his two daughters died. Another man in Illinois, however, followed the directions of the letter, sending out copies anonymously to twenty people, and a wonderful fortune befell him.

May must have read the letter upwards of twenty times when Gruff was at his meeting, each time the picture the words made coming in clearer. Finally, she saw what she had to do and she folded the letter, gathered up her address book, went to the pine board, and pried the board away. The maps were still there and she took one of them, leaving the rest of the sheaf, thinking Gruff wouldn't miss the one, thinking this was what the letter meant. And then she quit the shack for good.

Just as she did when she came out of the river, May went south. The three things she brought with her—the address book, the letter, the map— were bound together in a magic knot, a golden chain.

And as May went south, down 3, the season changed and she left the

Klamath, crossed the Siskiyous, and came into the forests of the northern Trinity Alps.

In the light of the electric lantern hanging in May's tent at Goldfield, the stretched blue nylon ceiling was a curving phony sky in the cold November night. The campers at the adjacent campsites had settled down for the evening, their fire consuming itself, and May couldn't see the flames anymore from the screen in her tent, not that she was looking much.

What May was studying was the map of the Jubilee. There were a lot of surveyor symbols and language she didn't understand, even more geological words with callouts. It didn't matter to her she didn't know these words that she couldn't hardly get her mouth around. It proved what Gruff had told her the summer they worked Lucky Boy. "Gold has meaning," she said in the tent now, knowing it was something greater than she could fully understand.

Despite all this ignorance, she knew where she was on the map, could trace her progress inside the adit and down the crosscut. And that was enough for her. The old paper crinkled in her hands like folding money. The blue ink had turned in age to purple and brown.

Without fail, May looked at the map every night, her faith unshakable one night it would tell her more. "The letters have been sent," she said, saying what she had been saying nightly ever since handing the last of them to the little boy from Plano.

And after the map said nothing to her this night, she folded it up, switched off the light. May listened again, was always listening. The wind in the trees, the fast water in Boulder Creek running below the knob her tent was perched on—they told her the rains were coming soon.

After quitting Gruff and before setting up camp at Goldfield, May worked at Wyntoon for a year. The day she left him and thumbed south to the forests of the northern Trinity Alps, she saw a help-wanted sign at a gas station outside Trinity Center.

It was on the property of the Wyntoon Resort. With the spring and summer season coming, Wyntoon needed extra hands and May stayed on, working in the scullery at the restaurant, cleaning cabins, patching leaky canoes; whatever they would have her do, she did.

As payment, the owners gave her room and board and minimum wage, the room a small shack out by a stand of pines near the road. And that was enough, better actually than bunking with Gruff.

She kept to herself and she worked hard, nearly every day, although the work was much less taxing than working the hoists at Lucky Boy. And even if the owners thought she was an idiot that was all right by her, too. It meant they left her alone.

Anyway there were plenty enough things filling her head. The bruises and cuts and welts from Gruff healed in time but she would wake from sleep in the dim light of the shack, bolt upright from dreaming he was pummeling her again. Sometimes she got the dream mixed up, saw the rapids in his eyes.

Other times the man and the little girl visited her. It was around this time she got it inside her head that they were her husband and daughter, except she didn't feel any wifely or mother love for them and at the same time she considered they might be a trick.

It had been a year that she'd been delivered from the river, a year since this life began. May was one year old.

As time passed, the dreams of Gruff stopped and May missed him. This wasn't wifely love either. She liked the magic way he talked about gold during that summer before he fell off the wagon; she thought he understood what the river could tell a person. And to fill up some of the spaces inside her, she talked to him.

During the summer she caught a ride back to Coffee Creek, then walked the five miles up Coffee Creek Road to where the Forest Service trail was and hiked the mile to the Jubilee. She had been thinking about the address book, the chain letter, and the map in her shack and knew it was getting to be time.

Boulder Creek ran thin as it banded the trail. The trees stood stock-still in the heat, no wind to speak of. And May knew she would have to come back in the spring, when the river would be fat and muddy and the trees busy with blowing out winter, when they could tell her more. She stayed at Wyntoon through winter with the skeleton crew and left with the spring.

When she awoke at Goldfield her tent was hot with morning light despite the November chill, the two cars of the campers already gone. It was a handsome day, the purple underbellies of clouds sticking close to the higher elevations, the sun still strong even though it had already begun its sidewinder arc in the sky.

On the way to the Jubilee she watched Boulder Creek the way she always did. It was up a few inches, probably rained the night before higher up. And the wind confirmed this, carrying on it the damp and cold.

Inside the drift she fell into the comfortable rhythm of swinging, smoothing the face, swinging. She thought she saw a glimmer but it was flakes of quartz and she kept at it, the pickax marking time. "That was quartz, Gruff, not gold. But it's in here, the gold. They wouldn't have a map if there wasn't."

When her stomach started a conversation with her, May stopped for lunch, exiting the adit to eat by Boulder Creek. It was up yet another inch since this morning.

Settling back in the dark after she ate, her lantern making a little room of light in the void, she continued, her shoulders rolling with each throw of the pickax, her wrists flicking. She was getting close, she told herself between swings. "Just you wait, Gruff," she said to the darkness, "that gold's going to rise like a varicose vein."

And the darkness said back to her, "You thought you could fool me," in a voice full of rasps and nails.

At first May thought it was her head that was doing the talking and so she said, "I'm about to discover the meaning of gold, Gruff."

Out from the black, from farther down the drift, he stepped, Gruff, big and terrible. "You're about to discover something else."

He stepped forward and May backed up. She didn't know if this was still her head, a trick or something, until he pushed her, and when her head bounced off the wall, her teeth bit tongue, tasted the salt of blood in her mouth, then she knew he was flesh.

May rolled back to the wall, using it to help her regain her footing.

Gruff said, "It's best to mind that jackleg, girlie," and he laughed, more a deep rumble than anything else. "I was thinking you might have left for good and maybe I lost my map. But I knew better."

He pushed her again and again her head snapped back into hard rock. She struck with her pickax and this time she hit vein, not gold, but the carotid artery in his neck. He fell back, the blood spurting a good foot outward, and he made a horrible gurgling noise from deep inside. He was grabbing frantically, pawing the air like an animal. May could smell that he evacuated his bladder and bowels as he shook there.

Then she heard it. From deep inside the adit came the sound of the trees and wind and river—the chittering of Gruff's limbs, the air rushing out of him in gusts, the washing of his blood onto waste rock. And what she heard dissolved the gold, the letter, the links that bound them together.

The tremors slowed, then stillness, another throb, then nothing. May looked at what was Gruff no more, an enormous body stinking of piss and shit and the smell of death already. And she left, Gruff, her pickax, her wheelbarrow, the hand tools, she left all of it. She kept moving on the Forest Service trail, the sound of the rising river in her ears as she ran. And she saw that this is the way it would be, so much of her life happening in the dark, the river washing it away. And she kept moving.

Philip Levine &
Charles H. Webb

Santa Monica College Writers' Conference

L.A. seldom gets the credit it deserves for any-
thing, but in fact it's the home of a rich,
varied, wonderfully energetic group of poets, and I had the good fortune
to have one of the most resourceful as my student, Charles Webb. I'm not
sure what Charles was doing there, for he is his own poet and in terms of
mastery of craft and theme he is light-years beyond the need for a teacher.
In huge, disorganized L.A. perhaps he was just lonesome for other poetry
people. Whatever his motives, I was delighted to have him in my class for
one afternoon, for he brings to the study of the poetry of others the same
gifts he brings to the page when he's composing: intelligence, generosity,
wit, originality, and a fierce devotion to the art he practices. As you'll dis-
cover reading what follows, he has caught the unique qualities of life in
Southern California, and surprisingly he's done so in very elegant poems
which possess a fine tension between their formal exteriors and the inten-
sity of the emotions raging under their cool surfaces. This is American
poetry as it should be: available, smart, finely crafted, and steeped in our
great tradition from Dickinson through Frost and Berryman to the present
moment. If you'd like to hear how American poetry of the future will
sound, here it is.—**Philip Levine**

Philip Levine won the 1991 National Book Award for his collection of
poems *What Work Is*. He is the author of numerous books, including
his two most recent, *The Bread of Time* (essays) and *The Simple Truth*
(poems).

Charles H. Webb received his M.F.A. and Ph.D. from the University of
Southern California. His work has appeared in the *Paris Review, Plough-
shares,* the *Gettysburg Review*, and the *Antioch Review,* as well as in *The
Best American Poetry 1995*. He has also published a novel, *The Wilderness
Effect*.

Holy Son and Mother of the Projects

■ ■

In this new place without elm tree, without rooks
nesting in stone turrets, the squat barracks stink
of pork fat and worse, here his mother is about her work.
She will return with a loaf of Wonder Bread, a sausage,
and six eggs spotted with blood. Were human life
what it should be he would speak the Latin of Augustine,
interceding with heaven on our behalf, for he
is our hope, the resident wonder of the projects
Ford built to house the workers up from West Virginia.
Outside the day is breaking over the crusted mounds
of last month's snow filling the rutted road, outside
a car starts up, a door slams shut, a shrill whistle
addresses the stained and many-colored dome of earth
so that Thursday night's shift might enter history.
This is not another day in an industrial neighborhood
in the city of man in 1948. Inside the air
is warm and still, and all men do nothing. Outside
the actual mother of blood picks her way carefully
across Mud Lane to the front door with a sack of morning.
Face flushed she enters in a cloud of steam and tears,
she casts her cloak aside, she mutters, "Christ, it's cold!"
She brings to you the ritual meal, courtesy of eight
long hours of assembly, so bow to kiss the proffered hand
of the only one who serves you more than you deserve.

My Given Name

■■■■■■■■■■■■■

My grandmother missed the midnight train back
and walked home to our village. The day broke
over a sleeping world. The sparrows rose
one by one to wait in line to eat shit.

Thus some months later was my father born
in a year without numbers, in a house
nailed together with smoke, in a land
no one dared to name. My life is his.

I was told to worship the first book I read,
the book of waters written in a dry year.
"Memorize it all and say it back to me,"
said the bearded servant of the bearded lord.

Instead I counted out the letters of my name,
the name I gave myself, Fishel Efroyim.
They total lucky thirteen, forward or back,
from the middle vowel to the consonants.

These are truths told with a good intent,
little secrets I want to share, like the bread
I hid from Abraham, the delicious piss
against Adam's tree in honor of our God.

The Letters

■ ■ ■ ■ ■ ■ ■ ■ ■ ■ ■

My friend Arnold wrote me how his life
changed the night he sat up in a car
speaking with a woman he'd met
while picking cherries. The woman
was unafraid of the future, she wanted
to live as much as Arnold, she had nothing
but the money she earned picking cherries.
Oregon in late June, the light hanging on
long past nine, the sky a radiant blue.
She reached one arm out of the car window
to gesture to the night sky as the stars
began to emerge. The car was her brother's.
The three of them would wander the whole
Northwest in search of work and settle for
an autumn outside Billings where Arnold
built fence and Bailey, the woman, waited
tables in a small cafe on the Crow reservation
taking crap from no one. Winter just behind.
They never waited for spring and the cloudless
great spread of sky and the fields running off
in all directions yellowed with clumps of broom,
they never bent to the wild orchids hidden
in grass or the spikes of phlox at the roadside.
They headed south and spent two nights trapped
by snow in a mountain pass. The brother
dropped out, not—perhaps—out of their lives
but out of the letter, and when they got
to West Texas there were only the two
crossing the bridge at Juárez to find
the bus to Guadalajara. The story gets fuzzy
just here. They sold wood sculptures weekends

while Bailey painted and Arnold wrote
his first stories. I could go back to search
out the letters, six in all I kept that arrived
within a few weeks probably twenty years ago
when Arnold and Bailey were living in Oakland
two blocks from the freeway. They'd married
so many years earlier they'd become one person
in my mind. I know I won't find the letters.
I know it hardly matters. In the dark
I can see Bailey's hand, dark itself, stained
by the juices of the sweet cherries, reaching
out to speak to the stars clustered above,
I can see the sky deepen and disappear before
the early dawn stills the two of them,
stunned by how much they've shared
in just this one night and with words only.

The Seven Doors

■ ■ ■ ■ ■ ■ ■ ■ ■ ■ ■ ■ ■ ■ ■

The waiter carries a white towel over
his left arm; when the couple enters
he bows his head before leading them
to a corner table. They ask for menus,
so he bows again. Instead he brings
a flagon of such dark red wine
it appears black in the candlelight
as he pours it, first into her glass,
then into his and goes off in silence.
There are seven ornate doors leading
into the large room, but no one leaves,
so the new couples that enter must
stand by the solemn doors waiting
as the candles burn slowly down, so
slowly it appears that moment by moment
nothing has changed. Nothing has changed.
One hundred years ago Gustavo Muntaner
borrowed a modest fortune at low interest
from his father-in-law and founded
The Seven Doors using his daughters
as collateral. Ships sailed from distant
ports bringing saffron, bananas, tea.
Later sealed trucks ground up the heights
where they executed the small businessmen
and their clerks in 1936, one bullet
for each as a new dawn bloomed upon
the perfect bay. Then there was peace,
the dark night of decades of utter peace.
This long day's last light breaks through
the high leaded windows, staining some
couples red, some blue, some nothing

at all. The menus arrive. The waiter
stands at attention, humming a song
not even he can hear. The candles blink
on and off playing their silly games
with darkness. The kitchen fires up.
Now we can smile. Everyone eats tonight.

Good Monday

■ ■ ■ ■ ■ ■ ■ ■ ■ ■ ■ ■ ■

The long day breaking over the rooftops
    of heaven. The sparrows
waken, one at a time, shake the dust
    from their feathers and go
in search of a coffee and cigarette.
    Yesterday was Easter,
and two days before that the weekend
    began at noon
when I punched out, a free man released
    into the smoky air
of my hometown. Celebrated with lunch
    of thick barley soup
and slabs of rye bread. The waitress
    called me by the wrong name
and shared my table and her secret wish
    to master tango dancing.
She threw her head back and let the smoke
    trail slowly from
her dark little nostrils as she sang
    seven unintelligible words
in Spanish to the ceiling. Thus I told her
    my true name and shared
my secret desire to live in Philadelphia
    where poets are paid by the hour
no matter how badly they write. This before
    one, with hours to go,
hundreds and hundreds of years after the day
    got its odd name. At home
I ironed my good wool pants and the white shirt
    I wore on special occasions,

shined my black shoes, and practiced my steps:
    one, two, three, four,
side to side, forward and back, side
    to side, forward and back
until the room spun with so much music
    I had to rest my head.
Oh, how this tight little heart of mine
    can fill with song by day
and by night live the long hours alone
    a moment at a time
until day breaks over the rooftops of heaven
    where the pigeons punch in
at 8 or 9 or even 10:15 on stormy Mondays.

The Dead

■■■■■■■■■

A good man is seized by the police
and spirited away. Months later
someone brags that he shot him once
through the back of the head
with a Walther P .38, and his life
ended just there. Those who loved
him go on searching the cafes
in the Barrio Chino or the bars
near the harbor. A comrade swears
he saw him at a distance buying
two kilos of oranges in the market
of San José and called out, "Andrés,
Andrés," but instead of turning
to a man he'd known since child-
hood and opening his great arms
wide, he scurried off, the oranges
tumbling out of the damp sack, one
after another, a short bright trail
left on the sidewalk to say,
Farewell! Farewell to what? I ask.
I asked then and I ask now. I first
heard the story fifty years ago;
it became part of the mythology I
hauled with me from one graveyard
to another, this belief in the power
of my yearning. The dead are every-
where, crowding the narrow streets
that jut out from the wide boulevard
on which we take our morning walk.
They stand in the cold shadows
of men and women come to sell

themselves to anyone, they stride
along beside me and stop when I
stop to admire the bright garlands
or the little pyramids of fruit,
they reach a hand out to give
money or to take change, they say
"Good morning" or "Thank you," they
turn with me and retrace my steps
back to the bare little room I've
come to call home. Patiently,
they stand beside me staring out
over the soiled roofs of the world
until the light fades and we are
all one or no one. They ask for
so little, a prayer now and then,
a toast for their health which is
our health, a few lies no one reads
incised on a dull plaque between
a pharmacy and a sports store,
the least little daily miracle.

Marilyn's Machine

■ ■ ■ ■ ■ ■ ■ ■ ■ ■ ■ ■ ■ ■ ■

She bought it because her baseball player didn't want her to,
because her playwright and her President and her Attorney
General disapproved. You're a star, they said: the one
thing they agreed on. Stars don't wash their own clothes.

Too timid to defy them, she rented a little room
and left her machine there, safe in its cardboard box.
Disguised in a black wig and flowered muumuu,
she sat and stared at the machine, imagining the famous

bras, nylons and panties, tight sweaters and skirts
sighing as they rocked, settling down into the warm,
detergent bath. Sometimes she cried, thinking
of the men who dreamed about her clothes and what

went in them. How many orgasms had she inspired,
who'd never had one of her own, her breathy voice
warding off "Was it good for you?" She loved
selecting temperatures: hot/warm, warm/cold, cold/cold,

and her favorite, hot/cold. She loved the brand name
"Whirlpool Legend." She loved the cycles,
especially "Rinse" and "Spin." She whispered their names,
thinking of a man thinking of her some distant day

when she is nothing but an image made from movies,
photos, gossip, exposés—an image thinking of him
thinking of her in her black wig and flowered muumuu,
rinsing, spinning till the dirt is washed away.

The Dead Run

∎∎∎∎∎∎∎∎∎∎∎∎∎

Vampires and zombies, being liveliest, start first,
shambling, jogging, sprinting as their condition
permits. The freshly dead in hospitals and funeral
homes totter to their feet (if they have feet)
and, embalmed or not, start running. Corpses claw
up from the ground, in the order they went in:
skeletons and rotted horrors hobbling and clattering,
stooping to pick up parts that fall. The long-dead rise
as human dust clouds, and run with the rest:
a dark, stinking wind that crosses water as easily as land.

And now the oldest rise, the ones whose atoms
have mixed with everything. The Watson house,
the Pomeroy's sweetgum, Dottie Tang's azaleas
dissolve to let them out. Robert Ufman, Jan Nash,
Tiffany the Schneider Schnauzer disintegrate,
along with the still-solid dead, their molecules
joining the marathon that circles the earth
like a jet stream, until only I am left, remembering
how this always happens—how, in despair,
I pull a rib from my side, and begin again.

Health

■ ■ ■ ■ ■ ■

You wake each morning in a satin bed—
the air caressing, temperature, humidity
just right—but the mail comes. You suck
down ripe papayas on your balcony
as lemon finches, scarlet tanagers,
black mynahs flicker through hibiscus
and the sea shrugs its white shoulders
in the sun—but wind keeps messing up
your hair. You swim through ocean
warm as skin, drifting with fish vivid
as the sunsets here, violet, orange,
claret, indigo, watching golden cowries
flow on black mantles across white coral—
but you scrape your hand on lava outside
the room where your love waits, limpid with sleep.

"Be ecstatic," you remind yourself
every so often, but you're peeved at potholes
in the street; and one day your left arm is numb;
you lose your balance for no reason, or feel faint,
or wake from bad dreams with a headache
that won't quit, or take your yearly physical,
leave feeling fine, then get a call
from a nurse who won't say why, but insists
you see the doctor right away. And right
away you're on a plane, one among rows
of faces watching desperately the last
green mountains disappear, and clouds close
over turquoise seas the way a woman
you still love, whom you betrayed, shuts
her robe in front of you for the last time.

Flying Fish in the Jet Stream

■■■■■■■■■■■■■■■■■■■■■■■■■

One minute he was beside me; the next, he was gone.
—Army buddy of Charles Casey Webb, 1880–1916

I pictured him bombed into a red mist
rising above the battlefield, filling the air.
Other kids' grandfathers took us fishing,
or to state parks in their mobile homes,
but mine was like God: everywhere.

His sword and sergeant's helmet
shone like sunlight high in the loblolly pines.
I heard his voice when redwing blackbirds
screamed and flashed their epaulets.
He had an English accent—said "I say!"

and "Cheerio," and called things "bloody,"
which colored them bright red. Summer nights,
I'd lie in the warm current of the attic fan,
and feel his fingers in the sweaty wind.
When anything was made in Germany—

a clock or Christmas ornament or Pfeffernusse—
I felt him there. His one thin comma
of black hair seemed glued onto his shiny head.
Pushing, bald-pated, between heaven
and earth hurt his brain, he said.

"Be a strong groundhog," he whispered
in dreams. "Flying fish in the jet stream."
I interpreted that for days. When Mom
sent me to my room, he taught me looks
to make her feel sorry and give me ice cream.

Crouched on the john, my twelfth birthday,
I saw a lone hair sprouting
like a black scratch above my little wang.
"Bye, Charlie boy," the pines,
the breeze, a redwing blackbird sang.

Buyer's Remorse

■ ■ ■ ■ ■ ■ ■ ■ ■ ■ ■ ■ ■ ■ ■

I'd hate to take a job teaching,
then spend my life trying to get out of it.
                                 —Mary Oliver

No sooner do the ruck of us declare
"I do," than we don't anymore. Go out
for football, and we who never dared
to stand up on a pair of ice skates, pout
that we can't play pro hockey too. The ink's
still wet on our tickets to France, and we
wish we'd picked Japan, or come to think
of it, Kauai, New Zealand, or Tahiti.
Open any one door and we're deafened
by the roar—loud as the sea swallowing Atlantis—
as other doors slam shut, and their wind
knocks us down. The serpent didn't hiss
    to Adam and Eve, "Hide your nakedness!"
    He wore his best suit, and whispered, "Look at this."

Four-Wheeling

∎∎∎∎∎∎∎∎∎∎∎∎∎∎

Driving off-road, watch for rocks out of the corner
of your eye. If you focus on them, they're like magnets;
you'll think boulders have minds, and all hate you.
It's like climbing a cliff, then wanting to jump;
like seeing a woman you know will wreck your life,
and saying Hi. The Imp of the Perverse,
Poe called it. New Agers call it psychic law:
You move toward what you think about.

The paper screeches BEIJING FLU POUNDS L.A.;
an hour later, my throat's raw. (Yet I often think
of winning the Publishers Clearing House Sweepstakes.
I visualize their block-long caravan swarming to my door,
champagne popping, to a brass band, as cameras roll,
Are you Charles H. Webb, Ph.D.? Last time I checked.
You've just won 10,679,533 dollars. Are you kidding?
No, I've got your check right here. It never happens.

Maybe if I sent my entry in?) Therapists cite the self-
fulfilling prophecy: Fearing Claudia will cheat,
Ted treats her as if she has—snarls over dinner,
comes home drunk, avoids sex until she's so miserable
that when Frank at the office says, "How about coffee?"
she walks to the divorce court, straight from his bedroom.
Homer was blind but sensed the presence of fanged sirens,
whirlpools, Cyclopes, witches who turn people into swine.

You have to know danger is there, but not dwell on it.
Gorgons can't do a thing unless you stare.
Trust your mirrored shield. Trust your third eye.

Trust your instinct. Trust The Force. Stay loose.
Easy does it. One day at a time. Turn and accelerate.
Feather the wheel. Watch the dust fly up behind you.
Don't think *boulder*. Don't think *ripped oil pan*.
Don't think *Goddamn it, stranded*! Don't think *Wham*!

Michael Pettit &
Julie Kamrowski

Mount Holyoke Writers' Conference

Perhaps most striking about Julie Kamrowski's poems is the distance between their emotional sources and their eventual music. Johnson said, "A simile may be compared to lines converging at a point, and is more excellent as the lines approach from a greater distance." Julie's ability to make painful experience a pleasure—haunted and haunting—for *us* is what makes her an artist. Not pain itself, not simply music, but transformation. To say much more about her poems—the richly detailed imagery, the narrative gift, the sure voice—is to risk saying less. Her poems say it best, in the only way adequate to her spirits. We are lucky to listen to them.—**Michael Pettit**

Michael Pettit's books include *American Light* and *Cardinal Points*, which won the Iowa Poetry Prize. He lives in Shutesbury, Massachusetts, and is director of the Open Road Writing Workshops.

Julie Kamrowski is a past recipient of the Writers' Conferences & Festivals poetry scholarship, selected by Charles Simic. In addition to Mount Holyoke, she has attended the Wesleyan University Writers' Conference.

A Dog's in Heat

■ ■ ■ ■ ■ ■ ■ ■ ■ ■ ■ ■ ■ ■

A dog's in heat up Leonard Road, my dog
paces the house, howls on his chain outside,

drives me crazy. I do not hate this heat
he feels, I feel that same yearning myself,

on my chain of pride, or inside this house
of silence. Could we both tear free to run

up the long roads, shedding tears of desire,
gulping the burning air, what would we find?

Our selves there, in the elemental night,
wet fur, sweet funk, the female, the other?

Last night he stood for hours at her fence
in the rain, in pain, and why not, why not

I ask you, through the silent door, my blood
on the wood, my knuckles raw, why, why not?

Leonard Road

■■■■■■■■■■■■■

I'm learning all the dips and rises,
the half-mile up and half-mile back
between the pines and ferns, learning
the five houses, the four barking dogs.

I'm learning rainwater in the ditches,
weeds blooming, deer flies appearing
in cool shadowy stretches, learning
telephone poles, doves on the wires.

When you walked alone in the evenings
did you dream endlessly of becoming
the anonymous goddess of Greenwich Village,
the cold hot blond of Carmine Street?

I'm learning to walk my sorrow early
and late, when the changing light
seems unbearable, learning to walk
this one road over and over, mantra

of footsteps and enduring mystery.
I wonder whether you ever felt
this road might offer answers,
or free you from questions they'll ask

on every corner of Houston Street,
in New York, London, Rome—
wherever you might wander, looking
to banish doubt, to take control.

I'm learning this washboard gravel road,
its silence, its occasional passing car,
the gravid woman who walks her dog,
the old stone walls overgrown with lilacs.

I'm learning how little I'll ever know
of the heart, systole and diastole,
left, right, man, woman, here, there,
I'm learning, slowly, slowly, to let go.

Matins

∎ ∎ ∎ ∎ ∎ ∎ ∎

So the seed falls when wind vibrates the stalk
to just such a pitch, and it is music
which reproduces these speechless grasses.

This is dawn. Lola calling her cows in,
frost on the fields melting as light brightens
and the air warms one critical degree.

Now, dew, thick over clover, alfalfa,
green pastures from which rise, like bits of dreams,
scattered white asters, cool blue chicory.

This is dawn. Fog down in all the valleys
the Kickapoo River twists through the hills,
draws filled with fog, world emerging from fog.

Shagbark hickories on the ridge take shape
and shreds of clouds change color—red, pink, gray.
This is dawn. Lola calling her Holsteins,

a lone man picking wildflowers and weeds,
grasses packed with seeds waiting for the wind
to rise, waiting for song to scatter them—

purple thistle, red clover, packed clusters
of pink smartweed, flowering campion,
tall long seedheads of sunlit timothy.

Here. I've walked over the cold grass, my tracks
a shadow from flower to flower,
my hands full as I stand dumb in the dawn.

Lola calling her cows. Old rituals
at sunup, before the world goes silent
and still and we wait for the wind to rise.

One Drum

■ ■ ■ ■ ■ ■ ■ ■ ■ ■

Never shake hands across the threshold.

Today the sun will not count me among the dead.
   No ghost drifting dream worlds,
I will stand in my doorway facing east at dawn
   to hear the sun's first words.
And birds will follow, swooping down to the feeder,
   wings beating like soft drums.
Among the living I will listen to each sound
   light scatters as it comes
through the bare trees: chickadee, cardinal, junco,
   dove that mourned all last night.
I listened then too, long, unable to let go
   of thought, terrible noise
the heart, a hole in the heart, old and new blood
   confounding, the sound wrong.
Let go, let go, then or now, of thought or your dreams,
   both in great disarray,
let go and walk among the ghosts—your old lovers,
   beloved grandfather—
then let them go, close the hole in your heart, at dawn
   stand in your doorway, face
lifted, eyes closed, gold light and birdsong all you know,
   one world at a time, one
drum someone will hear, distant, calling her to rise,
   light, among the living, now.

Lost Gloves

■ ■ ■ ■ ■ ■ ■ ■ ■ ■ ■

A lost glove is a happy glove.
—Neruda

If so, then what a happy world. It's spring
or will be soon. Snow will recede and leave

its secrets scattered across the pale grass:
a black glove, for the left hand, half-frozen,

but sunlight pulling steam from the fingers
now beginning to curl inward, beckon

some mate in the bottom of a closet
in a house so still all song's forgotten.

Back in deep winter there were other songs:
child's turquoise glove on a snowy hillside,

red knit mitten fallen to the sidewalk,
old leather hand propped on a newel post,

chorus from the lost and found box, voices
without hope or real need for harmony.

A brown one tacked to a bulletin board
may look deflated, defeated, alone—

wrong. There's thumb, index, middle, ring, little
fingers and the palm, front and back, the wrist

that breathes, sings now no hand reaches inside
for warmth. There's the past to sing, the future,

pairs and solitude, unforgettable
and yet to become memorable ones.

Lost glove, happy glove, glove that loves its life!

Magnolia

■■■■■■■■

Spent magnolia blooms lowered themselves onto our lawn,
petals sheltering grass like abandoned pink-skinned tongues.
In sunshine they melted into the tarred sidewalk and driveway
until no broom or boot toe could tear away their liquid veins.
Climbing low gray branches, we'd shake defiant blossoms loose—
our dog, Cheyenne, leaping and snapping at floating flowers.
With work gloves too large, trash cans covered in kick-dents,
we were sent to rake the yard though it was late May
and maple, mountain ash, lilac leaves hung firmly on trees.
Scratched into piles, the softest breeze sent them scattering
like escaped children we'd have to hunt down beneath evergreens,
in foot-ruts under the swingset, impaled on pickerbushes,
snarled in our hair. Undressing at night we'd find fugitive petals
slipped in our socks, tickling like shirt tags at our necks,
curled in pantcuffs, pastel coins falling from pockets.
Once we found a petal grafted like skin on my brother's back,
thin and translucent among freckles, seamed hockey scars,
clinging there through three weeks' worth of sweat and showers.
Peeled off whole, the petal left behind faint traces rough-edged
as a kissmark along the spine—we took turns draping it on our arms,
washed white, still darkening our skin, like a birthmark we all wore.

That June

■■■■■■■■■

Before she had a child, she was a child
with her back against the wall that was her family,
the wall that crumbled every night,
showering debris so thick she could not breathe.
That June, she would climb out her bedroom window,
quiet as footsteps coming down the hall,
carefully trimmed evergreens scratching her ankles,
pulling her blouse, tattooing her face.
She would run, run down the street
to the waiting Chevy warm with the smell of a man
who cradled a bottle of Bacardi between his knees.
They would drive to the reservoir, watch stars fall,
listen to sleepy bullfrogs call each other back to the mud.
Leaning against the car, she drank until she wasn't there to touch
that old familiar ache. All she felt
was a fire in her throat swallowed down hard
until it caught in her smooth white arms, legs,
wrapped around a body that was this man, this man.
The drive home ended in front of a house dark as a secret.
In the cool before an early summer dawn,
she would watch his Chevy grow small,
her mouth filling up with night.

Reservoir

■ ■ ■ ■ ■ ■ ■ ■ ■

Through light snow we drive slowly to Quabbin Reservoir,
Eric Clapton on the radio, windshield wipers beating,
looking beneath gray ice for a buried black road
that runs right into the water, continuing on under reeds and rocks,
black road where you stood, said you loved me, and I believed you.
They drowned four towns for this you know,
people of Prescott, Dana, Enfield, Greenwich forced to pack up
their babies and dogs, pull up clotheslines, swings,
lift glass from window frames, brass knockers off doors.
Women wrapping china in newspaper, clocks in dishtowels,
silver tea sets and dried wedding flowers cloaked in bed linen.
Men came to unearth bodies from every family graveyard,
kids swinging on the gates, watching them raise dirt-caked caskets,
each one tagged, piled one atop the other like firewood,
heavy wagons pitching in rutted roads leading out of town.
Husbands stripping shingles, wives pulling and potting rosebushes,
planning to put it all back together in Brookfield or Belchertown,
they were so careful, trying not to leave any life or love behind.
But today widows still gather at Tuesday teas and remember—
Mrs. Roberts's prize calla lilies, Father Neal's golden retriever—
as today we stand in the snow watching our life together
spill through our opened hands like wild rushing water.

Canals

∎∎∎∎∎∎

They empty the canals into the river every season
so the paper mills can work on their waterwheels,
pick them free of car parts, reed-tangled eels,
branches dripping off like a woman's long black hair.
Rodney at Parsons Paper found a body one November
hooked on the massive frame like a child dangling across a swing.
He could still make out red and green checks of a flannel shirt
twisted up under blue, bloated arms held outward.
The cold keeps flesh firmly on the maze of bones.
Police, following skid marks in the road, pulled a Toyota out in April,
found a man on the bank curled among litter and brush.
He told through numb lips how his friend was driving,
lost control, how the car didn't float as he'd imagined it would,
he couldn't feel his fingers, storm-colored water sealing doors, windows,
he couldn't find his friend, he must have been dreaming,
the muddy bank sliding smooth and cold under his skin,
he told how he felt like a salamander writhing in the muck.
In July, bait-mongers arrive with their battered trucks
to scrape the oozy bottoms of the freshly drained canals,
rich in eels and trash fish for Provincetown fishermen.
Drowned to the knees, they pile slime into barrels, stinking.
As they leave town, gulls circle and dive from the sky.
Last September, kids cutting school to search the sticky earth
discovered a lower mandible poking up between their feet,
its teeth solid and straight. Daring each other to touch it,
they invented a history of Indian burial grounds and ancient curses
as they tossed it back and forth, gold fillings glinting in the sun.

Nora

■ ■ ■ ■ ■ ■

Nora, you believe every time your husband pulls his shotgun
down from the top pantry shelf, takes his heavy boots from the porch,
announces he's hunting deer with Dean and Ed from the shop,

he's driving to the Auditorium Pub and smelling red permed hair
waving over pale shoulder blades of a waitress younger than you
by three kids, a Toyota with transmission trouble, an unscrubbed tub.

You see them fucking in the Cleopatra Room of the Pines Motel
in your mind as you wash plate after glass, pan after baby,
resentment hardening in your bones like marbled stone.

So you start to check out the curved ass on the kid who pumps gas—
imagining his thumbs on your throat, teeth at your breast
as you grip the grocery cart's handle, selecting grapefruit and potatoes.

Soon you're filling the tank every other day, taking the long way
to work, using up gas, dirtying the windshield, all so you can watch
him stretch his long frame over the hood, shake his hair

from his face inches from yours as you tune the radio
to a station you both can dance to slowly in a room, in a town,
in a country so far you can't even make out roof peaks from here.

But on Tuesday night he gives you change for a twenty and you see
a tattoo—fresh and red—an eagle in flight on his left forearm,
notice his nails—black, bitten, the smothering smell of oil and gasoline.

So you tell yourself it's over, drive carefully home, cry in the bathroom—
toothbrush in your fist, toothpaste foaming in your mouth like pain.
Nora, it's late. Go to bed, circle your husband in your arms.

Heathen Bed

■ ■ ■ ■ ■ ■ ■ ■ ■ ■ ■ ■

When it all becomes too much for him, God comes to my bed
and quietly, his slim hands by his side, asks if he might stay
at least for a little while where no one can find him.
Maybe because I once heard my aunt call me a heathen
when I was a child and she was closer to death than she knew
and I believed enough to believe I was a heathen
with my heathen bones, my heathen blood roaring
beneath my heathen skin, maybe because my heathen heart
beats so quickly at the very thought of God seeking peace
beneath the covers of my heathen bed, I always answer
Sure, pulling back the covers so he can slip his weary body in.
Only when I feel him settle on his back, hear his soft breath
become sure and slow, my own heathen heart calming
within the cage of my heathen ribs, do I climb from bed and go,
searching for a place where even he can't find me.

Francine Prose &
Michael Byers
Bread Loaf Writers' Conference

What's impressive about "In Spain, One Thousand and Three" is how much like life it is. That is, it takes a series of seemingly random elements— opera, *Don Giovanni*, the death of a lover, sexual politics in the office, kids' computer games—and fits them together in a way that artfully suggests the untidy collection of puzzle pieces that make up ordinary (and extraordinary) existence. There is a naturalness about this: none of these elements seems willed or forced to coexist in the same story. Michael Byers has taken on a large and dangerous subject: our inappropriate human responses to the mysteries of sex and death. Neither moralistic, sentimental, nor self-regarding, this is a dense, ambitious, admirably complex story.—
Francine Prose

Francine Prose is the author of nine novels and two volumes of short stories, most recently *Hunters and Gatherers* and *The Peaceable Kingdom*. Her work was included in *The Best American Short Stories 1991* and *Pushcart Prize XVII* and in many magazines and journals.

Michael Byers's story "In the Kingdom of Prester John" appeared in the spring 1995 issue of the *Indiana Review*. He also has a story in a forthcoming issue of *American Short Fiction*.

A Coincidence at the Vet's

■ ■

Twice this summer rabid raccoons have crawled down people's chimneys and in both cases bit old women, in both cases on the face. This is the reason that A. has brought in her cat, B., to the veterinarian.

The waiting room is crowded, but A. can't tell how many pet owners have brought in their pets for rabies boosters. For one thing, no one mentions the article that appeared yesterday in the local paper and that focused—wrongly, it seems to A.—on the second raccoon attack, when the real news, it seems to her, is that the same thing happened twice, though this fact was only mentioned once in the last paragraph of the article.

Also, many pets in the waiting room seem to have something seriously wrong with them, or rather many pet owners seem to believe they do. The office is very crowded, and during the long wait A. sees a woman announce to the whole waiting room that her dog is deaf, but when the receptionist calls them, that is, calls the dog's name, the dog turns its head and barks. A. also sees a man tell the receptionist that his cat is blind even as the cat paws with cruel accuracy at a ladybug on the counter.

So even here at the veterinarian's, things are not what they seem, even here where it should be so simple: pet lovers and loving pets. Partly what's caused the long delay was the young couple, much too young to own the old cat that—you could see on their faces—was dying. The receptionist took them first, ahead of everyone waiting, all of whom understood at once that this was an act of mercy. It strikes A. that this must be regular procedure at this office, which tips her feelings briefly on the side of the veterinarian, Dr. C., whom on the one hand she admires for how good he is with B., even though she knows he will not give B. a rabies shot without insisting on feeling his lymph nodes and checking for many nonexistent conditions while A. looks on in panic at how much this is going to cost.

The couple returns—without their cat. The receptionist says, "No charge." The couple is weeping, both of them—but you cannot tell. Just as, watching A. stroke B.'s orange fur, you could not possibly tell that this pet owner and her pet have been having a little trouble. In past weeks, B. has smashed A.'s favorite vase, shit on her best black dress, killed a squirrel—a squirrel!—and left its headless body at the foot of A.'s bed. A. removed the corpse with a shovel. The rabies shot is a must!

For years B. has been a good cat, affectionate, even loyal. A. knows it is stupid to imagine an animal capable of something like human malice. One thing animals teach you is to accept things for what they are, and anyone can see that B. is simply being catlike. It is crazy to think that this is happening because A. laughed at a photograph in a supermarket-tabloid article about a woman whose sweet white kitty began to resemble Hitler: the diagonal shock of dark hair, the little black brush mustache. And finally it is paranoid to imagine that the trouble A. is having with her cat is in any way related to the trouble she is having with people—specifically, with her boyfriend, D. Your warm understanding with your pet is supposed to remain constant, comforting and sustaining you throughout your misunderstandings with people. Your pet, A. thinks, shouldn't turn on you when it sees that you are wounded, though of course A. has to wonder if that is animal nature, too.

Eventually A. is the last one left in the waiting room, though others—and not just the owners of the cat who was put away—came in after her. Once they're alone, the receptionist compliments A. on what a smart thing she is doing, how few people watch out, really watch out, for their pet's well-being. Clearly she has no idea of A.'s new ambivalence about B., or maybe if she did she would say it doesn't matter, what absolves A. is that she is here, getting B. a rabies booster, when most people don't even know that they and their pet need not actually be bitten but can get infected merely from blood or saliva. A.'s stomach lurches sickeningly as she tries to remember if the squirrel B. beheaded could have bled or drooled on the rug, and she is preparing to hide her dread by bringing up the two old women bitten on the face, weeks and dozens of miles apart, both by rabid raccoons . . .

Just at that moment the phone rings. Answering, the receptionist says, "Oh, hello, Mr. E."

A. knows the rules of politeness: she should pretend not to listen, but feels that at this moment the rules have been suspended, because Mr. E. is the last name of A.'s boyfriend, D.

D. is not, strictly speaking, her boyfriend. Or maybe he is her boyfriend. He used to be her boyfriend but hasn't called for two weeks, and she fears that they may have broken up, but without her knowing. In fact she doesn't want to know, which is why she hasn't called him, and the longer this goes on . . . well, it could go on forever.

From hearing the receptionist's end of the conversation, A. concludes that something is critically wrong with D.'s (Mr. E.'s) parrot, F. In the year that A. has been in love with D., this parrot has suffered and recovered from several life-threatening ailments that caused all its feathers to drop out and a milky film to cover its eyes. A. has heard, from the other side, several such conversations—essentially the other half of the conversation that the receptionist is now having with D. And yet, surprisingly, it never came up that A. and D. have the same veterinarian. A. always preferred to say as little as possible about the fact that she has a cat and D. has a bird. It was supposedly one of the reasons for their not living together.

A. is only mildly surprised by the coincidence of D.'s calling the veterinarian while she and B. are there. After a week of D.'s not calling, A. happened to phone her brother-in-law, G., a friend of D.'s—and D. was there when she phoned; this is how she knows he's not dead, just not calling. At the start of their love everything was coincidental—their meeting, their both dropping by N.'s party though each had a cold, their having the same thoughts at the same time even with their small city between them, and of course A. always thinking of D. the second before he called. Lately she has been thinking of him at many seconds when he doesn't call. So his phoning the vet while she is there may be a step in the right direction, back toward a time when destiny seemed to have nothing to do but fling them together.

At last the receptionist calls B.'s name, and A. carries her cat into the vet's examining room. Dr. C. is a plump little wombat of a man with a curly red beard and hair and strong stubby hands into which A. gratefully surrenders B. The doctor sets B. on the table and shines a light in his ears as A. struggles against the desire to shout out loud that all B. needs—that all A. can afford—is a rabies booster.

But now the doctor is complimenting A. on her concern for her pet, most people don't know you can get infected merely from blood or saliva, just as people don't want to admit how much Lyme disease is around. Dr. C. never goes hiking without rubber bands around his cuffs. But A. is hardly listening, she no longer even worries as the doctor checks B.'s teeth and gives his testicles a squeeze. She is thinking that having overheard the news of the parrot's illness is a perfect excuse to call D. She would call a friend—a distant friend—in a similar situation.

Dr. C. pinches B.'s fur and sticks it with the syringe. The cat recoils from the needle. A. is overcome by a wave of love for B. that intensifies as she realizes that her cat could not have been purposefully cruel, at worst he was acting out the pain he'd felt streaming out of A. Her cat would never have hurt her just because she'd been hurt by D.

That evening A. dials D.'s number and then turns out the lights; she sits in her dark kitchen, stroking B.'s fur—sleepy from the vaccination, he's dozing on her lap—and listening to D.'s phone ring. Finally D. answers.

There is no way for A. to convince herself that D. sounds happy to hear from her.

"How is F.?" she asks.

"What do you mean?" D. says warily.

"I'm worried about him," A. says.

"What do you *mean*?" D. repeats.

Already they have gotten off on the wrong footing—this is not the tone a man uses when his lover calls to ask after his ill pet. "I'm worried he's sick again," says A.

"What makes you think that?" says D.

Why can't A. just tell him that she's overheard his call to the vet? Why can't she point out this coincidence signals a return to that happy time when what seemed like pure chance was in fact a conspiracy of fate to knit them tighter and tighter? It would probably annoy him—he might think she was making it up about being at the vet. Something is terribly wrong! A nice gesture, an ordinary act of human kindness and concern has been made to seem inappropriate, pushy—sexually aggressive!

"How did you know he's sick?" asks D.

"I dreamed it," A. hears herself saying. "It was the strangest thing. Last night I dreamed a parrot was perched on my hand and all its feathers started—"

"Oh, Jesus," says D. "He's convulsing again. I'll call you back, okay?"

A. is still holding the phone long after D. has hung up. The most humiliating part is that she feels herself mouthing the question: When? A siren blares inside her head, set off by the knowledge that D. so clearly loves a dumb bird more than he loves her. In the very beginning, she'd mistaken this for a good sign, a sign of his ability to care about a parrot.

A female voice—a computer voice—tells her: please hang up. Startled, A. leans forward to replace the receiver and, in doing so, forgets about B. Abruptly woken, B. cries out and bites A. on the hand. Now A. cries out, too, and, half rising, spills B. onto the floor. B. makes no effort to cling to her lap. As A. sinks back into her chair, she hears B. pad out of the room.

The pain is so searing, so terrifying A. thinks at once of rabies. Did she get B. vaccinated too late? Or, by some freak accident, too early? Could B. be harboring the rabies bacillus, a result of the vaccination, and in a one-in-a-million coincidence have transmitted it to A.? And *could* A. have somehow dreamed all this? Everything is so familiar. She should get up, call the doctor, get antibiotics, hot water—but she remains in her chair.

Sitting in the dark kitchen, cradling her injured hand, A. considers the two old women bitten by rabid raccoons. And now at last she understands how wrong she was about that. The real news was not that it happened twice, but that it happened at all, that someone was shocked from a deep sleep in her own bed in the middle of the night and looked up into those dark masked eyes and those spitty razory teeth, and almost, almost saw something there, something she recognized, in the moment before the pain flared up and burned everything else away.

In Spain, One Thousand and Three

■■■■■■■■■■■■■■■■■■■■■■■■■■■■

The little blue axe hung in the trees, flashing, and the monkey grabbed
the axe with two fingers, as if he were plucking fruit, and then the axe
was gone, and the monkey ran on, hunched, compact as a raccoon. He
skimmed low along the ground; but when a stone wall rose in front of him
he went floating up and over the wall gracefully, like a balloon. Martin
watched him with a detached affection, the way he might have watched a
neighbor's child.

"So it's the first left after the turtle farm," he said.

"How can it be after? There's nothing after the turtle farm."

"Yes," he said, gently, "you're on the *second* level, okay, and then you
turn *left* after the turtle farm, and then you grab the axe and you can go
over the wall."

"Do I need anything?"

"No. Just the axe."

There came a pause. Martin heard the boy's house rattling behind him:
a dishwasher, maybe, something throaty and mechanical, and then a dis-
tant door closing. It was late afternoon.

"And what else can I do for you." Martin entered the time in his log.

"Nothing."

"I need to know how old you are."

"Nine," said the boy.

"Calling from where."

"What?"

"Where do you live?"

"Sacramento."

There came another pause. Martin heard a siren and the boy's heavy
breathing.

"What's your name?" the boy asked.

"Who, me?" Martin said. "My name's Martin."

"How old are you?"

"Oh, I don't know, about a hundred and fifty, I guess," Martin said.

"Do you have a girlfriend?"

"No, I don't, actually."

"Why not?"

"I'd rather not say, buddy."

"She dumped you."

"Nope."

"*I've* got a girlfriend," said the boy.

"Well, good for you."

"*Fuck* you," the boy said, giggling, and then he hung up.

Martin sighed, not bothering to be bothered. Who can blame children? he thought; and then, who really finds children interesting? Fifteen seconds later the phone rang again; it would be a different boy, asking a different question. He heard other phones ringing far down the hall.

Martin's office with its black carpet had a dark, clandestine feel, as if in keeping with the conspiratorial nature of his job—these little planned betrayals of the programmers' codes, the toll-free numbers, the cynical days of gentleness training: *they're young, but they're customers*. Ignis paid him well—forty thousand dollars a year—but his office was stuck off in a far corner of the building, with a brief view of an alley and a dumpster. He sat at his desk all day and answered the phone when it rang. But everyone on his hall did this, more or less, and the weeks passed quickly enough; and on most days Martin actually enjoyed his work. He kept the lights off and the metal blinds drawn against the glare, and people said *You'll ruin your eyes!* so he squinted and fumbled for his coffee. He played along. But really he *liked* the darkness; it felt, to him, protective. "Hey in there, Mr. Caveman," Ms. Brendan would say, bumping her round hips against his doorjamb; but everyone knew Ms. Brendan was sleeping with Jack Halloran, the boss. "You're *hiding* from us in here," she'd say.

"Oh, not from you," he'd say. "Never from you."

She'd click her tongue. "*Martin*," she'd say, peering into the dark. There's a time and place for *this* sort of darkness, she meant. She'd shake her head, and then Martin would watch her walk away down the hall, her body compact and strong. Recently he'd imagined her big hips far too often, what they'd be like, and her pudgy feet in the air, and her face, how it might become contorted during sex, riven and dramatic. He'd sigh, and people would laugh, not knowing how often he thought of this and how ashamed he was of himself for thinking it. But they were all nice to Martin; and they had to be, considering.

Martin was a tall man, blond and young—barely twenty-five, though that sort of youth wasn't unusual at Ignis. He was handsome and he dressed well, and like many people at Ignis he had mixed feelings about the games themselves. They had some graphic moments, of course; some horrible things, if you really stopped to consider them, but there were worse things in the world to worry about, and most of the kids who called him were avid and healthy. And why not? Ignis had created strange and detailed worlds that seemed to expand as you explored them, as Martin had been made to do, as part of his training; and as he'd explored them, details of strategy had revealed themselves, and he'd come to understand these worlds' deeper mechanisms, a healthy thing for children to do, he believed; but at the same time, he understood, these worlds were really only *half*-created—all the street-fighter games appeared to take place on stage sets, like westerns, with the false fronts of office buildings and warehouses scrolling past in the background—and then of course there were always places you couldn't go, and things that didn't move; and Ronron the Monkey scampered over landscapes that were jungle-bright but depthless and that gave no hope of escape—Ignis had in effect contrived a batch of little hells, where your enemies kept coming, as relentless and dispassionate as the forces of nature, places in which you died over and over, by machete or bullet or snake, or in which you endured a neat simulacrum of death, a slow fading away as you were erased from the universe; and he could understand some of the protest against such things.

An hour later the Sacramento boy called back. "It's not working," the boy said.

"You swore at me, kiddo."

The boy said nothing.

"You apologize to me," Martin said.

"I'm sorry."

"Good. What's not working."

"He still can't get over the wall."

"Then it's a defective cartridge."

"It isn't working."

"I think it is," Martin said. "I think you're lying to me."

After a moment, the boy said, defeated, "Yeah, it's working." He hung up.

"Ha," Martin said, slamming the phone. "You lying little shithead."

At home Martin had a glass of wine and opened the balcony door. He looked out over Lake Washington, at the white boats and the far gray populated hills. Alone now in the apartment he felt its size and ostentation, the white walls that met perfectly with the white baseboards, the heavy doors. His furniture was all glass and steel piping—the coffee table, the low-slung chairs—and his refrigerator still clinked with Evelyn's tall colorful jars: her fancy jams, her French sauces and spreads. All of these were rotten now, or so he suspected. He had resolved to move, soon, as a matter of principle, or in the interest of making a clean break, but it hadn't happened yet. And on his salary he could certainly afford the place, and quite a bit more, too.

He brought the phone to the balcony. He called his mother across town. "So I've got this extra opera ticket tonight," he said, when she picked up. "I need some company."

"I was wondering when you'd call."

"I wasn't sure I felt like going," he said.

"This is pretty short notice, you know."

"I know it is."

"Well," his mother said, evenly, "I guess I've got nothing to do."

"We could dress up," he said.

"Sure." She cleared her throat. "That's good, Martin."

"Whatever."

"Pick me up in your fancy car," she said.

"All right," he said. He leaned on the railing. "Make it seven."

"I'll get dressed," she said.

For several years Martin's mother had kept college girls as boarders in her big timbered house. She felt safer with them there, she said, and she liked the company. There'd been dozens—all vegetarians, as she'd requested, and all women, and sometimes three or four boarded at once. Over the years these women had tromped up and down the dark stairs, and swept the yellow cherry leaves off the deck in back, and hung their crumpled nylons in the shower; and before he'd met Evelyn, Martin had entertained fantasies in which he'd crept into these women's bedrooms and hidden in their closets, and he'd imagined them peeling their stockings from their legs, and their various breasts falling into view, smooth, and then their hair coming unbound, spilling.

But Maria Relzina was now his mother's only boarder, an Oregon girl who was studying biology. Maria had lived with his mother for years, and the two of them were great friends, often to the extent that Martin was made uneasy. Maria and his mother were not lovers, he was almost certain—Martin found such a thing really unimaginable, his mother was too loopy for any such elaborate deception—but they did spend a lot of time together. Now Maria stood on the porch in a white dress, sweeping dust into the yard. "Hey," she said. "Long time." Her dress glowed in the dusk.

"How've you been?"

"Oh," she said. "So so." She leaned against the broom. "You look okay for once. Dressed up."

"I'm okay," he said.

"She's very excited," she said, tilting her head toward the house. Maria's neck was slender, and her black hair was long. Martin watched her jaw become defined, then softened, as she moved her head. Her breasts were small beneath her dress, like eggs bundled in cotton; she was wearing sandals, and her feet were dusty.

He looked away. He watched the sprinkler hissing onto the sidewalk. "That's a nice dress," he said.

"Oh, ha!" Maria twisted her hips. "This is my summer night dress."

Martin watched the hem settle around her ankles.

"You shouldn't stare like that."

"It's a hell of a view."

"You," she said, "are a flirter."

"Sorry."

"Oh, hoof, don't apologize." She leaned the broom against the railing, then took his hand. "Come inside."

His mother patted his leather dashboard. "That is just *fine, fine, fine*," she said. Her dress was bunched and crumpled under the seatbelt, and she smelled pleasantly of leaves and dirt. "I love this *car*, Martin."

"You should get one."

"Oh, it's so *quiet*. Mine's always *bumbumbum*."

"Maria doesn't have a boyfriend, does she," he said.

"Maria?" His mother pursed her lips and put a finger to them. "Oh, no, I don't think so. I think I'd know about that."

Martin rolled the steering wheel left.

"But you know she's not up to your sort of *style*," his mother said.

"I don't know what you mean."

"She's *my* friend," she said. "And I'd happily *kill* you if you laid a *finger* on her."

"Yes, I bet you would." The car hummed around them.

"She's becoming interested in my studies."

"Oh is she."

"She *is*. She's really very *skeptical*. In a good way, I mean. She doesn't take my word for anything. Which means really she's *already* a Buddhist. A Buddhist-in-waiting."

"She's from Eugene."

"Don't laugh, Martin, it's the only sensible religion there is. The fundamental principle of the world is its illusory nature," she said, staring out the windshield at the traffic. "And yet the world is holy, and God lives in all things."

"You understand how that might ring a little hollow."

"Well, yes, I do." She patted his hand. "I know you think I don't understand, but I do."

When it began to rain he closed the sunroof with one finger. In downtown traffic the lights through the windshield were blurred and brightened, and near the white-brick opera house he thought—again, as he did every day, and many times a day—of Evelyn, of her high bed and its aluminum rails, and he felt again the pit that had opened in him, perhaps forever. It was a horrible thing that couldn't be avoided, or gone back upon; her death—cancer—was, in its way, embarrassing, as any public infirmity might have been, obliging people to be sympathetic and understanding, though he felt he did not deserve any such sympathy, or understanding, because he felt he was not mourning her properly, that he had never been properly sorrowful. In fact he was filled with a raging lust, so overwhelming that at times he felt unstable, as if he might grab a passing woman's breasts before he could stop himself. Were his lusts apparent, just by looking at him? He thought not; but they saddened him nonetheless, because he believed they marked him as less than faithful. Women in the crosswalk, and then in the lobby of the opera house, appalled him, held his attention too long. He watched hips and legs climb the red-carpeted stairs ahead of him, and ankles with their tapering Achilles' blades, and hundreds of little conical breasts, and he felt great loathing for himself, and he was saddened, too, by his faithlessness. But then at once this sadness embarrassed him as still another thing he did not deserve. No one scolded him anymore—though if he'd ever deserved it, he deserved it now—no, everyone was polite and accommodating. Evelyn would have scolded him. Turned up her little chin.

It was *Tycho*, one of Offenbach's minor operas. They had loge seats. The ushers in their gray suits recognized him, and they nodded politely at his mother. Before the lights went down Martin plucked the staples from his program and tweaked them out over the audience. "Oh, Martin," his mother said, scowling. "You ought to be put in *irons*."

"Maria's got another year before she gets her master's, doesn't she."

"*Yes*," his mother said, whispering. "But it's none of your business."

Then the lights went down and the overture swelled, first perky, then doomed. His mother patted his arm once, in encouragement. The curtain lifted and showed a heavy Danish castle, and murky Danish fens, and stars in the purplish sky. Kepler was at his desk, his floppy hat asymmetrical. *O my eyes*, he sang. *The sky spins before me, teeming with light*.

"He's very good," his mother said.

Martin nodded. Kepler sang and sang.

Brahe loomed out of the wings, huge and majestic in his purple cloak. *Johannes*, he sang. *My friend, my mentor. I have news from Vienna.*

Ah, Tycho!

Ah, but Johannes, you look no better than a ghost.

Martin rolled his program into a telescope and put the telescope to his eye.

"Stop it, Martin." His mother smiled and batted his hand down.

It was a familiar view: the red ornate ceiling above, the soft loaves of rising breasts below. He could not avoid thinking about sex, and he didn't want to *avoid* it, exactly, because he thought this would be unhealthy; but at the same time it shamed him to want women so desperately when Evelyn had died, especially when he still felt her presence so palpably in the world, a pressure in the air, as if she were beside him, in her old seat. And what, really, was so strange about that? There were, perhaps, fragments of her body still here—flakes of her skin, or an eyelash—in the folds of the velvet chair. He had opened a book recently and found one of her hairs, brown and thick, curled like a serpent between the pages of *The Long Day Wanes*. He had taken it between his thumb and forefinger and lifted it gently, like a piece of parchment, a delicate document from an unimaginable age. He had gone stealthily to the bedroom and set it on his pillow, as if he intended to conjure her; but by that night he had forgotten it, and though he had remembered it at once in the morning, it was gone. Of course it was gone, he thought now. And what would he have done with it? What envelope would have had dignity enough to hold her last hair? What wooden box, what silver case? He looked down at the stage. Pyramids and cubes drifted like ghosts across the scrim, left to right, unreachable, and Kepler had his arms out, singing to them. *The universe lies within itself*, he sang, *nestled, delicate*. His mother was asleep beside him, snoring delicately.

Martin spent the weekend at home. He read the newspaper in the sun, and he watched a baseball game on television with the balcony door open, and he watered the plants on the deck in their clay pots. He stared at the telephone and thought of calling Maria, but did not, afraid that his mother would answer. He lay awake on the oak floor, in the indoor sun, naked, and the unfamiliar warmth on his groin aroused him. He thought of his own odd childhood: his mother's chamomile tea, the thin bronze gong in the living room where late at night when he was thirteen he had seduced a neighbor girl, Constance Tiptin, his first, on the carpet. It had not been *her* first time, and she'd peered at him through narrowed black eyes as he worked above her. Then there'd been scores and scores of women, too many to count, really: dozens in high school, and then in college he'd averaged three or four a month, very often sleeping with them only once. Their nakedness, always original in some particular, had thrilled him in his rented room, in the dark, with the streetlights playing over their bodies. They told him he was handsome, which he supposed he was, and he told them they were adorable, a word they'd have used themselves had they felt more comfortable with him.

He met Evelyn in one of his English classes. She was a musician, and her cluttered apartment was piled with musical scores and old records. "Sit down," she said, after their first movie together. She hefted a box off the sofa. "Listen to this." She put on a recording of Casals, suites for cello unaccompanied, she said; Bach. Martin, though he knew nothing about music, suspected he was being seduced; and of course he would acquiesce. He admired this woman's particulars (though in those days he could honestly say this about almost any woman), and he liked the creaking and groaning of the cello on the record, like a ship tossing joyfully at sea, and the nubbly texture of the record sleeve, coffee-stained and worn thin and hairy at its edges, and Evelyn leaning against one end of the sofa, watching him. She hummed, her big goofy teeth resting on her bottom lip, and Martin wanted her: her thighs in her jeans, her solid upper arms heavy in her green sweater. The cello creaked on, dust popping in the seams of vinyl. She held her finger up as the music climbed, joyfully; then she put her palm down and looked sad as the music descended and became somber again, like a horse in a field, chestnut-dark, corralled. "All right," she said, when the record ended. "You can go now."

"Go?"

"Please go," she said. And he went out, a little puzzled. This rarely happened. But then that weekend she called him again and asked him to the movies, and the marquee lights on her face reminded him of those other women's bodies lit through his window. Over coffee she pushed up the sleeves of her sweater. Her forearms were thick and brown. Her hands were heavy and strong. "I *play* cello, actually," she said, and in her apartment after coffee she lifted the thing from its black case. It was brown and sculpted as a body, but light, and she spun it deftly on its stand and then sat with it between her knees. "What to play?" she said, staring over his head.

"Whatever," he said. "I'd like to hear anything you've got."

"I'm trying to impress you," she said. "But I don't think you're easily impressed."

"I'm already impressed."

"No, I've heard about you," Evelyn said, squinting at him. "I know what you do."

"And here I am."

"You've got a reputation," Evelyn said. "Quite a shameful one."

He said nothing.

"I shall play *The Flight of the Bumblebee*," she said. "Transposed for cello unaccompanied."

She began to bow very rapidly, rapt, ignoring him. He smiled uncomfortably and tried to nod with the music, but it was much too fast for him to keep up with. Her fingers flashed on the neck of the cello, and she gritted her teeth, and her hair hung into her eyes. When they moved in together after college he remembered this night; and it wasn't so much that he'd fallen in love with her music or her passion but really with her *scolding*, and with the sudden sense that all he'd been doing since Constance Tiptin had been foolishness. It was a relief, really. He felt he had learned, if rather late in life, at twenty-one, to appreciate a woman's soul, though he knew this was a little silly, that he was still quite young. After graduating they shopped for pots, and commingled their books, and in this new life of his he thought only of Evelyn's body: its dips and hollows, her solid, round rump, her underarm hair swishing against his fingers. She had filled his hands; but now he had begun imagining the bodies of his mother's boarders again, and Ms. Brendan's body, and his own body had begun betraying him, wanting the surfaces of things, the pale appearances. Appalling, appalling, he thought; and of course his mother was right; paradise was the absence of desire, and hell was desire let loose, desire forever satisfied.

The Sacramento boy called back on Monday. "I got to level four," he said.

"You again. Why aren't you in school?"

"I'm sick. I have the flu."

"You don't sound sick."

"I am, though."

Martin tipped back in his chair and turned on the Ignis. From far away down the hall he could hear someone laughing. He keyed himself into the fourth level. "What's your name?" Martin asked.

"Oscar."

"All right, Oscar. You promise not to lie to me."

"I promise."

"You promise to be polite."

"I do."

"Good," said Martin. "Then I've got more secrets for you."

"Wait! Let me get a pad." There came crashing in the background, and Martin imagined the boy's plastic vomit bowl, the Kleenex box, the metal cars and helicopters, the Ignis black and solid in the yellow blankets at the foot of the bed. "Okay."

"There's a blimp that flies over on level four," said Martin, quietly. "It's got an extra life in it. Throw a Barterball at it."

Oscar breathed.

"Also, try to fool around with the porcupines for a while and see what happens."

"What happens?"

"Something good."

Oscar said, "You'll never guess what I did." His voice was thick and conspiratorial.

"What."

"Me and my girlfriend did it," he said.

"Did what?"

"*It.*"

"Oh, really."

Then Oscar laughed, wickedly, and hung up.

"Well," Martin said, and hung up. He looked uneasily at the phone. Was this how people had seen *him* in the old days—as unnaturally avid, and wicked? Oh, it was, it had to be. He got up from his desk, unplugged the phone from the wall, and pulled open the shades. In the alley the dumpster was open, and above him he could see a blue slice of sky. Children had called him before with confessions—they'd killed cats, stolen candy, hit their brothers. Now Martin stared into the alley and imagined both children in bed, sticky, impudent, smelling like meat and candy; and then the boy's older sister coming in with her loose adolescent blouse, undressing, observing, giving them tips. He knew he should not be thinking these things.

Halloran knocked on the doorjamb. "Martin," he said.

"Halloran."

Halloran was barefoot, and his toenails were dirty. Halloran was thirty-one and had a raggedy beard like a railroad hobo, and he was so thin that Martin had once worried for his health. But Halloran ran marathons. "Listen," Halloran said, shutting the door. "I was talking to Mark down in receiving."

"Mark who."

"Mark Macom. Said he went to college with you."

"Mark Macom works here?"

"He does."

"He's a sleazeball."

"Well, he says you've got a reputation," said Halloran, picking his toenail.

"A reputation for what."

"You know for what." Halloran pinched his beard. "For getting it whenever you want it. In college, anyway."

"Jesus."

"I know." Halloran shrugged. "It just came up."

"Maybe it doesn't occur to you that I might be embarrassed by that sort of reputation."

"He sure didn't think so."

Martin sat down behind his desk. "Macom's an asshole."

"Yeah, well, Martin, I need some advice."

Martin sighed. "Jesus."

"I'm getting the feeling she's bored with me physically," said Halloran.

"Who is."

"Ms. Brendan."

"Ms. Brendan is."

"Yes, Ms. Brendan, who the hell else?"

Martin shrugged. "I don't know, maybe you're working around a little."

"No," Halloran said.

"Well," Martin said, sighing again. "So she's bored, get yourself a haircut."

Halloran stirred uncomfortably.

"If she's bored, give her a change. Start working out."

"I run a lot."

"Yeah, so start lifting."

He made a face. "Cuts down my times."

"Look, you asked," Martin said. "You came to me. Spend a little money on clothes once in a while."

"Yeah, she likes your clothes," said Halloran. He grimaced. "She talks about you an awful lot. She likes that checkered jacket."

"There you go."

Halloran steepled his fingers. "You really don't give a shit what I think, do you?"

"Not really."

"You just told your boss to get a haircut."

"Yeah, well, you asked."

"No, I know. But you answered."

"Well," Martin said, "you *asked*."

"Do you mind if I ask you something?" said Halloran.

"What."

"I'm wondering if you're seeing anyone these days."

"No," said Martin. He looked at the ceiling, the porous tiles.

"Just gossip, I guess," said Halloran. "Mark said he'd seen you out with someone."

"Yeah, I don't go anywhere he'd go."

"Well, I was just wondering, sort of on a personal level," Halloran said. "But I guess not."

"No."

"You must miss her," he said.

"Yes, I do."

"You never really talk about it."

"Not really."

"I guess you stop thinking about that sort of sex thing for a while, after something like that, I mean. More important things to think about."

"Something like that," said Martin, looking down from the ceiling. Though of course this was just the way his body was betraying him: *oh, the body's just a dirty jar*, his mother would say, kindly; *just a dirty jar for the soul*. In fact he had wanted Evelyn's body even on her worst days, not expressly against doctor's orders but rather skirting them, as surely the doctor knew they would do, being young. The medicine had weakened her heart, and it was finally this that would kill her, though of course they couldn't know this; but they'd gone slowly at home anyway, because she was often dry and uncomfortable, and she'd had to lie still with her eyes closed, as if finding the pleasure of sex was a trial, a task of concentration—like a dark passage underground, she told him, later. She held her head back, studying the movements they made. He had wanted her constantly, and it had shamed him to want her when she weighed a hundred pounds, or less, or when she was sick and dizzy, or when, in the early days, her purse clicked with vials, or when, in February, he cut off her hair. Then in the end he had taken sexual interest in her hands, and her face: he put his tongue in the dry spaces between her fingers and she stirred, breathing carefully; and then her forehead, which he would kiss, and breathe on, and then her ears, stiff and waxless. He had never stopped wanting her. And then after she'd died sitting up, and there had been a week at home, in his old bedroom, in the dark, he had woken up in the morning and wanted Maria, and he had listened to Maria padding back and forth to the bathroom upstairs, and the water running in the shower, and he had imagined the soap sliding over her belly, and the wet slap of her hair, and he had been ashamed and had thought himself low, hiding in his mother's house, uncaring. But of course it had continued, this imagining—with Maria and then, later, with other women. And though he had done nothing yet, Martin knew, as Halloran left his office, that he soon would do something, that his body would demand its satisfaction, and that Evelyn would be gone, then, for good, and the memory of her body would be forever absorbed into the feel of another woman's body, as a twin absorbs the tissues of its twin.

After work on Monday he drove to Evelyn's parents' house. They'd been in Mexico for six months, and now they wanted to see him. They met him at the door; they smelled of liquor. "Well hell, Martin," Peter said. He had big shoulders, and rough hands, and sandy hair, a Swede. "It's good to see you."

"You too," said Martin.

"Oh, Martin." Josephine was skinny and overtanned. She had short brown hair. They embraced, and the big yellow beads around her neck clacked like teeth. She held Martin out. "You are so *pale*."

"I think I'm about right," he said.

Josephine laughed and then began to cry, mildly. "Martin," she said. She clawed a tear away with a brown hand. She sniffed and recovered. "Whoops," she said. "Didn't see that one coming."

Peter patted her shoulder. "It's all right," Peter said.

"We were just having a drink," she said, and sighed. "We're turning into drinkers."

"No we're not," Peter said.

They moved into the living room: small, gray-carpeted, with fringed lamps. "We haven't talked to your mother in ages," Josephine said. "She's all right, I hope."

"Well, you know my mother," Martin said. "Nothing quite gets to her."

"Yes."

"But she's fine."

"She's a very strong woman," Josephine said. "I admire her for that."

Martin took a whiskey. "Thanks," he said. They all sat. The room reeked of booze.

"Gackie," said Peter. A dog, brown and leathery like a suitcase, trotted through the room, then out again. "Gackie," said Peter, more loudly, but the dog ignored him. Peter stuck out his tongue.

"Well, I'll be teaching again soon," Josephine said, fingering her beads. "In Shoreline. They couldn't get along without me."

"That's good," Martin said, drinking.

"Back to the kiddies." She curled her lip.

"Yeah. I've got a story for you. Had a kid tell me today he'd had sex with his girlfriend. Nine years old."

"Oh, no," she said.

Peter shook his head. "This world," he said.

"Couldn't believe it. Just came out and told me. And the same kid told me to go screw myself a couple days earlier." He was angry now, for the first time. "Just called right on back. No compunction."

"Punks," Peter said.

"You didn't take much time off, did you?" Josephine said.

"A month."

"We took six months," she said. "But you know that. Ran up the credit cards."

"You guys look great."

"Thanks," Josephine said.

Then it seemed there was nothing else to say.

"You were so *good*," Josephine said.

"Oh," he said. And there was another odd silence.

"We have some things of yours upstairs," Josephine said.

"You do."

"A shirt, I think," she said, waving vaguely. "Up in her room." She stood, unsteadily, and took his arm, and the two of them padded upstairs.

The smells of the house: the metallic smell of rain, somewhere, as if the roof were leaking, and a thick smell of onion and oil; the gray dusty carpet; the rough unpolished banister. Now upstairs in her carpeted room: the bed, the shelves cleared, most of them, though here was her picture, and here, indeed, was his, with his arm around her. "Yes, that," she said. "That's nice, isn't it." Josephine was standing at the door behind him, and he could hear her breathing, and the little rustle of her breasts, certainly, beneath their blouse, little downturned teardrops they'd be, and her hips slack and tanned and liquid in his hands. Brushing past him she put a warm hand on the small of his back, and then to the closet: "Your shirt," she said. The vials were gone from the dresser, the stacks of folded towels, and the bowls and syringes, and the telephone and television had been removed; it was a silent room now, looking out onto the wooded backyard, the fir trees, the window where he had cupped Evelyn's breasts once, from behind, and she'd twisted her hips back against him, a day when the house had owned that delicious weekday afternoon sexuality, the ease and arousal born of quiet, just the jets passing over occasionally, and the distant rainy whish of traffic.

It was a heavy white cotton shirt, a good shirt, almost formal, dirtied long ago by Evelyn's vomit, and laundered and forgotten several times. Now Josephine held it to him on its hanger, ducking her head, a little embarrassed: this was a specific thing, a specific memory of a particular time; and Martin then remembered the room, not as a death room but busy and filled with activity, the radio always on, and magazines folded and discarded in a rush, and a fan blowing from the dresser. Josephine held the shirt to him as if testing its size in a store; and then she hugged him, holding his big shoulders and tucking her head beneath his chin, pressing against him. "Oh, Martin," she said. She was warm and soft against him. Like shy dancers they stirred their hips against one another, just a brush at first, then deeper, harder; then they separated, looking away.

Ms. Brendan stopped him by the elbow the next morning. "Martin," she said, whispering, and dragged him aside, into the coffee room. "What exactly did you tell Jack yesterday?"

"I'm not sure."

"He shaved all his *body hair*," she said, looking both ways, then behind her. Her eyes were dark with mascara, and her mouth was big and easy. "He's like a sausage now."

"*All* of it?"

"Every bit. He came out of the bathroom last night and he said he had a surprise. I almost burst a vessel."

"Not his head."

"No. But the beard's gone."

"Holy shit."

"It wasn't bad, though," she said, licking her lips. "I'm not complaining. He was very *smooth*."

"I bet." Martin cleared his throat.

"You must be about ready to get set up, honey."

"I don't think so."

"I've got a friend."

"I don't think so," Martin said again, blinking. But she was close to him, so close he could see the fuzz on her chin, the black crumbs of mascara in her eyelashes. He really couldn't be blamed for this sort of thing, he thought, and he couldn't be blamed, either, for the way his eyes darted down to her breasts, which were big and solid in their flowery blouse, or her hips, which would crash against his, muscled and demanding. He had gone home the night before, mortified by what he'd done but hopelessly aroused by Josephine's satin pants, by the experienced grind of her hips. He cleared his throat again. "You're not looking so bad yourself," he said.

"I know I'm not," she said.

"Old Halloran doesn't know what he's got."

"Oh, I think he does," she said, and raised her chin. "I think *you* know what he's got, too."

"I think I do."

She looked away.

"You know I have to confess," Martin said, still whispering. "I've been thinking about it constantly. Sex, I mean."

"Oh, Martin," she said, "that's understandable."

"I mean *constantly*. I can't stop thinking about it. Everybody. My mother's roommate."

"Well," she said, "that's a good sign, maybe."

"It's not a sign. It's been going on ever since."

"Since what." She peered at him.

"Since about six months ago," he said. "Right after the funeral."

"Really."

"Really."

"Well, I don't think that's all that unusual," she said, but she was guarded now. "It's like people pairing off at weddings, you know. It's life-affirming."

"I got aroused by her *mother* yesterday."

"Her mother?"

"Yes." He pinched his tie and sniffed. "But you don't think it's too unusual."

"Well, no, that's a little unusual, I'd have to say."

"I'm not sure why I'm telling you."

"That's all right."

"It's not really something I can talk to anybody about. Not her parents. Not my parents, either."

"No."

"Listen," he said, "don't tell Halloran any of this."

"You know, he told me a few things about you last night." She pursed her lips. "Said he heard from somebody you were sort of a playboy in college."

"Oh, god."

"Don't be coy."

"No, I'm not," he said. "It's just not who I am anymore. Or I guess it's not who I *want* to be."

"I see."

"I mean, I miss her," he said, desperately. "I really do."

Ms. Brendan smiled and patted his shoulder. "It'll be our secret," she said.

He walked down the hall to his office, his hands shaking. He felt foolish; he had not in fact meant to say any of that; and what did she mean, *our secret*? What, exactly, would she keep as their secret? He took one deep breath and slapped his thighs when he sat down behind his desk. Things, he felt, were becoming unpredictable. He plugged in his telephone. Thirty seconds later it rang: a boy from Memphis was stuck in *Uplands*. Oh, Christ, he said, jump on the playing card, it slides away, reveals the tunnel. He told a boy in Toronto to keep the sword and drop the potion bottle, which was wrong, backwards. But then after a while the work calmed him, as it often did, and he felt trustworthy again. Children asked him questions to which he knew the answers: touch the statue; ask the robots for the keys; knock twice, then once.

Then Oscar called back. "Hey, Marty," he said.

"Oscar. How do you keep getting my line?"

"I call lots of times," Oscar said. "When it's not you, I hang up."

"Why?"

"Because you're the one I talked to first."

Martin leaned to look down the hallway, then said, "Hang on," and got up to close the door. Back at his desk, he said, whispering, "Oscar, listen."

Oscar breathed.

"Oscar, you want another secret?"

"Sure."

"What level'd you get to?"

"Seven," Oscar said.

There was a girl's voice in the background.

"Who's that?" Martin asked.

"Nobody."

"*Oscar*," Martin said, ferociously. "You've got to stop playing these *games*."

"Why?"

"Because they're a *big fucking waste of your time*," he said. "Throw the fucking thing out the window. You're not learning anything. You're fucking up your little *head*."

Oscar gasped and hung up.

Martin hung up, smiling. He got up and opened the door and went to the coffee room. He saw the back of Ms. Brendan disappearing down the hall, her solid rear packed beneath her skirt. Before he knew it he had whistled at her; and she waved back at him. Halloran would surely hear of this, and he began to anticipate punishment from various people—the call from Halloran, or Oscar's parents, or Peter, and when he imagined these things he felt a little thrilling clutch in his stomach, the same thrill he had once felt with a new woman, the immediacy of her soft new skin in all its naked particularity. But the afternoon passed uneventfully; Halloran showed up, rubbing his pale naked chin, and he gave Martin the thumbs-up around the door jamb. Even Ms. Brendan waved at him and shook her head. *Naughty naughty*, she meant to say; but she didn't really seem to mind.

In their two good years together, when he hummed her songs—and he would often find himself humming in front of the Ignis screen, or on the phone—Martin could almost imagine what it was like to inhabit Evelyn's head, to occupy the wet grammar of music and its gentle repetitions. When he was alone in the apartment he played her LPs and heard, occasionally, the click of a bow against a music stand, or the shuffle of someone's shoes, and he liked these moments for their fallibility, and he suspected, too, that when Evelyn's musician friends talked about the old days, and about their nostalgia for vinyl records, they were really just being nostalgic for an age when things seemed achievable, when music was noticeably a human endeavor, not polished and electronic but warm and liquid, the black record revolving like a puddle of oil.

And Evelyn still played the cello, too, though not as much as before. She was a teacher now, and often worn out from work; but every so often she invited her teacher friends to the apartment. These women, who had round, heavy rears, set their violins down on the dining room table, gently, as if setting down platters of delicate food; then after drinks, and after the dinner was in, they'd snap open their cases like businessmen, and the expressions on their faces would become serious, and fearful, as if they were admitting they could never be perfect at this thing, that they would always be slow for a certain cue; and Martin loved the rueful cast that came over their faces, as if they were bringers of bad news. They would put down their wineglasses and play, their chins tucked into their instruments. "Shit," they'd all say occasionally. "God damn it." To Martin the music sounded seamless; but he liked them swearing, well-dressed and holding their polished instruments in his big apartment.

At dinner they asked him about his work, and he told them about Halloran, and Ms. Brendan. The women smiled and glanced down the table at Evelyn, *good for you*, they meant; and Martin felt strong and decent. He could keep his attention on these women's faces, off their bodies, and only occasionally when they were playing did he watch their bodies and only then as part of the whole, he thought, as an anthropologist might, or a technician of some kind, interested really in how the music contorted them. He was proud of himself for this, and of course he felt silly for being proud, and he couldn't tell anyone about it; but that again was another pleasure of maturity, having pleasures which couldn't be related without being distorted. When it rained he'd take the women out onto the spattering balcony and huddle with them under the overhang while Evelyn cleared the table, and he'd point out the gauzy lights on the other side of the lake.

During these two good years he felt he had conquered himself. He felt he had considered the patterns of his own life, which had been lascivious, and changed them. And Evelyn was understanding, if only because she'd done some of the same things in college herself: she'd slept with men whose names she'd hardly known, for whom she'd had no love, certainly. She described to him how she would seduce a man, and to Martin's surprise this aroused him: he liked to imagine his plump Evelyn calculating and considering frankly the aims of her body. And she still looked at men, she said; she still considered what it'd be like sleeping with the principal, the bus drivers, and she'd elaborate for him the fantasies she had—their slack middle-aged bodies, their sudden hopefulness in her arms, the way their breath came in puffs, their sweet inept bodily release. Daily in the kitchen, in the steaming car parked beneath the building, leaning on the midnight balcony, she and Martin fitted themselves together; and he found he was still aroused by that illicit sense of abandon, all pretenses dropped, this and only this the real reason for everything, her breasts filling his hands; because wasn't sex behind everything, the point of manners, the point of art, commerce, luxury? Everything else, he said, was adornment. Even music, he said: birds and their territory. He didn't quite believe this himself; but he saw how Evelyn liked him to be odd, sometimes theoretical, or didactic. It made him more hers when they had sex, he supposed, and he felt a little guilty, too, when she looked sad and touched his face, after he said music was only adornment, and this guilt bound him to her, too.

This faith in her, this conversion, had been genuine, and he was proud of those days, those two good years. She brought home her students' papers, and they spilled around the apartment, burst out of her filing cabinets; sometimes in odd corners she'd find a paper from months ago, a stowaway, and she'd look at it guiltily and fold it once and throw it away. When she corrected tests at the dining room table she puffed out her cheeks and her red pens squeaked across the pages—she did not have the best students, being a new teacher. They talked about marriage, but never did anything about it; and then suddenly it was their third winter, and she became increasingly tired, though at the same time she was unable to sleep well for weeks, sitting up in bed: *I feel funny*, she said, and her eyes grew thin gray bags, like hammocks. And then on a rainy day they went to see *Don Giovanni* (they were her tickets, of course) though she'd said she'd felt dizzy, unearthly. In their loge seats he held her hand, mildly concerned, stroking the wide strong bones of her wrist. The strings sank away at the end of the overture; and then Leporello sang, roguish and importunate: *Madamina; il catalog e questo*. I've compiled a little list, he sang, of the don's conquests. The Italian hills rolled sandy away from him in the distance; there were colonnades and, in the valley below, red-tiled roofs. Leporello held the paper out for inspection, propped his glasses on his nose. *In Italia sei cento e quaranto; cento in Francia, in Turchia novantuna; ma, ma, in Ispagna, ma in Ispagna, son gia mille e tre. Mille e tre.* That profligacy, a thousand and three in Spain alone! A point of pride for Leporello, the don's servant, bearded and jolly, and surely he got some scraps now and then; but even he seemed unsettled by it, by this bursting arrogance: washerwomen, duchesses, the elderly, the infirm, the virginal. And perhaps in alarm, but fascinated, as one is fascinated with a horrible infection, he kept the list, which gave proof and certainty. "Ah ha," Martin said, and tapped her knee. "See? It's not so unusual."

"Don't," she said.

"The don's my kind of guy," he said, and she swallowed, uneasily.

And it wasn't the next morning, or the one after that, but the next weekend when she went to the doctor, and it all began: the speculations, the mystery, the organic food, the thought that toxins were everywhere—that they were, in fact, the real purpose of the world, the world's revenge, killing those who had killed it. The surgery, the chemicals; weaknesses. Had he actually pushed her over the edge, he wondered, sometimes, pushed her by bringing up his old libertine self, resurrecting himself in front of her, for her to consider? But he loved her, and her bodily weakness compelled him as nothing had compelled him before, as did the desperation with which she looked at him, the unimaginable envy she must have felt for his body, sound and solid. Like something left outside in summer, she became gradually more fragile, more brittle, grayer. But he continued to imagine only her body—first as she used to be, round and full and tight; and then, as she grew sicker, he accommodated himself to her new body, to its sags and fragilities. He couldn't then conceive of his old sexual treacheries; his former self, he thought again, had been finally abolished; and in a way he was right, for he found he wanted no one else until she died; but it was small consolation, and now he was right back where he'd begun. He had admired himself in those days, he thought now; and he no longer admired himself.

The front door buzzer rang. It was Maria. "Martin," she said, dryly.

"I think you've got the wrong apartment."

"Stop fooling. Let me in."

He buzzed her in. He stood at the top of the stairs and watched her come up, her black hair in its band, her blue dress soft on her shoulders. "You look wonderful," he said.

She passed into the apartment, scowling. "You're bad, *bad*, Martin. You're making your mother feel terrible."

"I know."

"So stop pretending you feel so good."

"I was kidding about the boyfriend thing."

"Don't kid! She doesn't know what to think."

"I know."

"You shouldn't be living over here all alone anyway," said Maria. "You should be with us."

"No thanks," he said. "I like being alone."

"Oh, Martin, you don't like anything. You don't care about us at all." She looked at him, disappointed.

"Sure I do," he said. "Of course I care about you."

"I'm thirsty," said Maria, and she went to the refrigerator. It was rancid. "Well," she said, bending. "You're growing thallophytes in here." She began stacking bottles on the counter.

"Don't do that," Martin said. He approached her from behind. "You look like a maid."

"You could use one." She examined a jar of chutney.

"That's Evelyn's."

"It's moldy."

"I know it is."

She put the jar on the counter and he looked at it, balefully.

He sighed. "I'm going to take a shower," he said.

"Stay right here," she said.

"All right."

"Josephine called me," she said, sniffing. She stood and took a sponge from the sink, and Windex from the cupboard beneath it. "She said you weren't quite yourself."

"Josephine isn't herself either."

"No, she isn't," Maria said, her voice contained in the refrigerator. "She was very drunk."

"She made a pass at me."

"It sounded like it was almost successful," Maria said.

"No."

"That's what Josephine said."

"Well, it could have been," Martin said, and suddenly he was aroused again.

"That is not healthy, Martin," Maria said, squirting the Windex. "That is really very very sick."

"Why's it sick? She did it."

"Peter called us, too."

"He did?"

"He sounded *very* angry. He said he's coming over here to pick you up and have a talk."

"I've had sex with older women," Martin said. "Several, in fact. Dozens." He took an egg from the rack and slipped it delicately into his mouth, then out again, as if he were birthing it. "You don't believe me," he said, putting the egg back.

Maria sighed.

"You won't get angry at me," he said, sorrowfully. "Nobody gets angry at me anymore."

"I *am* angry," Maria said. "I'm very angry. You're being disgusting."

"You're still here."

"You don't deserve me, though," Maria said. "I am doing this for your mother. I am not a maid."

"Let's have sex," he said.

"*No*, Martin," she said, still facing the refrigerator. "You don't touch me."

Sixty years from now you'll wish you did," he said.

"Martin." She turned. "In sixty years you'll wish you deserved me, Martin. You'll dream about me, and you won't ever have had me, not ever. I'd cut your penis off with a clippers," she said, calmly, still kneeling, with the sponge in her hand. "And I'd shove it down your throat."

"Oh, Maria," he said. "I'm sorry."

"Don't you call me by my name," she said. "Don't you look at me."

"I won't," he said. He looked away, terrified.

She stood and took his throat calmly in her hands. Her hands were cold, damp, the fingernails sharp and precise. "You won't ever say those things again."

"No."

"You have been dreaming," she said, and he closed his eyes, involuntarily. "This is the world," she said, savagely. "Live in it."

Peter drove stiffly, his arms out like poles, his head back against the headrest. His jaw was set; he hadn't shaved, and a fine gray stubble sanded his cheek. They drove over the Ballard Bridge, the metal seams banging *ta ta ta ta* against the wheels. "Gotta love this city," Peter said finally.

"I can't stay out for long," Martin said.

"Yes, you can."

"I've got my freezer defrosting."

"It'll keep."

"I don't want to stain the floor."

Peter steered suddenly right. "You know I'm cold," Peter said, holding out his hand. "Feel my hand."

Martin felt it. Cold and stiff.

"I'm a statue," Peter said, gravely, his jaw clenched. "My circulation is shit. My blood pressure's *dropped* fifty points in six months."

"That's something."

"This is hell," Peter said. "This is it, right here." He gestured at the traffic with his white, bloodless hand. He steered onto a side street. "This fucking day-to-day bullshit nothing life we live. Hell on earth."

"No it isn't," Martin said.

"I believe in purposes now," Peter said. "I think there are purposes to things. Nothing makes sense otherwise. I sit down at the fucking docks all day and people go in, come out, and I think, Why the fuck am I painting the bottoms of boats that nobody's ever going to see? What the *fuck* am I doing here? But now I know the reason why I'm there."

"What's the reason."

"Because I deserve it," Peter said. "We deserve what we get. I was a fuck-up in school, that's what I get. You were faithless in spirit to my daughter, and she died. You were rude to me the other day, and now you deserve to sit here next to me wondering if I'm about to kick the living shit out of you, which I should, and you deserve worse, in fact, if you ask me."

"I was faithful to Evelyn," Martin said, somberly.

"Oh, God, I'd see you ogling around. Obvious, obvious. Shitty as hell."

"I never ogled," Martin said.

"Oh, you did. You thought you were hiding it, but I could see it. You wanted everything you fucking saw. Everything that walked the fuck by."

"That's not true. I used to do that, but I stopped."

"Like hell," Peter said, and turned the rearview mirror to look at himself. "People still talk about what you used to do."

"Used to do, sure," Martin said. "Before."

"Bullshit. You always wanted to."

"No, I want to *now*. *That's* the problem."

"Coming into my goddamn *house*," Peter said.

"You think I was rude to you," Martin said.

"Oh, shit."

"What'd I say?"

"God. What'd you *say*. You didn't *say* anything."

"Well, what, then."

"Jesus," Peter said. He rubbed his face. "Oh, *what*. We were both drunk. We walk around the house all day drunk and naked," Peter said. "All the shades down. Drunk and naked. I'm drunk now, in fact."

Martin nodded.

"You don't believe me."

"Sure I do."

"You like thinking about us walking around like that? Naked?" He pulled up at the curb and undid his seatbelt. "I bet you do."

"She approached me," Martin said.

"The hell she did."

"She put the shirt against me."

"I want you to understand something," Peter said, calmly. "Okay? You know nothing. You know nothing about me or Josie or anybody. You're a selfish little shit and you always have been, and the more I see you the more pissed off I get that my daughter ever met such a monumental piece of horseshit as you."

"You're not so great yourself," Martin said.

"*Exactly* what I thought you'd say," Peter said, still calm. He tipped his orange cap back on his head. "Just a little horseshit answer from a little horseshit guy. She was my *world*. *Every*thing. The rest of this is just nothing." He gestured out the windshield. "Shitty job, shitty weather, shitty car. Shitty house. And the rest of my life I'll be thinking about how she spent five years with *you*"—he began crying, his lips mashed out of shape—"and not *us*, where we would have taken care of her, and given her what she deserved."

He punched Martin half-heartedly on the chin, but it was without force and didn't hurt. "The *rest* of my *life*," Peter said, still crying. "I am going to be in this city for the rest of my life until I die, and I don't ever want to see you again, ever, not even by accident or anything."

Martin got out of the truck. He was not quite sure where he was: he recognized none of the buildings: warehouses, equipment sheds. Nothing looked quite familiar.

"Josie hates you," Peter said, getting out of the truck too. They stalked across the street, facing each other. "Apologize."

"For what?"

"For making her *hate* you."

"No," Martin said, still backing up. "She doesn't hate me."

"She does, she does, she does," Peter said, grinding his jaw again. "Apologize."

"I can't apologize for nothing. I didn't do anything."

"You did," he said. "You fucking made a pass at my wife, goddamn you."

"I did not."

"Apologize."

"I didn't do anything."

"Yes, you *did* do something, goddamnit. You fucking *humped* her."

"That's not what happened."

"The hell it isn't."

"I'm not going to apologize."

"Well, then goddamn you," Peter said. "Goddamn you to hell."

But then Martin was filled with a glorious calm. Trees stood out against billboards. Paper cups rolled back and forth in the gutters. The soft rushing city sounds around them grew gentle, caressing. A green station wagon rolled by, honking, and Peter kicked at it, missing wildly, one drunken spin on his work boot, then a stumble, then recovery. Martin was sorry, of course, not that he'd admit this to Peter—actually Martin *liked* seeing him this way, drunk and ridiculous, it made Martin feel solid, and dependable, and rational—but he *was* sorry for so much, for his lustiness and his trespasses, yes, but also he was suddenly sorry for himself and Josephine and for sad abandoned Peter, and for Evelyn, most of all, who could not be here to see any of them, her father's paint-flecked clothes, his graying, unfocused eyes, the flat, false world they'd all inhabited since she'd died; and

162

all at once this sorrow filled him, and he wasn't ashamed by it, and it made him heavy, as if he were a bucket filling with sand. It was a moment Martin would remember for the rest of his life when he felt small, or uncaring, or unsure of what to do—he would remember this scene, every bit of it, this particular industrial back street, the gray sky, the blank warehouses, the blue truck awkward at the curb, Peter crying into his hand—for years it would come to mind unbidden, this long back street heavy with sorrow; and then much later, in his long slow adult happiness, and surrounded by those he loved, Martin would remember all this purposely, over and over again, in its every peculiar detail, these sad men lost in an anonymous landscape, and his sudden weight, as if the sky were pressing him into the earth, at last; and with a little shiver of his old selfish pleasure Martin would be reminded of the man he had been before this moment, and the proximity of hell, and of his old lusts for the false things of this world.

Bob Shacochis &
Tom Paine

Bennington Writing Workshops

Tom Paine's "Will You Say Something, Monsieur Eliot?" poignantly demonstrates the literary fact that other worlds put America's reality into perspective; lives other than our own make for fascinating mirrors, illuminate the dimensions of our own context, our own imperative, our collective destiny.

What I find most aesthetically compelling is that while it certainly must be considered a classic adventure story, its subtext is politically panoramic, inferring the day's headlines without depending on that topicality to graft depth and meaning onto a narrative where they might otherwise not exist. The story is solid and autonomous, yet resonates with the global pulse of the times—a perfectly crafted geopolitical parable that so devastatingly personalizes the American identity, the American mythology.

Throughout the drama, the prose is unostentatiously gorgeous. The seductive cadence of the language, the velocity of the narrative, the vividness of the physical universe, the stunning economy of emotions—all of these writerly virtues converge in Tom Paine's undeniably powerful work.

Everybody clap.—**Bob Shacochis**

Bob Shacochis received the National Book Award for *Easy in the Islands*. His other books include *Swimming in the Volcano* and *The Next New World*. He is a contributing editor of *Outside* and *Harper's*.

Tom Paine has published fiction in the *New Yorker, Story*, and the *Boston Review*. Winner of the O. Henry Award, he is currently an editor for *Columbia* and lives in North Ferrisburg, Vermont.

Going Back

■■■■■■■■■■

Someone once wrote that twenty years of distance gives you not just an event or place to return to, but also your former self. Or, I might add, *somebody's* former self, not especially recognizable as your own.

Van Britton's younger brother was certain he remembered me, offering as proof the details of my residence on Old Providence Island, when I lived there in the early seventies.

"Mistah Bob, you used to live in Freshwater Bay."

"I lived in Old Town," I gently corrected him, "near Raimundo Lung."

"You used to ride a white horse," he continued, undaunted.

"No, my horse was red."

"Your wife's name was Sherrie, no?"

"I wasn't married," I felt obliged to tell him. "My girlfriend was Marta, the *panya* girl who lived with her mother and sister and brothers in Old Town."

Van's younger brother paused, momentarily subdued, trying to untwist this piece of information. After a minute his head slowly bobbed, his face brightening into a shy expression of the pleasure that comes from remembrance. "Mistah Bob," he insisted. "Back then, you didn't have the beard."

Back then he was only thirteen or so, what the *isleños* call a sprat, a sardine. I had never fished with him, as I had with his older brother, up on the Serrana Banks, and I didn't know whether I knew him or not, since his affliction—a right eye that rolled back into his skull when he shifted his line of vision—was peculiar to more than one Britton. At least as I recalled.

"No," I had to tell him, "I had the beard."

"But it was black, eh? Now it is white."

"That's true."

"Yes," he concluded triumphantly, his eye rolling blank, "I remember you, Mistah Bob. It is very nice to see you again, mahn."

"It's very nice to be back," I said, acquiescing.

Throughout the exchange, Van had been giving me knowing looks, studying me with a wry half-smile. I had come upon the two brothers at their compound—sort of like a Rasta daycamp for lost travelers—in the middle of a jungle clearing, enjoying a quiet summer day, sitting across from each other on two log benches muscled into position on both sides of a long log table. I sat down next to Van, who automatically reached behind him for a calabash gourd filled with dope.

"Do you remember me?" I had asked Van. We had not seen or spoken to each other in almost twenty years. He peered into my eyes for a second before he answered, resolutely, "Yes," and then remained silent while his kid brother, exercising his right as an islander, constructed a past for me that wasn't even remotely true, yet nevertheless plausible. Providence is a small place—*small*, not a daylong walk end to end—and the smaller the place, I've learned, the more it thrives on mystery, intrigue, conspiracy, shadow play, myth. No one is quite anonymous, but no one's story is ever quite reconcilable with the facts. Now I suspected that Van himself was bluffing, that he didn't know who I was either—until he suddenly spoke up.

"Mistah Bob," Van began, squinting through the smoke of the ganja stick he brought to his lips, finalizing his appraisal. Behind us, a woman stirred a Dutch oven set over a wood fire, boiling rice. "Mistah Bob," Van began again. Apparently he had scoured his memory to his satisfaction and I was there, loud and clear, yet once again transformed, another variation on the theme of my island identity. "Mistah Bob," he said a third time. "What did you do with the gold?"

Gold, the breakfast of empires.

There once was a golden highway in this part of the western Caribbean Sea—these days resurrected but snowblown with narcotraffickers—running from Cartagena to Campeche, whereupon it doglegged eastward with the Gulf Stream toward Havana, turned north along the coast of Florida, and cast again below Cape Hatteras to direct its trade across the Atlantic to the royal court of Madrid. This route was the legendary Spanish Main, and throughout the sixteenth and seventeenth centuries on its prevailing winds and currents sailed the fabulous wealth of Mexico and the Americas, treasure-laden galleons forever at the mercy of God, hurricanes, uncharted shoals, and, of the utmost relevance to my tale, those rogue seamen and cutthroat adventurers known as the buccaneers. Multicultural long before it was fashionable, the pirates of England, France, and Holland bivouacked primarily on three strategic islands scattered along the Main: Jamaica and its blasphemous Port Royal; Tortuga, off the coast of Haiti, where barbecuing was invented; and, 455 miles northwest of Cartagena and 143 miles east of the Nicaraguan coast, the island then named Santa Catalina—St. Catherine—known today as Isla de Providencia, or, as its Afro-Anglo inhabitants have always called it, Old Providence. (Its colonial designation, Catalina, has been passed on to its tiny sister island, now connected to Providence by a footbridge.) Regardless of its far-flung obscurity, tiny Providence was considered prime real estate by the privateers, for virtually all homebound ships sailing north from South America passed within sight of its timbered peaks, like fattened geese adrift on a pond, offering themselves to be raided and sunk or plowing into the island's thirty-six square miles of barrier reefs to end up permanently established on the bottom, their ghosts counting the centuries until the invention of the Aqua-Lung.

It was a Welshman named Henry Morgan, though, who placed Providence on the bloody map of history. The future Sir Henry greatly desired, wrote his Dutch surgeon, John Esquemeling, in *The Buccaneers of America*, "to consecrate it as a refuge . . . unto the Pirates of those parts, putting it in a sufficient condition of being a . . . storehouse of their preys and robberies." Which is precisely what Morgan did—or so say the islanders today—when he arrived in Providence in 1670 with two thousand fighting men aboard thirty-seven picaroons to stage his most daring and brutal exploit, the sacking of Panama City. The fleet proceeded from Providence to the Caribbean coast and off-loaded twelve hundred banditti, who marched across the isthmus and marched back three weeks later, leaving Panama's seven thousand houses, two hundred warehouses, eight monasteries, two cathedrals, and one hospital burned to the ground. Of rape, torture, and cold-blooded murder there was plenty. "Of the spoils thereof," said Esquemeling, "[Morgan] carried with him 175 beasts of carriage, laden with silver, gold, and other precious things." The contemporaneous value of the loot, it has been estimated, was between three and six million dollars. Back on the coast, Morgan secretly reboarded his flagship and put out to sea, followed by three or four vessels containing the greatest part of the treasure. Contrary to the historical record, Providence islanders argue passionately that Morgan stopped there on his return, sailing into local waters with three ships, though only two went on to Jamaica, either because one of the treasure ships hit the reef on its approach or, most insist, because Morgan unloaded its golden cargo and buried it with several slaves to enchant the trove. Then the pirate hoisted sail for Port Royal and, caught up in the volatile politics of the day, never returned.

After Morgan, Old Providence experienced, like Gabriel García Márquez's fabled Macondo, one hundred years of solitude. A refuge for out-casts, fugitives, and escaped slaves, it was resettled in 1787 by Francis Archbold, the Scottish captain of a slave ship, who established a cotton and tobacco plantation on Catalina, where the Archbolds—or Archi-bols—reside to this day. This explains why the people of Old Providence speak a vaguely Elizabethan patois—*You vex me, mahn. Tis as I say, Alphonse*—with a Scottish accent—*Gid mairnin, sah*—but it doesn't ex-plain why the islanders claim, rather emphatically, that they are descen-dants of Henry Morgan, his beautiful red-haired mistress, and his crew.

Of course, I didn't know any of this stuff when, in December 1973, fresh from a university miseducation, I decided to head south. I didn't know, for instance, that Providence islanders, in the words of one anthropologist, were keen on generating hypotheses concerning the whereabouts of Mor-gan's treasure, or that over the years they had dynamited and dug up the length and breadth of Catalina and a good many sites on Providence, or that the Colombian government itself had sent soldiers to excavate the old ruin believed to be Morgan's fort—that everybody down there, in effect, was running a high fever searching in vain for pirate's gold.

Actually, I had never even heard of an island named Old Providence when I boarded the cheapest flight from Miami that would deposit me, at least technically, on Latin American soil. The flight's destination was San Andrés, the main island in an off-the-map archipelago and a budding Co-lombian resort. From there I planned to boat-hop to the continent in pur-suit of a romantic's itinerary, the adventurous dreams of youth; I wanted to sweat in the oceanic jungles of the Amazon, scale the Andes, surf in Peru and Brazil, smell the fires of revolution igniting. Free and restless, I had just turned twenty-two and wanted out.

I never made it, though, to the South American mainland. On the flight down, fate's ever-playful travel agent booked me a seat next to a fellow I had observed in Miami checking an egregious amount of excess baggage: footlockers, duffel bags, scuba tanks, an air compressor that nobody could lift. He had gleaming eyes, a brush mustache, and hair like a clown's wig, and from the start he impressed me as a genius of self-importance. As we entered Cuban airspace, he began to fiddle with a long cardboard tube, extracting nautical charts, which he rudely unscrolled in my face.

"Here," he said cavalierly. "Hold the end of this."

With the index finger of his free hand he tapped three or four meaning-less spots clustered in the archipelago we jetted toward, mumbling to him-self and behaving like an ass. Impatience, not curiosity, got the best of me.

"All right, already," I said. "What's your story?"

Howard was a dive instructor from Chicago who had once worked on Mexico's Isla Mujeres, where he had befriended an American couple—Tay and Linda Maltsberger—who now lived on Providence and were somehow in possession of an exclusive license from the Colombian government permitting them to salvage old shipwrecks. Before we parted ways, Howard made a casual, quasi-serious invitation: Should I happen to be in the neighborhood, he'd teach me how to scuba dive. The impulse to take that forty-eight-mile detour, I have since thought, was tantamount to trading a mammoth illusion for a small unknown. In my imagination the continent struck an obscene pose, pursed her lips, and beckoned me with a gesture of unlimited possibilities, yet here I was contemplating a blind date with an unheralded island I felt no special interest in. I'll go for a week, I told myself.

When I landed in Providence two weeks after Howard and tracked him down, I was grateful for his effusive welcome, only partially tempered by his announcement that if I went halves he could now afford to rent a launch.

"Let me get this straight," I said, amazed. "You're going to salvage a galleon, but you don't have a *boat*?"

My career as a treasure salvager began and ended with our third dive, which also was my last with crazy Howard. My journal entry, dated January 24, 1974, begins: "Our object was a Spanish galleon sunk 300 years ago ¾ of a mile off Morgan's Head on the island of Santa Catalina." Reading this today, nearly twenty years after it was penned by my adolescent hand, I wonder, however briefly, whether I made it up. Is it early evidence that I was already being influenced by the islanders' habit of thought that aggressively blurred the lines between fact and fiction? For instance, what about those details? How did I know the wreck was three hundred years old, a galleon, or even Spanish? Did Linda or Captain Tay tell me, or are these morsels of verisimilitude my own invention?

Whatever the case, we did indeed dive that day on the visible remains of a ship lost during the colonial epoch—a scenario that would have produced yawns in Hollywood. After snorkeling all morning across a grid of reef off Catalina, we spotted what we were hunting: a prosaic mound of ballast rock, round as the cobblestones that paved the alleys and esplanades of the New World. We skin-dived down four fathoms to inspect a brass cannon nestled in the sand and an enormous fluked anchor, nearly twice my length, canted against the rock pile. I recovered a page-size sheet of whitened lead, an oxidized iron or silver rod with four symmetrical nodes on its crown, coral-encrusted shards of amphorae. Fixing the exact location in our memories, we moved up the reef to spearfish and then returned to Providence, where a small crowd had gathered on the dock, anxious to learn whether we had found Morgan's treasure. No matter what we said, it was assumed we were hauling up gold by the bucketful. My journal advises me that I was too excited to speak and that someone commented on the wild, lusty look in our eyes. After lunch, Howard and I returned to the site with tanks and crowbars. The journal entry ends anticlimactically, but with a trite and grandiose flourish: "We found nothing of great significance—except to me—but we know of two more galleons, and these have never been dived on—so there is this possibility called tomorrow."

Yikes. We were the most hopeless bunch of treasure hunters the world has seen, our naiveté exceeded only by our incompetence. I'm not entirely sure why, but I never dived on a wreck again. Any time we took a boat out to the reef, however, it seemed the entire island grumbled: *Dem fellas takin' we gold*. We were chronically half-assed, but that trait seemed to elude the *isleños*. We had the license, the scuba gear; we were gringos. In their minds, two plus two equaled millions, equaled Morgan's treasure.

Meanwhile, a better story unfolded, far richer in potential; the island itself, its astounding beauty, and the fascinating singularity of its people. I rented a house on the beach in Old Town, on the other side of the harbor from Town (which no one called by its actual name, Santa Isabel). The house had no furniture and, like everyone else's, no running water (we bucketed water out of a cistern), and though it was one of the rare houses in Old Town with electricity, the power plant managed to function only three hours in the morning and two more in the late afternoon, keeping the fishmongers' freezers in a state of perpetual thaw. I purchased a kerosene stove and lamp, unhinged the kitchen door for a table, with seats made from driftwood, ordered a hammock from Moraduck the hammock-maker in Lazy Hill, and began to feel at home—a feeling that my new neighbors, welcoming me with fresh-baked johnny-cakes and plates of food, did not discourage.

For twelve dollars I became the owner of Reeva, a spirited Paso Fino, and explored the island, galloping bareback on the palm-lined beach at Southwest Bay, reining the horse into the turquoise ocean until the bottom fell away and we swam together in liquid air, my hand wrapped in Reeva's mane. In rum shops I sipped the local moonshine—called Jump

Steady—and heard the braggadocio of fishermen. Ingesting the mushrooms called duppy caps—*duppy* meant "ghost"—I climbed into the mountains, whacked out of my mind, to stand on the peaks in the raging wind, the sea glittering like foxfire and jewels below me.

Howard moved in and set up his air compressor on the veranda; so did a woman named Beth, from Friday Harbor in Puget Sound. I began courting the only available Latina on the island—twenty-year-old Marta, transplanted from Bogotá with her younger sister Clara, two little brothers, and her beautiful but slightly crazed and overprotective mother, a relative of the archbishop of Colombia, who exiled herself to this alien paradise upon learning of her husband's infidelity. Marta's mother despised me—I was the first boyfriend of her oldest and favorite child. She'd come pounding on my front door to rescue Marta from my caresses; her shrieks would send Marta dashing out the back door, scurrying across the mud flats to be home waiting not-so-innocently for *madre*'s stormy return.

Life for all of us grew more immediate, less goldstruck, more devoted to daily survival, island dramas, the textures and subtleties of a community where poverty intensified, rather than corroded, the honest joys of existence. Assimilating, we flared with modern schemes for short periods, then relapsed into slothful bliss, taking to our hammocks with a book, savoring our *cuba libres*. The Maltsbergers' efforts to lure investors into the wonderful world of treasure hunting never got off the ground. Linda and I came up with the idea to write a cookbook, but the project lost momentum and nothing ever came of it. I pitched articles to magazines, collaborated with photographers, worked tenaciously, ran out of money . . . and nothing ever came of that, either.

After a few months I went native, joining up with a pair of Old Town spearfishermen, Raimundo Lung and Gabriel Hawkins, leaving before dawn each morning to sail out of sight of land in Mundo's lateen-rigged catboat, learning the labor, fear, and glory of their profession and bringing home dinner to a house now crammed with a revolving-door variety of wanderers, outcasts, and expatriates. Then the collective, magnificent weave of a year unraveled, and overnight, it seemed, we were all gone, riding away on the currents to our separate futures, leaving in our wake a small but nagging contribution to the island's mythology, another installment in Providence's leitmotiv of gold.

To tell the truth, I did not want to go back.

Coming back, however, was part of the ethos of Providence, as was the act of leaving. "What defines islanders," says writer P. F. Kluge, "is not the way they live on islands but the way they move between them." The islands—all islands—depend on the human flow. On the profound restlessness that leads to self-exile; on remittance; on the magnanimous return of the prodigal son. Travel as rite of passage.

This is what happened when you lived on a remote island, an unimaginable distance from the push and shove of things, the commerce and convenience of the temperate latitudes. An island where men still went to the sea each day for their living, challenging its caprice in the smallest of boats. Where families took to the sea on holidays to visit and to celebrate. Where obtaining a government permit, or buying a bag of cement, or keeping a doctor's appointment, meant risking the hazards of the sea. One day you were talking with someone, playing cards with him, dancing with her. The next day they were never to be seen again, and you were dreaming of them falling, slowly, with macabre beauty and grace, through the blue ever-darkening thickness of space, and the dream never stopped, but at its bottom lay all your missing friends, looking up through the water at the moon.

This is what I remember: Shortly before dawn each morning, Mundo would send his little girls down the beach to wake me. "Mistah Bob," they'd whisper cautiously. "Mistah Bob," they'd whisper, their melodic voices barely audible over the lap and hiss of the lagoon. "Me faddah say you sleepin long enough, mahn." I would growl theatrically, they would giggle. "Mundo say git up, Mistah Bob. Is time to go fishenin." They were beautiful cherub-faced girls with gap-toothed sunny smiles. I could see their silhouettes in the lavender light of the window, their long wavy tresses braided, and I knew they'd be wearing their school dresses. "Mistah Bob," they'd persist, "Mistah Bob," until I threw open the door and stooped for the quick kisses, and that would be the end of the game.

The last time Mundo and I exchanged letters was 1976. His read: "Bob, I have a sad story to tell you. My two daughters went to San Andrés for Christmas and on their way back the *Betty B* [an interisland cargo and passenger boat] burst open and more than half the people drown. You must just know how I feel. Margarita and Virginia died."

With great reluctance I had sailed on the *Betty B* myself, and I had sailed on the *Acabra*, too, which was even less seaworthy than the *Betty B* and proved it by sinking first, only a few months after I had left Providence, overcrowded with passengers but close enough to shore for all hands to be saved. And a month or so later, my friend Ibsen would disappear one night in the passage between San Andrés and Providence, washed overboard his boat in heavy seas. However you got to Providence, your faith in everything—God, man, technology, yourself—was severely tested by the voyage, and never so wantonly as when you flew Cessnyca and its nine-passenger twin-engine Beechcraft, apparently maintained by obeah priests. On my inaugural flight twenty years previous, the pilot had knelt on the tarmac, crossed himself, and prayed before boarding the plane in front of me. Airborne, we roller-coasted through tremendous thunderheads, my surfboard levitating in the aisle. On my second flight to Providence, the pilot lost control of the steering as we touched down, the dirt runway slick with mud from a recent downpour, and we crashed sideways through a low stone wall, coming to rest in a mangrove swamp. Another day, a friend arrived at the airstrip to find the flight crew wrapping a rope around one propeller and yanking it, the way you would a lawnmower, to start the engine.

Twenty years later, getting on or off Providence still seemed like risky business, psychologically if not statistically. By the time I arrived in San Andrés from Bogotá I was understandably wired and struggling against a creeping sense of depression. No surprise to see that San Andrés hadn't changed much—its fate was to be a teeming, overbuilt tropical shithole, eternally engaged in the process of making itself uglier, a low-lying featureless freeport roamed by sunburned hordes of Colombia's equivalent of Kmart shoppers, loading up on appliances. The only difference seemed to be that now the mafia—meaning the cocaine cartels—was doing its laundry here, building tacky mansions and chintzy resorts apparently designed by architects using the Jersey shore for the aesthetic model.

On the other hand, the frenetic shabbiness of San Andrés had always been the perfect foil for the unassailable beauty of Providence, multiplying a traveler's sense of thanksgiving and wonder upon seeing for the first time its exotic peaks, its stunning cobalt reefs, its raw charms, experiencing the midwestern hospitality of its people. The kind of destination you connected with only in your imagination, because its existence was often too good to be true. A place endangered, ultimately, by your desires.

If leaving was a mistake, I figured coming back had the potential to be an even bigger one. Why break my heart reconfirming the trend, proving to myself that Providence was, after all, neither a quirky utopia nor an idyllic glitch, but a doomed fragment of a fragile, shrinking world? When the developers and speculators deployed (as surely a battalion had by now), who was going to be the fool who played Diogenes, rejecting their temptations?

As I sat eating my lunch at a little makeshift restaurant near the San Andrés airport, waiting for the SAM flight to Providence, I fretted that I was coming back too late, but I didn't know, I had lost touch absolutely, and since Providence was so vital a part of my past—had performed in fact a catalytic role in my self-definition—it was time I found out. As if in judging Providence, I would also be measuring the life I've lived against the life I might have lived, had I remained behind. What of Marta, whose mother had denied her the twentieth century by flinging her into the primitive world of a colonial pioneer? What of the two fishermen who had allowed me to share their lives as well as their boat: Gabriel, who had made me his brother, and Mundo, in so many ways my father? Long ago I had heard that Gabriel went to Jamaica looking for work, then shipped out on a freighter headed north. Had the northern ports bedeviled him, turned him into something as rare as murder on Providence—a racist? Had he ever raced back to marry his sweetheart? And what of Mundo? Robertson Davies once wrote that a man in his youth has several fathers, and his biological one isn't necessarily the most significant. I had three: the one who fathered my body; a professor in Missouri who fathered my passion to be a writer; and Mundo, the third and most adroit, a poor black spearfisherman, the father of my spiritual point of view, who taught me how to persevere past hardship and never be afraid of life. Mundo, I was convinced, was dead.

It didn't really eat at me, the life I never chose, though Providence is the only place I've ever lived where I envisioned myself not leaving. But years ago my island fever metamorphosed directly into an obsession for writing and swept me off into another life. I had never been homesick for Providence, though I often felt as if I had been born there, but I was aware of it always, there in my existence, like a phantom limb. I was never homesick for Providence, but more to the point, I was utterly bewitched by it. I was haunted.

My past on Providence wasn't ice but fire, burning with indelible images that kept reappearing in my fiction; the last thing I wanted to do was mess with the mojo or spoil a dream year's delicate aftertaste by indulging in the overrich confections of nostalgia or the thin broth of pity and disillusionment.

I finished my lunch but not my despondent mood. I ambled back across the road to the airport and asked a taxi driver whatever happened to Cessnyca.

"It dropped," he said, an answer that required no further elaboration.

As I sat in the departure lounge watching the weather deteriorate, I kidded myself into believing I'd been through too much over the years to feel trepidation about the flight. Even buckled in, finally, on the sweltering, claustrophobic nineteen-seater, I was more or less fine, a little jittery maybe, but the jolt of takeoff reawakened the religious conviction of the woman across from me, who began crossing herself and stuttering prayers. With horrific noise, rain blasted against the cockpit windows; a downdraft slapped us into a steep bank. I closed my eyes—here was the old dread, an overwhelming sense of déjà vu—and when I opened them again we had busted through the squall. Below us spread the inside reef like a celestial swimming pool, and in front of us humped the musky, verdant mountains of the island that had gotten deep inside me, so deep it seemed to have rearranged my DNA. I had flown back, not into time, but into my imagination, into my literary collaboration with place, my own symbols, themes, and fictions.

I jumped into a taxi. The road—the only road—had, like the landing strip, been paved some time ago, and already it begged repair. Larry, the amiable driver, smiled when I told him I wanted to get a room in Town. Alvaro's *residencia* was a general store; the Hotel Aury housed the bank and some municipal offices. The hotels were all in Freshwater Bay (Aguadulce, in Spanish), and having to rely on them underscored my unfamiliar status as a tourist. Driving through Rocky Point, through Mountain, and down into Town, I was cheered to find that at least on the surface Old Providence had not been inspired to recreate itself for profit.

"There was a fisherman in Old Town, Raimundo Lung . . ." I said, tentative, providing a lead.

"Yes, yes, Raimundo. He was our most famous diver on Providence. Guys would come from all around—Cartagena, the Caymans, the States—to dive against him. But they never beat him, you know. He was our best man with a speargun."

Was he still alive?

"Livin right there in Old Town still," Larry told me. Suddenly I was euphoric with relief, and coming back made sense. But then, just as suddenly, our conversation had a trapdoor, which sprang open underneath me. I asked about Marta and her sister Clara: What had become of them?

"Them still here," Larry said. This was unexpected, wonderful.

"No," a passenger we had picked up along the road corrected him. "One of them is dead."

On December 1, 1979, Marta and eight other passengers boarded the flight to San Andrés and that was the last anybody saw of them. No trace of the wreckage was ever found.

I was numb with sorrow when Larry pulled over in front of Mundo's house. What I had attained, exactly, by my return to Providence was an invitation to an emotional slam-dance. Through the greenery, I could see down the path where Mundo stood, leaning over a work table. Age had sucked at his muscles and carved into his face. His hair was graying . . . but then so was mine. When he realized it was me, we embraced, tears in our eyes, and finally I was back among the living.

"Mistah Bob," said Mundo tenderly. "I thought you were dead. I am a grown man, but when I received your last letter and then no more came, I lay in bed at night and cried, telling myself them rough fellows in St. Vincent killed you, and you was dead."

We held each other's hand like lovers, reluctant to let go.

"But Bob," Mundo continued, "just last week I was fishenin with Armando, and I tell him, 'Somehow I feel Mistah Bob is alive.'"

Anyplace else, coming from anybody else, Mundo's declaration would have struck me as a mannerism, the exaggerated rhetoric of a good friend, but Providence had a way of forcing the supernatural down your throat, and twenty years ago Mundo had startled me with his clairvoyance, again and again, until years later, as a student at the Iowa Writers' Workshop, I was compelled to write about it, fictionalizing the truth of events I was unable to comprehend, and although I had crafted an alter ego for myself I was unable to give Mundo any other name—or reality—but his own. In life, he had always been larger than life. The same goes for duppy-haunted Providence, rubbing itself so intimately against nature. The island had always played Twilight Zone tricks on me, suggesting, among other things, that there were moments of mysticism inherent in the human act of expression, including the act of writing, moments that would reach out to tear a souvenir off the coattails of the future. Where does an imagination come from, I found myself asking on Providence, but the island always answered back with a riddle—where does reality come from?—and a biblical reproach: In the beginning was the Word. It's the language, dummy. There was no other link between real events and the imagination but language and nature.

Our reunion drained me. I was both exhausted and exhilarated, heartbroken, remembering Marta, and remembering her, chilled by the fact that an image of her death had been with me—I could date it in my notebooks—since 1979. I needed a room, a shower, stiff drinks, food, and a bed. I promised Mundo that I would return tomorrow and we'd go fishing Monday. Not Monday, he said. We'd be hung over Monday. For a few minutes more we said what needed to be said between us. Then, as I was poised to re-enter life under the microscope in the nineteenth-century village that was still Providence, Mundo paved the way for me. "Mistah Bob," he said, his tone a mild warning. "When you left, everybody said you took the gold. But I told them no, I knew you well, you were not that type of man. That was not you."

The Monday after Sunday's fete at Mundo's, I couldn't determine whether I was actually hung over from *aguardiente* or my beaten-up, vulnerable feeling could be written off as emotional decompression. My former self chastised me for renting a *moto* in Freshwater Bay to tour the island, opting for two-wheeled convenience over the old-fashioned rewards of putting one foot in front of the other. But even though the number of cars and pickup trucks had doubled to about sixty since I was last there, as had the population—about 4,500—the island's underlying pace was still dictated by the start-and-stop stroll of pedestrians, whom I didn't overly blame for not stepping out of the way as I puttered past like a mechanical mosquito. Before I could click into third gear, I had left behind Aguadulce, Providence's only bona fide tourist zone. In my day, I would ride Reeva here from Old Town or walk it with Marta—an hour-and-a-half Spanish lesson, one way—to sit on an empty beach in a prolifically empty landscape. Now the paradisiacal expanse of sugary beach had eroded to a narrow crescent, and Aguadulce supported a thriving but inoffensive village of restaurants, open-air bars, and lodging. No big projects, cash only—even your traveler's checks were no good. Providence simply lacked the infrastructure and accessibility for corporate greed to take root. In this insular nook of the world, greed was still the prerogative of individuals, the damage they caused less visible. A few kids knocked into outer space by drugs; luxurious hideaways for nameless kingpins; ruinous land speculation. ("The island will be totally private ten years from now," one of Providence's entrepreneurs told me. "A few of the large landholders will get rich, but everybody else will be fucked. They'll have to move up into the mountains or to San Andrés. Their children's children will never be able to afford to live here.")

Over a hill that dropped precipitously into blue-green water, I motored onward to Southwest Bay, once the island's grandest beach. Despite considerable erosion, it remained wide enough, I could see, to accommodate Providence's most colorful spectacle, the Saturday morning horse races. I'd come to find the Brittons—Van; his father, Burgo; his sister, Indiana. Mutual friends in Miami had asked that I take them a gift, a small amount of money, a fresh reminder of caring, of old bonds renewed. But Burgo, I soon learned, had fallen out of a sea-grape tree and broken his back, and Indiana, two years younger than me, had had a heart attack—they were both dead. I followed directions to a trailhead, parked, and hiked into the bush to scout Van's weird, serene tourist compound and give him the money. Hey, remember me? Yeah, you took the gold.

Back on the *moto*, I traversed the hilly southern tip of the island, dismayed by the sight of well-armed marine guards posted at compass points on the sun-scorched mountainside. The Colombian navy found itself high and dry here in a garrison ostensibly built to show the flag to those crazy Nicaraguans, who for some unfathomable reason were nursing a Falkland Islands territorial fantasy about Old Providence. That would be an interesting turn of events for a people who have no communal memory of institutionalized colonialism or slavery, only of being ignored and forgotten, thanks very much. Islanders wouldn't readily admit even to being Colombian. What are you then, I'd ask? Dumb question. *We is gyad-dyamn Englishmen, Mistah Bob.*

Down where the eastward slope flattened on the outskirts of Bottom House, I stopped to ponder an unpaved turnoff that I'd never seen before. Had someone bulldozed a road over the densely jungled hill to Manchineel Bay, only reachable by boat or a perilous horseback ride along the cliffs? Manchineel Bay was one of those spots reserved for lovemaking, one of those places where you worshiped sensuality, enslaved yourself to it, where you ended up contemplating, if you were male, the metaphor that if islands were women, tropical islands were women who riveted you with lust, and how many islands would it take to stop the itch, you licentious dog? How many islands before you came to your senses, settled down, and married Ohio? I couldn't imagine that a road, however rocky and washed-out, would enhance Manchineel Bay's reputation for intimate liaisons. Better go see, I thought, and what I feared was true: cook shacks, snack bars, thatched ramadas shading picnic tables, some tourists sunbathing, some Bottom House locals playing dominoes. I bought a bottle of beer and sat down, feeling irrational, feeling jilted. But things weren't so bad after all. The beach was still spectacular, peaceful, its atmosphere like a postcoital daze. So what if Manchineel had lost her virginity? That didn't make her a whore, at least not yet, and maybe never, even if the municipality went ahead, as promised, and paved the road.

Bitch, I thought, still in love with her. I began to brood, took a walk and a swim to sort out my thoughts, to ease the ever-increasing weight on my heart. Rather than disoriented, I felt surreally connected—more, perhaps, than I wanted or deserved. Come back to Providence and all of a sudden you're loaded up with dead people. My own personal ghost-fleet of souls, and the manifest was growing daily. The worst of it was, and not without a measure of tragic beauty, that I had become a medium between two worlds, the one here and the one not here, not just an emissary from the past but from the afterlife, toting around the images that survived beyond death. There they were, the bulge in my daypack. My books of course, and two carousels of slides, thumbed by a curious *National Geographic* editor twenty years ago and then returned. In this poor place condemned to poverty and isolation, no one had pictures of their dead, no one could remember the faces of their lost children, fathers, sisters. Last night at Mundo's we had tacked a sheet on the wall, turned off the lights, and begun the show. Neighbors crowded in the doorway. I was prepared for the bittersweet taste of peeling back time, but I hadn't counted on opening so many graves. Now everywhere I went, sad-eyed but hopeful islanders were flagging me down on the road. Like Miss Daci in Old Town, who waved me over because she had lost three of her four young sons on the *Betty B*. Someone at Mundo's had recognized the eldest, a handsome fourteen-year-old boy sitting up to his chest in slate-green water, fishing with a hand line. Her surviving son, Roy, now cashier at the bank, had only been a few years old when his brothers drowned. He had no memory of them, and Miss Daci herself couldn't quite recall their looks, it had all happened so long ago. So it was that I began making house calls, delivering the disappeared back to their families, and two nights later I set up shop in the town square, running an extension cord out of the bank, which had agreed to remain open for this purpose, and as twilight fell I paraded my mixed bag of ghosts and former selves across the wall of the old Hotel Aury. "Dupyshow," I would overhear someone in the enthralled crowd say matter-of-factly.

There's Oscar Bryan, my uncle, said the bank manager.

Three schoolgirls sitting splay-legged on the ground: *Oh God, mahn, the one in the middle is my wife!*

Ah look, poor Winston. He get crushed by a truck. Lookout House—it burn down, you know. Yes, I know, and Linda's dead now seven years, her ashes scattered off the Turks and Caicos. Margarita and Virginia, Raimundo's girls. Angels. Marta.

I turned to see who had identified her so quickly. It was the island's agent for SAM Airlines. "Bob," he said, extending his hand, "you don't know, but I'm Robert, Marta's youngest brother." He had been four years old when I left, had inherited my surfboard, which still hung on his bedroom wall. His older brother and sister moved to Miami; Roberto had stayed behind to look after his mother, who had not come out of the house since the day Marta had died. No, Roberto told me in answer to my questions, Marta had never married; according to Clara, she never even had another boyfriend, and as for Clara herself, she hadn't become the aviator she had once dreamed of being, a sixteen-year-old girl sitting in the moonlight on my veranda, staring at the sea, but she had read about my books in the *Miami Herald* and knew about my life. It meant a lot to Clara, Roberto said, that things had worked out for me.

There was only so much of this I could take. My stoicism collapsed into melancholy, and I began giving away the slides, shedding my collection of spirits like a retiring schoolmarm dismissing class, sending everybody home for the last time. I escaped to the boat bar tied up at the wharf—Glasford's boat, dead Ibsen's brother—where I could sink into a pair of island traditions as eternal as its ghosts: listening to country-and-western music, the more sentimental the better, and firing back a bottle of Medellín rum. Bullshit optional, but just as time-honored.

Mistah Bob, mahn, listen, Mundo's new wife, Concha, is going to say to me, the day before I leave again. *When we are bairn we are each given a destiny, not so?*

I want to answer petulantly, wearily, cynically, *I know I know I know.* But I don't really.

Or I want to say, Deaths, yes. Destinies, no. Destinies you wrestle with, until they shake you off.

I don't have a new revelation about Providence but instead a revitalization of my original one: time and chronology are two different animals, the latter tame, a beast of burden, the former wild, unruly, popping in and out of holes, coming at you from all directions, everywhere at once.

That Sunday, we sat at a table moved out to the yard to eat the stewed conch, beans, and rice that Concha had cooked for lunch. Chickens and cats scavenged at our feet; Jim Reeves crooned on the cassette player. Gabriel was there, returned from the world to marry his gal Vivian and take a government job, night watchman at the hospital. His domesticated paunch and burgher's affability made poignant contrast to Mundo's wizened poise. In went the food, out came the memories. I had first met them as a customer, wading out on the flats in front of Old Town to join the queue surrounding Mundo's catboat, trying to buy a fish. Mundo gave me a five-pound slab of red snapper but wouldn't accept my money, which made me uncomfortable. Next day, same thing. Who did he think he was, Santa Claus? Take my pesos, I urged, but on the baffling basis that we were neighbors, he kept refusing. Neighbors, according to my upbringing, were nothing more than the people next door, a hazy part of the scenery. So what? You didn't need them, they didn't need you.

Where did a white kid from the suburbs go in 1973 to develop an abiding sense of community, family, tolerance, and generosity? How would I know, I would have replied at the time. "Seek virtue" was not ranked on my list of Things to Do in South America. I would have regarded any suggestion to go live among poor black people in the Third World as dubious indeed. All I know is that it *was* my destiny to alight in Providence for a year, to rent a house in Old Town, to have Mundo as my neighbor and friend and then as my teacher. His pedagogy was basic: watch and learn. He rarely gave instructions or advice or reproach, except where danger was imminent. He allowed me my mistakes, and I accepted his affectionate bemusement with my awkwardness. Occasionally he would say, about something good or bad, wrong or right, "That is the black man's way." Occasionally I would say the same thing about whites, but generally the issue of race was so mundane and pointless that we never discussed it except as a joke. I could never get him or anybody else on Providence to stop calling me *Mistah* Bob—I even retaliated for a time with *Mistah* Mundo, with no success. It became my name, yet when Mundo requested my most earnest attention, he'd drop the formal, slightly teasing designation in a second. "Bob," he'd say in his soft-spoken voice, "I am a grown man and my father is dead but still I hate him for taking my future away from me to give me this life of hard work and suffering." In his youth, famous as a baseball player in Cartagena, Mundo had been scouted by the gringos and offered a crack at the minors, and an education, in the States. A good son, he returned to his father's house in San Andrés to ask permission, but his father said no, and in those days, Mundo emphasized, you obeyed your father.

Or we'd be out on the reef, I'd be rowing, Mundo diving, when suddenly he'd pop up to rest his elbows on the gunwale, his face a bowl of exuberance. "Bob," he'd say, "put on your mask and come look. This is a beautiful spot, bwoy. Beautiful." He didn't place a lot of faith in my nautical abilities, though he held to his conviction that since I had voluntarily crossed the threshold into his world, on land or at sea, under his protection and guidance I would endure, and that single belief became my own, became deeply self-defining. In return I trusted him, probably far too much, not to kill me when he went a-cowboying beyond the limits of seamanship in his livelihood, half profession and half blood sport. It was a most unusual alliance.

In went the food and beer, out came the memories. Mundo and Gabriel exhaled laughter, reminiscing about the first day they trusted me to row the catboat while they dived. "Mistah Bob come back saying, 'My hands! My hands! They are all bloody! What did you do to my hands!'" The first time they let me share the diving: "You swam ugly, Mistah Bob. *Ugly*. Like duck." My first encounter with a shark, which had just bumped me and wheeled around for a second pass: "I never see a fellow fly into a boat so fast as Mistah Bob. And him shoutin, 'Fuck this, fuck this, I ain't punchin no more shark. Fuck this you motherfuckers.'" More beer, more memories and hoots of laughter. Our two-week trip up to the Serrana Banks, where you didn't have to dive to fill a boat with conch, where the sea turtles were as plentiful as hummingbirds in a garden of bougainvillea. Where Mundo announced one morning he had had a "sign," had dreamed that night that he had had sex with a man and that meant this day he was going to shoot a big male hawksbill. And did.

Mundo's dream interpretations of the future, their accuracy—I'm at a loss for what to say about them. Or what to say about the almost psychic coincidence of a moment like this: In "Hunger," a short story I wrote about Serrana, there is a line about Mundo's mother, the only line I ever wrote about her, about how she looked at the white man "as if he had come to steal the toes from her feet." Naturally I wanted to know what had become of her. With great pain, Mundo told me that she had died only last year, after long suffering. She had scratched her ankle, contracted blood poisoning. Mundo took her to the hospital in San Andrés, where they amputated her foot. Just coincidence, I know, but one of many, offered as a novelty from a private collection. Like certain poems, the incident seems to beg meaning but eludes understanding, perhaps because I've lived so many years with these people in my imagination. After lunch, I unzipped my daypack and brought out my books, flipped through *Easy in the Islands*, showed Mundo and Gabriel their stories, later read aloud from "Mundo's Sign." A tribute. If, as Debussy said, "music is the space between the notes," then stories are the space between islands, between lives. Mundo's reaction was, well, demure; he regarded the books with a thin, aloof smile, and, disappointed, I returned them to my bag. There were other people I wanted to show them to, anyway.

Fishing again with Mundo brought another twinge of heartache, like watching a former winner of the Kentucky Derby being hooked up to a plow. Forget sailing, forget catboats, everybody's using motor launches now. The whine of two-cycle engines instead of the hum and slice of the wind. Free-diving's out, scuba tanks in. Cutaway Clorox bottles instead of calabash gourds for bailers. The reef itself is in robust good health, but you have to go farther and deeper to find fish. OK. Fine. What did you expect? Bad weather kept us inside the reef for two days, diving for conch and bottom fishing. We were unlucky, and the hand lining was an exercise in the boredom inherent in endless patience. Dazed by the sun flashing off the water, your mind turns into a toad. Still, when a fish he hooked ran under a rock in eight fathoms of water, he donned his worn-out, patched-together diving mask and fins and went over the side, returning with not just the fish but a five-pound lobster—his first, he said, in many years. On the third day we went outside the reef to troll for bonita, but only succeeded in getting the hell kicked out of us in six-foot cresting seas. "Rough," said Mundo, the first time I ever heard him admit it. The result of our hard day's labor: not even enough of a catch to pay for our gas. On the way back in, Mundo began telling me the story of another day he had spent in rough seas. A year after I had left, he built his first launch, took it eighteen miles up north, to the top of the reef, and went outside into blue water. Then his engine conked out, and the bad seas stove in one of the planks along the keel. He wedged his shirt into the hole and, with a piece of iron, banged the board back into place. Now they wouldn't sink, but they had to bail constantly. As night fell, he threw out the anchor to slow their drift through the open ocean. When the sun came up, he waited for Cessnyca to come looking for them and send a rescue boat, but there was no plane, and no rescue boat, and when the sun went down he told himself, "Fuck it, they think we're dead," nailed a sheet of plywood to the bow to catch the wind, pulled the anchor, and told his mate they were going to

Nicaragua on the current. And for three days and three nights, without food or water, that's what they did.

Mundo, I wanted to say but didn't, you're planting another story in me.

This is what I remember.

There are the lives I imagine.

These are the recurring images that haunt me, outside of place and time.

The ballet of man and turtle, their pirouettes through the sorrow-filled loneliness of a blue universe. Sharks like a whirl of gnats around the head of a diver. Boys racing horses on an endless gold beach. The spiral of a hurricane, like a serpent's tail, lashing against the coast. The sleepless eyes of killers and the grin of the barracuda. A quiet day, fishermen asleep in their boats. A naked woman eating a mango, juice dripping off her chin. Rain like a swarm of crystal bees. A catboat heeling into a squall and going under. A machete cutting the arched throat of a hawksbill. A man playing the jawbone, the bounce of the quadrille. An old black woman's frown of suspicion. An old black woman's prayers for my safe passage. The phantasmagoric light of the flambeaus, the slap of dominoes against wood, and children drowning. And this, written in 1979 and coming to rest in a story called "Easy in the Islands": A woman crawling along the ocean's floor, weightless as a feather, her hair in flames of phosphorescence.

On my last day with Mundo I gave him, as I had always intended, the book containing his story. I wasn't sure he wanted it, or what it meant to him, or if he thought of me, ultimately, as nothing more than a voyeur and a thief. "Ah," he said softly, "I finally have it. Here it is in my hand," and, to my astonishment, he raised it to his lips to kiss its cover and complete a twenty-year-long circle.

This is what I did with the gold.

Will You Say Something, Monsieur Eliot?

■■■■■■■■■■■■■■■■■■■■■■■■■■■■■■■■■■

After the eye passed over, the shivering Concordia yawl *Bliss* was picked up and tossed sideways down into a trough. For a moment in the dark that had been a brilliant noon two hours earlier Eliot saw a light on the horizon and knew it was the light at the top of his own mast. The light flickered and went black, and there was nothing but the white noise of the storm. The wooden yawl shuddered deep in her timbers, and Eliot was catapulted from the cockpit and landed chin first on the deck and heard his molars shatter. Weightless for a moment as *Bliss* dropped, Eliot again cracked down against the deck like a fish. The bow rose up the face of a mountain of water and Eliot fell head first toward the wheel. His heavy arms locked in the spokes, and his Adam's apple crunched on mahogany, and he was upside down, bare feet to the sky. *Bliss* paused at the crest before her bow came down hard, hurtling Eliot backward through the companionway onto the teak floor below, where he rolled in a soup of seawater and motor oil and caulking.

The creaking of the hull planks rose to a moan and subsided and rose again. The garboard plank was wrenching away from the keel and the sea overwhelming the pumps. Eliot caught his breath and lifted his head. The storm paused. In the pause Eliot heard a distant *plink*, the single sharp piano *plink* of the lower shroud snapping, and then the crack of the main mast as it folded at its midsection into the sea. *Bliss* rose and twisted against the storm. The seaborne mast buffeted, a battering ram still wired to the hull. Eliot was braced against the sink in the galley reaching for the bolt cutters when the mast rammed through the after-hull. He crawled behind the companionway toward the hole with a red flotation cushion for a potential patch and a broken paddle for a wedge. The sea poured in against his knees. The mast broke through again, and Eliot was driven backward on a river, into the cabin. He crawled to his feet and slid an orange life jacket over his head, and *Bliss* was thrown from the sea into the air and turned turtle and the sea rushed into the cabin and she righted again. Climbing up the companionway, Eliot saw in the west the vaporous glow of the end of the storm working toward him. He thrust his arms through the wheel and watched the light grow, and a rogue wave dropped from the heavens and drove *Bliss* down into the sea.

Eliot's shoulders and head bobbed in the sea like a red bottle. He was shirtless and stripped of his life jacket, and his face bloated from twenty-four hours of exposure and oozing from cuts and abrasions. His eyes were swollen half shut. The sharp nubs of his broken teeth lanced at his tongue and Eliot counted six—three to starboard and three to port. Once a dolphin flew out of the sea not far from Eliot, but it didn't come again, and the sea was mute. Eliot's lips fissured and the fissures spread red and raw. At night he watched the sky for a shooting star but never asked to be saved when he saw the first one, and there were dozens, as if every star in the sky was thrown down. He floated on his back all night and missed *Bliss* more than anyone because *Bliss* was perfection. Eliot exhaled and sank under, down to his blistered lips and nose, and when he filled his lungs the white island of his belly emerged, breaking the black surface, and he let the breath go in a gasp and sank down again and then pulled the night again into his lungs. It went on and on, this rising and falling. Morning pinched the stars from the sky one at a time, and Eliot watched them go, and slowly the gray turned to yellow and then gold, and the sun burned at the edge of the Atlantic Sea.

On the second day, Eliot saw something long and shiny in the sun, and he paddled to it. It was the boom of *Bliss*, yellow varnished Sitka spruce rolling in the sea. Eliot removed his belt from the tight loops of his bunched shorts. He tied the belt around the boom and looped his arm through the sling and fell back with a groan and hung in the water. He slid his burning face under the sea and looked up through its lens at a cloud quivering like mercury and blew silver bubbles to the surface. His face turned down toward the depths, and his puffy hand drifted before his face, and his Princeton ring sparkled gold in the airy blue. Eliot pointed downward and cried out with the last air in his lungs, and the cry warbled in the water, and his breath bubbled up his forehead. He broke the surface gasping and flopped up across the boom with his face in the sea. Eliot looked down into the water ten meters, where there was nothing, just liquid blue fading into black. He turned his head and sucked in a loud breath and searched the deserted sea. Skin shriveled off his shoulders and drifted down and away as Eliot held his breath and watched the sails of skin battered in the invisible eddies.

On the day before leaving for this singlehanded sail—out of the Bahamas and bound for St. Barts—Eliot had stood over his secretary's desk with his bag over his shoulder and written a check for fifty thousand dollars. Eliot told her to send it to David Mercer at Fleet, with best regards. Eliot's tenth Princeton reunion was in June and he had been taunting David—threatening not to give any money this year—and one night was watching David squirm in his chair at the Princeton Club when David said out of the blue, What if something happened?

What if something happened when?

On your trip, David said. Your sailing trip.

Like what? Eliot said.

Like something could happen.

Like *what* could happen?

David raised his mineral water to his lips. Eliot, don't you see something could go wrong?

I've singlehanded *Bliss* dozens of times.

So you're not afraid.

Not really.

You think it's impossible?

What?

You know.

I never think about that.

Never?

I think about dropping twenty pounds. Wasn't this dinner about money?

Eliot, do you mind my making a personal comment?

No more than usual.

That's kind of fucked.

Yes? You think so?

Yes. I do.

Let me tell you something, David.

I'm listening.

You won't understand this at all.

Say it, Eliot.

I don't really understand it myself.

Understand what?

The world loves me.

David stared at Eliot, and the waiter arrived and stood over their table looking from one man to the other.

Ready to order, sirs?

David shook his head and rubbed at the creases in his brow. He looked at Eliot, who hadn't aged since Princeton.

Eliot finished his drink and looked up at the waiter and ordered another. The waiter nodded and turned to David, who looked at Eliot and repeated, *The world loves you?*

The waiter's gaze swiveled back to Eliot. Eliot laughed and shook his beautiful strawberry head. The laughter rolled up out of him as if he were a child being tickled.

What, said David. What's so funny?

The third day the sea was glass, and then the wind whispered at noon and feathered the glass in running swaths. For hours, Eliot watched the swaths dapple in the sun, and once a dolphin rose against the horizon. Eliot hooked the belt around his head, using it as a sling under his chin, and slept lightly for a few hours with his head against the boom. When he awoke, his throat was on fire, and he wanted to drink from the sea and he swallowed, and the salt burned like acid down his throat. Soon the sun was slipping away and the breeze blew cool on the burned skin of his face and shoulders. The sun dropped out of sight, and Eliot saw the green flash, and the green flash was a sure sign to him. When he closed his eyes he saw the solar phenomenon lingering like green lightning on the glowing red interior of his swollen eyelids.

Tomorrow, said Eliot, nodding to the universe with closed eyes.

At dawn, Eliot took the metal edge at the end of the belt and carved a line next to the other three scratches. He tried to think of something dramatic to scratch in the boom for posterity and could only think of adding his name, Eliot Swan. He closed his eyes and saw the boom over the fieldstone fireplace in the pastel living room of his house in Locust Valley and saw himself standing under it telling the story of his shipwreck. There were many people in the room listening, but they were all strangers. Eliot tried to picture the face of his former wife, Claudia, or his former partner, Clive, or one of his former mistresses, Ilena or Mandy, or his doubles partner, Henry, or his broker, Dutch, but Eliot could not recall a single face. For a moment Eliot thought he saw the face of the green-eyed Florentine waitress he was screwing when the sink broke and Claudia came in screaming and he went on pumping and laughing on the floor of the *gabinetto*, tossing Claudia all the lire in his pocket—but it wasn't the waitress, and Eliot gave up and opened his eyes.

The wind started after sunrise and whipped a spray off the tops of the waves. Eliot's boom bobbled against his bruised ribs, and he looked up at the clouds filling the sky. He cinched his belt tighter against the boom so there was no gap, and rode the slap and bounce of the agitated sea. The clouds darkened during the day and soon a low front appeared and sheeted across under the cumulus in long raked strips of black. A drizzle fell, and Eliot opened his mouth and drank as the drizzle became a downpour and then a wooden pounding of raindrops, filling his mouth as fast as he could swallow. Then the rain stopped as if a conductor had sliced his baton through the air and with his white-gloved hand swept away the clouds and calmed the sea.

Eliot felt the life from the rain pass into his wilting body, down his arms to his hands, and he ran his fingers through his hair. The strawberry hair came off in clumps and spread on the water. It floated with him and clung to his chest when he rose from the sea. Eliot loosened a canine tooth for hours with his tongue, and it fell out when he was face down in the water. It waggled through the chalky blue, sparkling in the shafts of underwater light until it winked and was swallowed by the dark below. Eliot ran his tongue over the bloody, wet crater until the taste of blood was gone and his mouth was dry and he smelled bile in his throat.

Eliot raised his chin to the setting sun.

Tomorrow then, he said.

Eliot heard voices—not the voices in the wind, but voices from a radio far away that faded and then crackled again. He heard a splashing sound and the creaking of timber and was sure it was a boat. He cried out, but there was nothing, not even the sound of the waves slapping against his boom. Eliot pulled on the boom and twisted his head slowly like a radar receiver. It was morning. He lowered his head and shielded his eyes with his forearm.

Eliot heard muffled foreign voices, and wood splashing in the water. He tried to call out, but his voice snapped and there was only a croaking. The boat's waves splashed toward him, and Eliot heard a jumble of voices overhead. The shadow of the bow fell over him, and his boom was banging against the boat.

Eliot felt feet on his shoulders and toes searching under his armpits. He reached upward slowly. His hands touched thin ankles but slid down and fell back into the water. The voices were loud now. Eliot clung to the boom. A rope fell on his head. Eliot raised his arms and understood and pulled the rough rope over his burned shoulders. He was dragged up the side of the boat, wood against his belly. A woman yelled and Eliot felt something sharp on the side of the boat catching his foot. The sharpness pulled deeply in the skin of his instep as he was yanked upward and Eliot scraped over the gunwale and flopped like a large dead fish onto the deck.

The sun burned through his blind eyes. There were yellow spots on the backs of his eyelids. The yellow broke up and scattered into a thousand small suns, and Eliot saw ideas whipping around his head as if in a hurricane, taunting him and then fading. A woman's voice was in his ear. There was a cloth and warm water, and she was wiping his eyes tenderly. The woman was singing a lullaby. The others were quiet while she sang in his ear and wiped his eyes. Her breath steamed on his ear. The boat creaked, but there was no motion on the deck.

Eliot tried to get up on his elbows. There was a clamor of voices, and he lay down again. Water was poured into his mouth and it curled warm down within him. Eliot felt a thumb on his eyelid, pushing upward. His eyelid opened and Eliot saw a yellow eye.

Monsieur, parlez-vous français?

The thumb held his eye open, and Eliot saw a black face with cracked red lips and broken teeth. Eliot moved his head to the side, releasing the thumb, and blinked. He rubbed his eyes with his aching hands and he could see dozens of black faces crowded over him, waiting silently. A man in a torn light blue dress shirt with dirty white ruffles said, *Parlez-vous français?*

Eliot opened his lips and said, I am American.

The faces turned to the short man with the ruffles and he waved his hand like an impresario and pointed at Eliot and said triumphantly, U.S.A.!

The faces, open-mouthed, looked down at Eliot, and the man in the ruffles nodded like a king and pointed at him and repeated, U.S.A.!

Their faces floated down to him and bobbed in the air, and Eliot felt dozens of dry hot hands patting his belly. The old woman who had sung the lullaby to him cried, her hands over her face, and ran her wet palms lightly over his forehead. Eliot saw many in the crowd make the sign of the cross and raise their eyes to the heavens, and the man in the ruffled shirt cut through the crowd and his face drifted down. He took Eliot's hand and said, I am Alphonse.

Eliot.

Monsieur Eliot, said Alphonse. We are happy to see you now.

Where are you from?

We are left from Haiti.

How long at sea?

We are at sea twenty days.

Does this boat sail?

There is a storm, Monsieur Eliot. We have no good sails.

Shit.

We are very happy to see you now.

Eliot looked up at the mast and saw it was a telephone pole and the boom was a series of boards lashed together with black rope. A patchwork sail hung limp against the mast, and broken ropes hung loose like vines. The rough wood on the side of the boat was covered with the cryptic destinations of old shipping crates. Eliot could see the sea, flat and silent through the cracks. A small boy with a large head pushed through the crowd and looked at Eliot and poured a bucket of dirty seawater over the side of the boat.

Alphonse looked down at Eliot and smiled.

Now we are saved, said Alphonse.

Eliot looked up at the empty blue sky, and for the first time it seemed foreign and unknown to him. He looked at it and closed his eyes and retreated into the shell of his body.

Because you are American, we are saved.

Alphonse took Eliot's hand in his own and pressed it to his heart. You have a big boat? said Alphonse.

She sank.

You are very rich?

Eliot said nothing, but his throat burned.

Alphonse spread his hands wide and his face snapped into a fiery grin. He turned and spoke rapidly in Creole to the other faces. All the Haitians spoke at once, and some of the old women raised their hands to the sky, and a few of the men cried.

Alphonse raised Eliot's hand and kissed his Princeton ring.

What did you tell them?

I tell them you are a rich American and very big in America and now the President of the United States will make them look for you and we are saved. They are very happy to hear this good news.

The Haitians hugged one another and scanned the horizon and beamed at Alphonse. Eliot looked up at the sky and closed his eyes.

The sea was light blue ice. The sun was insolent and bitter. The Haitians were silent, sprawled on the burning wood of the deck as if struck down. They had placed Eliot on a platform in the center of the boat, and Alphonse had used his pale blue shirt to rig an awning over Eliot's head. An old man grunted from the front of the boat, and other voices were praying with a sound like cicadas. A woman stood in the bow, fishing with a string. When Eliot moved his head he saw faces twitch and look up at him from the deck with expectation. The sail quivered occasionally as if possessed.

Eliot's right foot throbbed for the first two days. A nail sticking out of the planks on the side of the boat had gashed jagged and deep. A faded little girl came to look at Eliot and ran her soft fingers down the length of his body until she came to his foot, where she stopped and lowered her face and sniffed. She went back to Eliot's head and knocked on his skull lightly with her hand balled into a fist. Then she pointed to his toe and pinched her nose. The girl looked at Eliot and Eliot looked at the girl. Eliot turned his head, and Alphonse, who was always watching from nearby, where he squatted inside a cardboard box, stood slowly and hobbled over. Alphonse took Eliot's hand and pressed it to his chest and squinted at the horizon with his yellow eyes.

Alphonse, said Eliot.

Oui, Monsieur Eliot?

My foot is infected.

Alphonse looked at Eliot's foot and held it between his fingers and twisted it from side to side.

Monsieur Eliot, said Alphonse. It is not bad.

It *is* bad, said Eliot. It is infected.

Alphonse looked out across the sea, still holding Eliot's toe.

You are big man in America, said Alphonse. They will come for you.

Alphonse let go of Eliot's foot and returned to his box. A wrinkled woman shuffled over and poured a few drops of water into Eliot's mouth from the good edge of a broken glass. A few minutes later a young girl carefully poured a few drops into his mouth from a rusty can. Alphonse watched them and nodded from his box. Eliot kept his mouth open, and one by one Haitians came to him and offered a few drops of their supply.

In the evening, the woman who had sung the lullaby in his ear hummed a song and laid her cool hand on Eliot's hot forehead and Eliot closed his eyes and nodded. She stopped and pulled back her hand and looked down at him and her hand in surprise. In the melody or the touch Eliot had remembered something, something as rare in his life as the green flash at sunset. Others came during the evening and spoke in Creole and touched his body, and sometimes they cried and wiped their tears on his chest. Alphonse came and took down the awning when it was dark and gave Eliot a few gulps of water. Then he went back to his box and watched Eliot look up at the stars.

On the fifth day no one brought him water, and he knew there was no water, and on the sixth day he heard the Haitians lying near him scuttle away. He knew it was the smell of his rotting foot. Alphonse stood over his foot and with his thumb traced the blue lines of poison up Eliot's calf to his knee. Eliot saw only a shimmering black form moving like liquid in the glare, but Eliot smelled the rot from his toe and had seen the blue lines of the poison creeping along his veins toward his heart.

Monsieur? said Alphonse.

Cut it off.

Monsieur, you know the Americans will come. He pointed out to sea.

Cut it off, said Eliot. Above the knee.

Non, non, Monsieur Eliot. We wait for tomorrow.

Do it today. You have a machete?

No, Monsieur, not today.

Alphonse.

Monsieur Eliot?

Take my ring.

Alphonse shook his head sharply and hobbled back to his box. The sun was eggshell blue through the shirt-awning above Eliot's head. The boat whispered with the sounds of scorched lungs, and Eliot wanted to say he was a skeleton bleaching in the sun. Eliot did not understand. With his eyes closed, he saw the skeleton lying on the deck, bleached and white. He tried to open his eyes and hold them open, staring at the strange sky; he tried to count to a hundred, but when his eyes fell closed he saw the skeleton. At dusk Eliot turned his head to the side in time to see a dolphin leap and the sea flat again.

The first Haitian died on the night of the sixth day. Eliot heard grunting and a splash and turned his head to see Alphonse and another man leaning over the side of the boat. In the morning when the sky was still pink Eliot heard another splash, but before this splash there was a sharp shout and another shout from Alphonse in the box. Alphonse hobbled to his side and said, It is the husband of the woman from the night.

Alphonse took Eliot's hand, and Alphonse's head and face were red and on fire.

I love America, he said. I teach myself to speak English. I listen to English on the radio for many years. We make this boat. We go to America. My daughter with me. You will see, Monsieur Eliot.

Take off the leg, said Eliot.

Tomorrow, said Alphonse.

Alphonse, said Eliot. Take off the leg or I'll die.

If you die, Monsieur Eliot, many will die.

Alphonse.

They see you, Monsieur Eliot. You are here. *C'est un miracle*. The sea is big and you are here from America. *Un miracle*. You see?

I'm going to die.

You will not die, Monsieur Eliot. Many pray for you. Do you pray, Monsieur?

Shit.

Alphonse stayed with Eliot and held his hand through the day. The sun hammered, and there was no air. The smell of his foot was strong and the two of them wheezed through their mouths. Alphonse held Eliot's hand and sat exposed to the sun on the edge of the platform. In the afternoon Alphonse wet a rag on a string over the side of the boat and wiped Eliot's forehead. Alphonse emptied water from below over the side of the boat and hobbled around the boat every hour and whispered to the Haitians the word "America" and pointed at Eliot. At dusk, Alphonse brought a little girl no more than five to his side, holding her up from behind as if teaching her to walk, and she watched Eliot. Her ribs showed through her torn shirt. She looked up at Alphonse, who smiled, and the girl smiled, and Alphonse walked her away.

On the night of the seventh day, Eliot heard more bodies going over the side. Those that went with a splash and grunts Eliot knew were already dead, but many more went with a sucking sound and Eliot knew those had jumped and some cried out and there was no question. Alphonse sat with Eliot all day on the eighth day and even found a few drops of water for his lips. On that night the bodies again jumped or were dropped over the side, and Alphonse came to him at dawn and held Eliot's foot gently in his hands.

How many on the boat? said Eliot.

I do not know. We are many.

How many? A hundred?

We are many. I know everyone. We are many, and many are family.

How many are gone?

They are gone, Monsieur. The others are alive.

How many?

Alphonse shrugged. It is too late for them. I pray for those who live.

The woman who had sung the lullaby to Eliot died at noon and was carried by three men to the side of the boat. Her body was rested on the railing and rolled slowly over the side, and her splash cut through the heat. The splash echoed in Eliot's skull and he closed his eyes and a green flash turned to black. Alphonse went to the railing and looked down at the sea and made the sign of the cross. A young woman with a scar on her nose stood on shaking legs in the center of the boat and sang in slow Creole. She swayed and sang with eyes closed, and other voices from the floor of the boat rose up in the sun. The woman collapsed after hanging like a puppet with a look of surprise. Alphonse hobbled to her and he carried her in his arms and dropped her over the side of the boat. On the way back to his box he stopped and looked at his feet and said, My daughter.

Eliot closed his eyes.

Monsieur Eliot, my daughter.

Eliot turned his head away.

Alphonse sat with Eliot and cried with no tears and asked him to say something please about the President of the United States and how the boats would come to take them all to America.

Tell them, Monsieur Eliot. They believe you.

At night the Haitians flew over the side like black ghosts and Eliot heard their footsteps as they passed his platform and heard them go into the sea. Eliot heard the feet pass him and then the hands on the edge of the boat and only once a shout and a loud splash, and in the morning watched a body floating near the boat. A foot stuck up stiff in the air. Alphonse was sitting in his box with his face in his hands, and Eliot thought Alphonse was dead.

Eliot heard a fly. He tried to see the fly but he could not turn his head, and the sound of the fly grew louder. Eliot looked up, and the sound of the fly became the sound of an engine, and he heard the helicopter coming and the helicopter was right over his head, whooshing over the boat. The helicopter swung around again and blocked the sun. Eliot saw the American flag on the side. Two seamen in white helmets looked down from the wide door, and one waved. The men swung a net down to the boat with dozens of plastic jugs, and Eliot could feel feet moving on the boat toward the supplies. Eliot felt the cool wash from the blades. An aluminum gurney rocked down from the helicopter. Hands slipped him into the gurney, and it rose swinging in the air.

Eliot was pulled into the empty cave of the helicopter. The pilot turned his blue eyes to Eliot and raised his thumb as he spoke rapidly into a small rectangular microphone over his lips. A seaman hanging from a strap leaned forward and yelled into the pilot's face, motioning with a jerk of his head toward the boat below. The pilot shook his head and with two flicks of his forefinger pointed to Eliot and the horizon. The helicopter suddenly swung around, banking hard, and Eliot's head rolled to the side and he was looking down at the deck. He saw them waving up to him, five Haitians standing and supporting each other, passing a jug of water. Many others were crawling toward the water jugs, and even some of those on their backs were waving and smiling. The helicopter circled around again and slipped down, and Eliot saw Alphonse emerge from his box. Alphonse stood stiffly, face raised, and turned slowly on his bare feet, watching the helicopter circle. The helicopter circled again, and Alphonse swiveled on the deck, never taking his eyes off the helicopter, his arms limp at his sides, and when the helicopter circled a final time Alphonse slowly raised his arms. Eliot blinked and Alphonse collapsed on the deck and Eliot looked down at the crumpled form until his face was pulled around gently by the chin. A smiling medic looked down at Eliot. The medic stuck an IV into Eliot's arm and wet his face and dribbled cold water into his mouth from an eyedropper. Eliot closed his eyes and closed his stiff lips around the long plastic nipple. The helicopter leveled and shot low across the turquoise sea.

Kim R. Stafford &
Florence Williams

Fishtrap Writers Gathering

In a circle of writers reading a list of stories they longed to tell—our first move at the writing workshop at the Fishtrap Writers Gathering in Oregon—I noticed a brisk web of connections among the stories told by Florence: polygamy, a mountain wedding, a canoe journey, all secrets revealed without the confessional flirting with a reader that spoils. She had learned, somewhere, to go straight at the story without apology or claim. I would not have to say "Show, don't tell" with this writer. At the same time, her obvious talents with language and story did not intimidate the others. Her verve was pure, infectious as mountain water. We all wanted to give her what we got, and I watched the whole company rise toward the level of her work.

The clarity of Florence's approach to writing made me realize how much can get in the way. What a pleasure to teach writing with her, rather than to deflect ego, invite suppressed knowledge, *explain* the joys of telling straight. There was simply a life of lively work to do, and she was eager, alert to the gift.—**Kim R. Stafford**

Kim R. Stafford is the director of the Northwest Writing Institute at Lewis and Clark College in Oregon and the author of *Having Everything Right: Essays of Place*.

Florence Williams received an M.F.A. in creative writing from the University of Montana in 1994. Her essays and articles have appeared in the *North American Review, Outside, Mother Jones*, and the *Los Angeles Times*. This is her first published poem.

Kim R. Stafford

The Good Son

■ ■ ■ ■ ■ ■ ■ ■ ■ ■ ■ ■ ■

So I'm climbing toward smoke on the fourth
floor, and the boss is still swinging the ladder
into place and I'm already climbing as fast as I
can, and I'm thinking just like I always do
on the way up, "Maybe I'm not cut out
for this," but at the same time I'm noticing the skid
tape on the rungs is getting worn again, and I'm mad
at the boss to let the truck get run down like this, but it's
bad to be thinking of anything but my immediate safety when I get
that high—third ladder section, and they get narrower as you
go up—but I always think of all kinds of things as I climb, I mean
it could be your last thoughts, so why not make them good,
and at the same time I'm curious what I'll see over the top,
like is it going to be someone dead, or passed out smoking in bed, or
(like this one time) these two making love behind closed doors
while the kitchen burns, so you get ready for anything, and about then
I notice the balcony I'm aimed for has the rusted railing about to
fall off, which is true half the time, and the smoke coming out the window
looks yellow, could be toxic, but I also notice this girl on the balcony
to the side, leaning on her railing watching me, and she's a good
looker, and first I notice she's calm, so that sets me at ease, because
my heart still races when I get near the top, and then through the grating
I notice how short her dress is, and I mean I'm not trying to see it or
anything, but I am coming up from below and it might be my
last time, because I could be dead in two minutes if it's bad, and if
the boys going up the stair can't break through the door once I tell
them to, some kind of explosion, some flare-up, and so the girl
smiles and I smile, and there's this sweet moment between us, just
the length of one breath, but then I'm climbing like mad again, climbing
past her, and then I'm over the railing and low in the room and guess

198

what, the smoke is only six inches down from the ceiling, and there's
grandma on the couch sleeping, and the neighbors banging on the door,
and I follow the smoke into the kitchen and it's nothing but
cabbage on the stove, so I'm on the radio to the boss with two
words, "burnt cabbage," and he shoots back, "what?" and I say,
"everything's cool," and I'm over and out, but I can't stop
thinking of the girl, will she still be there, and the grandma, is she
okay, and so I kill the gas at the stove, and knock the pan lid
into the sink and smother the burnt cinders of cabbage, and then
I'm padding out to the living room to wake her, and she's already
smiling, she's having a dream through all this, and I see in the smoky
light her face is beautiful when she smiles, and she must have
known some good times, and I can hardly bear to touch her, to
wake her, but she needs some air, so I put my hand on her
shoulder and she opens her eyes, looks up at me and says—
"Again?"—but she can't understand a thing I say, and I know
she must be deaf, so she didn't hear the neighbors pounding or
our siren, and I help her to the window for some air, and then
it comes to me we have been there before, only Pierre climbed last
time, and when he found the burnt cabbage he was so
disgusted he wouldn't say another thing about it, and I
see grandma is fine, the way she coughs and smiles and
looks down as embarrassed as a girl, but not exactly embarrassed, maybe
more like in heaven to have a visitor and all this attention, but I
have to take my leave, not touching the rail, but onto the ladder, and I
turn around and there's the girl, just below me, and I'm climbing down
past her, and as I go by so close I could touch her she asks me
if Madame is okay, and I say yes, and then somebody starts
honking—of course on this narrow street we have traffic backed up
everywhere, and the boss doesn't need the radio with me in view, he's
shouting for me to get down off the ladder if the situation is under
control, and I look at the girl and she's enjoying all the
shouting as much as Madame enjoys the attention, and she's
enjoying me, too, and I know exactly how slow I can go down
the ladder to keep the boss under control—one rung, two—and the
old woman is waving from her window, and the girl is
waving from the balcony, and the wind blows her
dress and her hair and there's just a little cabbage smoke, but it's
almost gone, and there's just a wisp of perfume, and the girl's

smile is wide open, and the old lady is so happy I came to
visit, and I'm going down slow—all that honking and
shouting on the street, and I'm thinking, like I
always do on the way down—I didn't die,
I didn't even die.

Mesa Flight 776

■ ■ ■ ■ ■ ■ ■ ■ ■ ■ ■ ■ ■

They tell her if she doesn't want to throw up, the best seats are the ones closest to the front and she gets on the plane and lo and behold! someone is smiling down on her because her assigned seat is the very closest one to the cockpit without actually being in the cockpit and that she wouldn't want anyway because they told her not to look out any windows but keep her eyes closed the whole time and hold this bag of ice to the back of her neck, so there she is strapped into the front seat and the tiny plane is taxiing and she's thinking hard she is ANYwhere but here perhaps a subway, yes, a subway like the IRT that she'd ride when she was a kid and she'd refuse to sit down because she wanted to hold the cold metal pole and shift her weight by feeling the pitch of the car through the bottoms of her sneakers and she's trying not to let her mind stop thinking she's not in the blissful safety of the Broadway #1 train but on this hiccuping 12-seater propeller so she says to herself, Don't open your eyes, DO NOT open your eyes and she concentrates on the ice on the back of her neck and the cold blast of air she's trained on her face she's getting cold but she knows it's the cold that's keeping her from getting sick she slowly moves the ice bag around to her breastbone but as she pulls the baggy from behind her it tears just a little catching on her ring and cold drops fall down her back and then down her front stopping a moment at her nipple she is so grateful the gate attendant gave her this ice she almost cried because the woman said, "I get sick too and this really helps" and it makes her love the whole world even the blond stewardess the kind she usually hates and the man in the seat behind her who is reading Ayn Rand not her favorite author but she overhears him saying the book is on his list, he made a list of 100 books to read and Atlas Shrugged was #74 what a dummy, she thinks, to read by numbers but then he says to the man across the aisle that he read all of Anna Karenina at 20-minute intervals on his lunch breaks for a whole year and so he can't be all bad and her eyes fill with tears again because she loves everyone and the ice water has now collected in her belly button she wonders how long it will take to warm up but meanwhile she's moved the dribbling bag back to the top of her spine and the plane is still sliding and hopping and if it's only the IRT it's one hell of a ride like when she read about that 12-year-old kid who hijacked the E train after he'd been watching the real guys do it for months and he was pretty good at it a little too fast but he rode all day and then brought it right back to the station and half the city thought he was a hero and the other half wanted him arrested and she opens her eye a crack BAD idea green fields slant sideways in the window of the cockpit so she squeezes her eyes shut again and thinks about the ice she wonders if she's getting nerve damage because you're not supposed to put ice right on your skin like that and she's barely moved it in 45 minutes and then through her feet she feels vibrations not like air but like something else and she knows they've landed and she's so grateful she wants to cry.

Gerald Stern &
Henry M. Seiden

Fine Arts Work Center in Provincetown

When I take a close critical look at this small body of Henry Seiden's work I realize how unified the sensibility is and how efficient the language is that expresses that sensibility, and I think that is one of the principal reasons I am attracted to his poems. It's not his realism, as such, nor his lucidity, though I like those things too, or mostly do. It's the maturity of his vision, the firmness of his grasp, if I can put it that way. I tend to trust what he says, and to believe him. Nor is it a simple matter of agreeing with *what* he says, for music is at work here and rhythm and pacing—a strategy, in short. I do want him to go a little farther afield, by which I don't mean changing the subject, though he may, and will, do that; I mean penetrating less visible aspects of that which he writes about, taking secondary, and tertiary, roads. In the meantime, I am delighted by what he does. I am delighted by the intelligence, the honesty, the knowledge, and the power of his presence. It is a moral presence, and moral most of all because of his good music, his good writing. I congratulate him.—**Gerald Stern**

Gerald Stern has published many books of poems, most recently *Odd Mercy*. For his work he has received the Lamont Poetry Prize, NEA and Guggenheim fellowships, and other honors.

Henry M. Seiden is a psychologist and a psychotherapist and has published in professional journals and co-authored the book *Silent Grief: Living in the Wake of Suicide*. His poems have appeared in *Poetry* and the *Humanist*.

Self-Portrait in His Sixties

■ ■

FOR LARAINE CARMICHAEL

Going wild in the batik shop
he traced the pink fishes with his one free finger
and swam through a blossoming sea.

He startled two half-dressed women
trying on silk and cotton,
shocked and flustered that he was still there.

All his life he loved to sit in an armchair
while those he loved walked back and forth
in their wool coats or their linen blouses

and if there was a mirror he slouched a little
with his thoughtful hand under his chin
so he could watch the two reflections at the same time.

Behind the fishes, upside down, in rayon,
there was a starfish, him of course, railing
against the oysters, a starfish going wild. He put

a blue bandanna on his head, the end of
a bolt of silk, a field of daisies; he dragged
the bolt of silk from room to room, but he

wasn't laughing when he brought it back. It was
for almost a second, a *shawl*, and he, the starfish,
half-bowed before he kissed it and put it in place,

apologizing a little to the daisies
in their unending rows, especially
the white leaves, especially the blue wayside.

Above Fourteenth

■ ■ ■ ■ ■ ■ ■ ■ ■ ■ ■ ■ ■ ■ ■

Somewhere above fourteenth he pulled up his shirt sleeves
the way he learned to do in Scotland. He found
two rubber bands and two feet of yellow string
in one of the metal baskets on Sixth. He smiled
at the color combinations but he was too stricken
to worry the way he used to. After he passed
Sam Goodys he opened his shirt. For thirty blocks
he thought of the upside-down bird; once he got
the name right he would stop in one of the restaurants
above Thirty-Fourth and write for an hour before
he went back down. Two girls wearing shorts
and yellow T-shirts made their fish faces and tried
their French on him. They wished he were dead, he ruined
their morning. Up in the sterile pear tree the bird
sang her heart out. She was a chickadee,
he was sure of that, and leaped to one perch
then to another and cleaned herself and chirped
a little more since it was the end of April
and it would never snow again. He sang
himself with his lips though there was a clicking heart
behind it and under the pear tree; across the street
from Blockbuster's there was such music, there were
so many pure complaints that when he whistled
to mark the ending, and to repeat, since who
could bear an ending, there was a quickening
and slackening in the blossoms—he even thought
he and the bird were working together, he even
waved to those girls—at least a gesture—he found
the harmony for that day, whatever you think
he was able to find his notes. He hugged
his ledger to himself—he carried a ledger—

and he adjusted his tie. When he turned left
into the forest, so to speak, those shoe stores
and ugly theaters and busy rag stores, he did
the rest of the trip in silence, that way he showed
respect for the dirt, though it was two feet down,
and for the stream that crossed there, maybe the west
side of Fifth, maybe in front of Fayvas,
and took his shoes and socks off so the muck
could bring life back into his arches and give him
back what he had lost. He put his shoes on,
he put his socks in his pocket, he tilted a stone
to see a snake, at least he thought so, and raced
past the sock store—that of all things—and past
the Moroccan cafe and up the forty-seven
steps to the right-hand door beside the flutist,
she who played all day and kept her cat
in a harness, all the time looking for clover—
that's what he said—and when she opened the door
he talked about the clover, there was no life
without it, clover the rabbits needed, her cat
if there were clover would roll in her harness, clover,
in maybe a month would cover the lawns, it was
the flower closest to him, after the blooming,
after the exchange, their petals turn brown
and drop, like a skirt, it is ironic that clubs
are black when clover is white, the ace of clubs
is only a flower, he has hope and he has
three leaves in his ear, he said these things, she said
she missed the country, upstate New York, the flats
of Nebraska, but he had taken one of the leaves
and put it in his mouth and turned the bolt
twice to the right and turned the light on beside
the second refrigerator and opened the window
and found some music, Dvořák in Iowa,
a town near the Mississippi, Spillville, his cuff
like Dvořák's, already full of notes, the sound
the same, the state abounding in clover, Irma
putting her head underneath his hand, the straps
twisted around a chair but she was so tired

she had to sleep and she was so trusting she had
to purr, for this is the New World and the doors
are both open the way they should be and music
from one place is mixing with music from another,
a flute with a piano, a flute with a violin,
the cellos now taking over, the horns taking over,
hope going down the stairway, despair going up,
somewhere on that plaster the two meeting,
the man in the busy cuffs, the cat in the harness.

This Time

■■■■■■■■■

That was his picnic table and those were his two
spruce trees growing so vertical you'd think
there was some desperation, say a roof
eating the light up, say a chimney, and those
two things that flew from gutter to gutter and perched
for only a second—each of them—were the black-streaked
white-faced goblins coming to eat and sing
above the noise of cardinals and the humming
of rubber and its echoes and the roaring
of the early train. Lord, he was here again
not far from the jungle gym beside the plastic
zebra. Lord, he would stare at the lightbulb
in front of the voltage box bolted to the untarred
telephone pole. He would study the guy wire
and how it stretched between the roses, the wire
that caught the earth just so that nothing fell there
and dip his face to suck his tea without
using his hands this time and say his chanson
in English and French the way they did six centuries
ago without one word of rage, with reference
to the lark this time and the white hawthorne, beating
one hand and one heavy knuckle, his tongue whacking
the roof of his mouth, his musical thumb scraping
across the dining room table, his pitiful slurs
in front of his metal quail, his fripperies
over his wooden-faced carp, his hapless rib cage
and nerveless fingers, his clumsy flutters
and three or four poor staccatos, hard time this time.

Someone to Watch over Me

■■■■■■■■■■■■■■■■■■■■■■■■

It is not knowing what a mulberry sidewalk looks like
in the first place that will start you up sliding, then dancing,
though if it weren't for my birdlike interior and how I shake
one foot and then the other I would have not seen the encroachment
myself; and if it weren't for the squirrel who lives in pure greed
and balances whatever he touches with one hand then another
I would have picked the berries up one berry at a time
and laid them out to dry beside my crinkled lily and my pink daisy.
In this decade I am taking care of the things I love. I'm
sorting everything out starting, if I have to, with the
smallest blossom, the smallest, say salmon-colored petunia.
I'm eating slowly, dipping one crumb at a time in my beer,
and singing—as I never did before—one word at a time
in my true voice, which is after all a quiet second tenor
that came upon me after my first descent into manhood
and after a disgrace involving my seventh grade music teacher
and a sudden growth of hair. If it weren't for my large lips
I could have played the French horn. If I didn't like mulberries—
one among a million, I know, and eat them—without sugar—
the way a grackle does his from the downtrodden branches
I wouldn't be standing on a broken chair, and I wouldn't be shaking;
and if I didn't slide from place to place and walk
with a bitter leaf in my mouth and touch one bush
for belief and one for just pleasure I wouldn't be singing.

Henry M. Seiden

The Story as I Understand It Is

■ ■

I am an accident that happened on a trolley car.
I'm a chance meeting. I'm my father's shy recognition,
his awkward passage down the crowded aisle,
his introduction of himself and my mother's serious
reply. I'm a funny warmth rising in his chest
and it won't cool down. I'm her caution. I'm a streetcar
just before it's called desire. I am the way she notices
his surprising red hair. I am a thought interfering
with her lesson plans. I'm the trolley on a familiar
track, the sparks jumping from the overhead wire
in the morning rain. I am the rumble of chance giving ground
to something like intention. I'm how he timed it after that
so he'd be there at the trolley stop when she was.
I'm what they talked about that morning and then
the next. I'm the ring of the heavy black telephone
when he finally got his nerve up. I'm how they like
the first play they see together and how she still
remembers who was in it. I'm how he likes
how serious she is, how cleanly she speaks the language,
what a mess her desk drawers are. I'm how his hesitancy
reassures her; how his clumsiness makes her feel lovely.
I'm how they worry about money. I'm her passionate
social theories and his skeptical questions. I am how
she refuses to believe in God. I'm how something
gets decided before anyone knows that anything's
been decided. And I'm the day it gets done:
the hotel wedding and the teachers' honeymoon
cruise. I am skin on skin and new pajamas. I'm a Bronx
apartment furnished from department stores, mothers,
mothers-in-law, a new fan for the bedroom humming
in the shadows, lights from the curtained windows

sliding across the ceiling on an August night. I'm the bad news from Europe and the outbreak of war.

I'm how they need each other's comfort. I'm their history and the history they create and the history of this world: chance piled on chance and accident on accident until inevitably we call it inevitable and certainly we call it us.

Looking for Lola

■■■■■■■■■■■■■

If there's something *dark* in this morning's light
there is an English word for it. But as Doctor Ramirez y Castilla
my second year Spanish professor explained (regretfully,
almost wistfully, I would say): there is no word for *mood*
in Spanish. I sat near skinny Vivian who never said a word
in Spanish—or in English—and didn't look like much
until I saw her one night in the Thespians' *Damn Yankees*.
She was Lola—Lola tango, red rose Lola—breasts,
body, hips, and she could get whatever she wanted
and, little man that I was, I wished she wanted me.
Let me put it this way—it changed the mood in Spanish II.
I kept looking sideways at Vivian that whole spring,
looking for Lola. Not that that was just a mood. It lasted longer,
like longing—for which there has to be a Spanish word.
No, mood is less than longing and you could say darker,
like a shadow, like a cloud, like the shadow of a cloud.
There's always a kind of darkness there. I don't know why
the Spanish can't say that.

Theology

■ ■ ■ ■ ■ ■ ■ ■ ■

I'm sitting on my consulting room floor playing War
with eight-year-old Jamie. He's here because he shits
in his pants when the nuns call on him in school
and I'm here to teach him to trust his mother's love
—and that it's no fault of his that his father's gone.
Both of us have our doubts. But we want to believe.
You Catholic? he asks me. I hesitate. Oh, he says,
you're Public. There's something about this he likes.

But I remember when theology was not so easy.
Not in 1950 outside the library on Morris Avenue.
I've got my arms full of books and my little sister
in tow. We try to cross the street because I know
enough to know what's coming: three sixth graders
from Saint Angela Merici's eager to revenge
the death of Christ—on me—and the fact that I think
I had nothing to do with it cuts no ice with them.
Hey kid, you Jewish? No. You Protestant? No.
You ain't Catholic. I'm Agnostic, I say,
having already learned that only my mother
thinks Atheist is the right answer to anything.
But this is about history and blood and not
about believing. The inquisition's judgment
is inevitable. I'm pronounced full of shit
and I'm nailed: I'm Jewish. And I'm on my back,
the library books are in the gutter, my sister's crying,
and the angels have taken flight.

Tinnitus

■ ■ ■ ■ ■ ■ ■ ■ ■

FOR MY FATHER

*A ringing, whistling, or other sensation of noise, which is purely
subjective.*
                    —Webster's New Collegiate Dictionary, 1953

                                        It's like a ringing in the ears,
a whistling, a kind of whisper—a sighing, a rising sound then falling,
like the ocean when you hear it in a seashell, except without the shell.
It's a murmur, a kind of gnawing. It's insistent like a hunger,
but receding like an echo, an echo that never quite fades to nothing.
I hear it in my sleep. I hear it now. It's a voice, but there are no words.
It's saying something or about to say something, but I can't say what
—maybe something someone on a Bronx street said
in another language, or I said it, or my father did, or it's a voice
on his tabletop Philco radio coming from another room.
Or it's the sound between the words, like the static in the station break
or the sound of the crowd under and around the broadcast voices
when the Yankees played the A's, in Philadelphia, in 1948
and there were thunderstorms between here and there. It's like a rumble
from somewhere in your chest, like exhaling changing to inhaling:
how the outbreath demands the inbreath demands the outbreath again
and that faint successive catching in the throat that is life succeeding life.
It's like a ringing in the ears. . . .

Kumquats

■ ■ ■ ■ ■ ■ ■ ■ ■

Only Aunt Rita and Uncle Billy go to Florida.
They fly in an "airliner"—it's just after the War when kids
still stop a street game to watch an airplane droning past
over the rooftops of the Bronx—because Uncle Billy
is an engineer who flew in Alaska during the War
and has rich parents who go for the winter to Miami Beach
where they visit at Christmas and send back a gift basket UPS,
a wooden crate of fruit packed in citrus leaves and straw:
grapefruits, oranges, and tangerines, and the spaces
between filled with kumquats which my father eats raw
—after the last grapefruit section has been eaten
and there's nothing more in the basket but the straw
and the bittersweet smell. He's holding a kumquat
and his mouth is puckering and he's in his undershirt
in the dining room, which after dinner is the bedroom
my sister shares with Grandma, and he's insisting:
This is one of life's good things. Oh Bernie, how can you
do that, my mother says. He turns to me, but I don't even
like them candied, which is what Grandma will do
with the last of them. A real love affair, Grandma is saying,
an engineer, the son of a rich man—retired, if you please,
a daughter playing golf in Florida and living, so help me,
like one of them now.

Joan Wickersham &
Deborah Kelly Kloepfer

Mount Holyoke Writers' Conference

I found a lot to admire in Deborah Kloepfer's "Exchange" when I first read it at the Mount Holyoke Writers' Conference. Her assured voice; her skillful accumulation of odd details that stick in the mind; her creation of a completely believable main character, Astrid. But a list of assets does not do the story justice. What distinguishes it is something that can't be listed or categorized. It transports the reader, literally and metaphorically, to a foreign place; and it has the irrational authority of a dream.—**Joan Wickersham**

Joan Wickersham's work has appeared in *Best American Short Stories, Story, Ploughshares*, and other journals. Her first novel, *The Paper Anniversary*, was a Book-of-the-Month Club selection.

Deborah Kelly Kloepfer has published many scholarly articles and a book, *The Unspeakable Mother: Forbidden Discourse in Jean Rhys and H.D.* Currently she teaches college writing courses and has recently finished her first novel, "Seeing Someone."

The Off-Season

■■■■■■■■■■■■

"Zip's getting married," Chase tells Marianne, coming into the bedroom and shutting the door behind him.

"Oh. Who's the woman?"

"Her name is Flora Ritchie."

"And when is the baby due?"

He narrows his eyes at her. "December." He pulls his shirt off. "But it was still a bitchy thing to say."

"Sorry." She watches him throw the shirt onto a chair. She is already in bed, propped up on a pillow against the rough wooden wall. She closes her book, keeping her index finger in to hold the place. "So, who is she?"

"Some girl he met in the schools. She's a traveling music teacher, I guess."

"I wonder what she's like."

"She's coming here tomorrow. You'll find out then." He lets his jeans slip to the floor and leaves them there.

"Does Zip seem upset?"

Chase shrugs.

"But you are."

"It's a half-assed way to get married."

"You think all ways of getting married are half-assed."

"Oh, Jesus, Marianne."

She gets out of bed and picks up his jeans, and folds them. "Were they serious, before she got pregnant? I mean, would they have gotten married anyway?"

"I didn't ask," Chase says, going into the bathroom and shutting the door.

The sportswriters call Chase Savoie the wise man of basketball. One year, early in his career, they tried referring to him as "Savvy" Savoie, but it wasn't a nickname that stuck. Mostly they content themselves with what they can do with his first name. "The Thrill of the Chase," said the *Sports*

Illustrated cover. The story in *Newsweek*, when the team was on the verge of winning the championship for the third out of four years, was called "Chasing Glory," and there was a separate little story, at the end of the big one, that compared him to Walt Frazier, Bill Russell, and Larry Bird. Then as he got older and kept playing, the stories had titles like, "Is the Chase Winding Down?" and "Chasing Thirty-Five." Chase has framed the clippings and hung them by the bed, so Marianne sees them first thing every morning and last thing at night.

She met him at a beauty contest fourteen years ago. She was Miss Oregon and he was one of the judges. He had seemed gloomy and depressed when he interviewed her, so she invited him out for a hamburger. It was unethical, but she didn't care; she wasn't going to win anyway. The contest was full of real killers: girls who owned dozens of beauty titles already at the age of seventeen; girls who had moved hundreds of miles away from their families so they could train with professional coaches in baton twirling or ventriloquism. The contest billed itself as a "scholarship pageant," and Chase, at twenty-two, was foolish enough to almost believe it; he rolled his eyes and told Marianne over a beer that he had half expected to see young ladies parading before him, solemnly reciting Wordsworth.

Where have you been? she asked.

On a basketball court, he told her, whenever I wasn't holed up in one of the Yale libraries.

Oh. She had never heard of him before—he had just finished his first year in the pros—but she knew enough to be impressed. She had never met anyone as smart, as big, as sternly handsome. He asked her what she was doing in the pageant, and she told him she wanted to be an actress.

Don't be a jerk, he said. Go to college.

He seemed so pleased with the idea of setting her straight that she didn't have the heart to tell him she was planning to go to college anyway. She went to bed with him in his motel room, and at the end of the week she collected her thousand-dollar check (she finished fourth) and followed him up to Maine, where he lived during the off-season.

The entourage then was pretty much what it is now. There was a secretary, a cook, and Chase's agent, darting in and out. Chase's brothers, Danny, Zip, and Doug, ranged in age then from fifteen down to nine, and there was a guy known as "the tutor" who took care of them, overseeing their swimming and sailing and tennis. When Chase was around, he coached them in basketball for a couple of hours every afternoon. Chase's mother, Mimi, wandered around murmuring about finishing her dissertation on learning disabilities in the inner-city schools, which she still hasn't finished. Chase's father had already been dead for six years when Marianne came. He'd been a doctor from a Boston family otherwise made up of bankers, so the infusion of Chase's basketball money didn't appear to Marianne to be throwing his family for a loop. They were already comfortable and discreet; Chase's astronomical salary only seemed to make them more so.

She settled in as Chase's girlfriend, but before long she'd taken on another role, as a kind of emotional business manager for the boys. Chase took care of them all financially, and Mimi provided a sort of vague spiritual guidance (she built a special pavilion, solely for the purpose of meditation and reflection, at the lakeside Maine tourist camp Chase had bought for them all to summer in). But it was Marianne who became the real parent in the family.

When Danny was thrown out of prep school for drugs, Marianne went around New England with him looking for another school that would take him, and she helped him write college application essays about how his expulsion (which was a big blot on his already mediocre record) had helped him grow as a person. When Dougie flunked seventh grade and got held back, and Chase raged and threatened to stop his allowance, she took Doug to Boston and got him tested and diagnosed as dyslexic, and then she hired a teacher to come to the house every day after school to work with him. When Danny, at nineteen, was found by the police on the middle of a railroad bridge one night, holding a gun, screaming that he had to stay right there, at the very center, or the world would end, she bailed him out of jail (Chase was out on the West Coast for a series of away games) and got him to a good mental hospital, where the doctors told her it was definitely drugs and possibly manic depression. Mimi brought a bonsai tree for his bedside table and read to him from *Zen in the Art of Archery*. Marianne brought Zip and Doug in for counseling and the doctor told her to watch out, she was going to have big problems with both of them.

In the beginning she assumed she and Chase would get married. He never brought it up, and whenever she did, he told her that getting married wouldn't make her any more a part of the family than she was already.

What about children? Marianne asked him.

We've got children, he said.

Not your brothers, children of our own.

We're still young. We've got plenty of time.

Now Chase is thirty-six and has one more season before he retires, and

Marianne is thirty-one and telling herself that it still might happen. She's made her peace with the fact that his stardom—a whole world of people a foot shorter than he is think he's perfect—has given him a kind of arrogance and also an undeniable power. He calls the shots in this household.

He has bought Danny a chain of sporting goods stores, helped Zip set up a basketball clinic which tours to schools, and gotten Dougie an entry-level TV sportscaster job. Mimi has her own money, inherited from both her father and her husband, but it is Chase's money that funds her more extravagant projects: the meditation pavilion, the Savoie Shelter for the Homeless, the grant to the animal protection league to buy cat and dog food for strays who would otherwise be put to sleep.

Marianne's dependence on Chase is absolute. She's never held a paying job in her life, never had her name on a lease or a mortgage, never had to worry about money. You could look at it another way and say that the Savoies depend on her, that without her Chase would have been lonely, and the boys' tangles with drugs and depression would have been far more disastrous. She doesn't mind their dependence, considering it a mark of truly familial love. Still, she would like to be married. She would like to feel more officially entrenched. And she would like Chase to declare, before a multitude, that she is utterly necessary to him, his next of kin.

For the most part she manages not to think about it anymore. Chase is right: it doesn't make any difference. But occasionally, to Marianne's own surprise, barbs slip out. The night Chase tells her about Zip and Flora, everything that comes out of her mouth is sharp and dangerous.

Marianne's first impression of Flora is that she looks like a girl off the wrapper of a chocolate bar. She has on a white blouse with puffy short sleeves, an olive green dirndl skirt, and a darker green chamois vest that laces in zigzags over her chest. Her cheeks are washed with pink (the glow of pregnancy?), her red hair is worn in a braid down her back. She smiles at Marianne when she climbs down from Zip's old Jeep, a bit tensely, unsure of her reception. Zip, beside her, is slow and reassuring, cupping her shoulders as he makes the introductions, and then rocking her gently, absently back and forth as they stand talking by the vegetable garden, where Marianne has been picking lettuce for lunch. Marianne is intrigued by Zip's air of sleepy confidence: the sleepiness is habitual, but the confidence she has never seen before—except when Zip is doing something with a small child or an animal. She thinks, watching him with Flora, of the day when

Chase saw a skunk run under their bed, and Zip managed to coax it into his hands and carry it out of the house without getting sprayed.

"I'll take her luggage around to the Bullfrog," Zip says. "Maybe you guys want to get to know each other."

"Sure," Marianne says, trying to sound comforting, picking up the look of panic that crosses Flora's face. Zip gives Flora a long slow kiss before he goes (Marianne looks away; it's like being in the first row at the movies), and then, surprisingly, he hugs Marianne. His body is damp and fruity-smelling beneath his blue T-shirt, which has "YES, I REALLY AM HIS BROTHER" printed on it.

"Well," Marianne says as soon as he goes. "How are you feeling?" She has decided that the best way to put Flora at ease is to acknowledge the pregnancy right off, but in a gentle, taking-it-for-granted way.

"Okay."

"No morning sickness, or anything?" They begin to walk toward the main house, where the family gathers for meals. Mimi has built her own house down by the lake, and the boys each have a cabin, with Pullman kitchens for morning coffee, but the biggest kitchen and dining room are in the main house, where Chase and Marianne live.

"I did in the first couple of months, but not anymore."

"That's right, you're pretty far along, aren't you?"

"Five months."

"You really don't look pregnant."

"I know. I was beginning to worry it meant a small baby, but the doctor said it's normal. A lot of people don't show at all till six months. You can see it without clothes, though." She stops walking to pull up her shirt and push down the elastic waistband of her skirt. Her belly swells white and round below the bulging navel, and there is a red crinkled line left by the elastic on her skin. "You want to feel?" she asks.

"Oh, no thanks."

"It's hard," Flora says, putting her own hand there. "I always thought it would be soft, but it's like a rock."

"Can you feel the baby moving?" Marianne asks, walking again toward the house.

"Not all the time, but sometimes." She smiles. "I was going to have an abortion, but now I'm glad I didn't." Her voice, even when she is talking about her own happiness, is cool and flat.

"Zip must be really excited about the baby."

"He's great with kids," Flora says. "That's how I first met him. He was running one of his basketball clinics at a school where I was teaching." She looks at Marianne. "You and Chase don't have children, do you?"

"We're not married," Marianne tells her.

"Oh," she says. "Oh. I thought you were. Zip always says, 'Chase and Marianne,' and I guess I just thought—"

"That's okay." She is beginning to find Flora's lack of artifice a little exhausting. Is it really possible that she could have reached the age of— what? Twenty-four? Twenty-five? And have so little finesse or protective covering of any kind? But then, Zip doesn't have much protective covering either. The two of them, she thinks, are going to get creamed.

"This really is a wonderful place," Flora changes the subject, gazing around at the old tourist cabins scattered among the trees.

"We love it," Marianne says.

"It feels so real, I mean, like real people live here."

"Gee," Marianne drawls, "how 'bout that?"

Flora blushes. Even her bare legs turn rosy above her galumphy little Heidi boots. "You know what I mean. The way Zip talks about Chase, I wasn't sure what to expect."

Her embarrassment is cut short by Mimi, appearing at the edge of the woods in a bathing suit and a big straw hat. She waves and trots over to them, her bare feet toughly oblivious of pebbles and pine cones. She holds out her hands to Flora. "It's so lovely to meet you!" she says warmly, and then she swoops in and embraces her. "We're just delighted about you and Zip. Really. And of course, the little one."

"Thank you." Flora swallows, looking immensely relieved.

Mimi turns to Marianne and hooks an arm in hers. "I've just had the most wonderful idea."

"What."

Mimi holds out her other arm to Flora and then begins to stroll, pulling them both along. "I think we should plant an asparagus bed. Right on that flat place, below the strawberries. The drainage is excellent, it's sheltered." She turns to Flora. "Don't you think it'll be marvelous—asparagus from our own garden?"

At lunch Mimi interrupts the general conversation to say, "Oh, and Chase, there's that trunk of linens in the attic."

They all look at her: What? Zip has been telling Flora the story of the tourist camp, how Chase bought it from a woman who had inherited it from her mother, who had run it as a summer retreat for Jehovah's Witnesses.

"You know," Mimi continues, looking at Chase a bit impatiently, as if she doesn't understand why his mind isn't running along the same lines as hers. "That stuff from your father's mother. Four sets of everything, for when you children get married." She turns to Flora. "We'll go up after lunch, and you can pick out what you want."

Marianne trails up the attic stairs after them, knowing it's masochism. The trunk is almost directly over the bedroom she shares with Chase. Inside the lid is a list, taped there so long ago that the paper makes a cracking sound when Mimi pulls at it, and it comes off leaving a frame of brown tape behind.

"Fingerbowl doilies," Mimi reads. "Well, some of this stuff is ridiculous. But let's have a look."

Marianne reaches out and helps Flora, carefully, to unfold the layers of white tissue paper. They lift out stacks of napkins, damask and linen, lace-edged and plain. "There are eight sets of twelve," Mimi says, looking at her list and calculating, "so Flora, you can choose two."

"How beautiful," Flora breathes, fingering lace.

Mimi picks up a stack wrapped in cellophane and pushes her reading glasses up to squint at a tiny white label. "Do you know, I don't believe these were ever used? Ireland. My guess is that Zip's grandmother bought these the year before she died. Ireland was one of her last trips."

"What was she like?" Flora asks, sitting back on her heels.

Marianne, despite herself, also hopes for anecdotes. All she knows is that everyone was tall; in all the old brown pictures that show them standing next to friends, servants, college teammates, the Savoies tower above everyone else, as though they belong to a different race or species. Chase doesn't seem to know or care much about his family's history, and Mimi is too vague to be much of a storyteller. Maybe the trunk of linen will cast some sort of spell on her, loosen her tongue or her memory.

But Mimi says, "Oh, not very interesting, I don't think. Bigoted. Stuffy. Dogs and horses. She always scared me to death."

Flora chooses, out of all the napkins, two sets with wide lace borders. Good, Marianne thinks, preferring the plainer ones.

They go through more layers of napkins, then linen towels, table runners, placemats cross-stitched in beige wool on colored canvases. ("Zip's

grandmother did those," Mimi sniffs. "Her only hobby.") Thirty-two li-
nen pillowcases. Everything is neatly organized into layers, in multiples of
four, ready to be divided.

Mimi seems unaware of any awkwardness in the three of them engaging
in this task together. But Marianne notices that as they make their way
down through the trunk and the riches accumulate, Flora seems to grow
more and more embarrassed, shrinking among the towering piles of white.
"Oh, boy, what'll I ever do with all this?" she finally says, placing six bu-
reau scarves on top of one of the stacks. "Really, Mimi, this seems like
plenty."

But Mimi is digging out tablecloths, lace after lace after lace. Finally a
few plain ones, damask and linen cutwork.

Flora shoots a quick look at Marianne. "Oh," she hesitates, and then
puts her hand on the two plainest. "This is fine, I guess, and this." Forgo-
ing the frills she is naturally drawn to, leaving behind some of what she
guesses Marianne may want, too.

"Oh—" Marianne says, before she can stop herself.

Mimi and Flora both look at her when that little sound of disappoint-
ment escapes.

"Well," Mimi murmurs finally, lightly stroking Flora's pink forearm,
"you must be tired. Maybe that is enough for one day."

Zip and Flora decide they want a big wedding, two weeks from Saturday,
on the lawn in front of the main house. They want to ask everyone they
know, everyone the family has ever known. They look defiant and proud,
announcing this. They decide there's not enough time to fool around with
printed invitations, they'll just call people. Chase lends them Trudy, his
secretary, to help with the calls and the arrangements. They get hold of the
minister who christened Zip; he's retired now and living on Long Island,
but he agrees to drive up to perform the ceremony. Zip calls a childhood
friend whose rock band is struggling to make it in L.A. and offers to fly
the whole band east if they'll play for the wedding. Mimi drives down to
Boston to get her own wedding dress out of storage and altered to fit
Flora's swollen abdomen. Even Danny and Doug, who go through cyclic
drunk/stoned and sober periods and who at the moment are both perpetu-
ally bombed, pitch in with the planning, volunteering to pick up liquor,
dry cleaning, people at the airport.

Through it all Flora sits on the sidelines, watching the Savoies tossing the wedding together, apparently having no preferences, no desires, no family of her own.

"Oh, sure, she's got a mother and father," Chase says, looking surprised when Marianne asks him. He's gone out of his way to spend time with Flora since she arrived, sitting with her in the living room after dinner, driving her into town one afternoon when she wanted to mail a letter. Interviewing her, Marianne thinks. Becoming, surprisingly, her partisan.

"Isn't it usual for the bride's family to plan the wedding?" Marianne has to be careful, make herself sound neutral, not bitter. She's been sitting on the sidelines too, as the wedding plans rumble along, and she's not sure if she's sitting there because she chooses to or because her position really has grown more awkward, now that a true wife and daughter-in-law is coming into the family.

"She tells me her parents are a bit overwhelmed by the whole situation," Chase says.

"By the baby, or by the idea of you?"

"Both, I guess. Anyway, they'll come to the wedding, but they don't want any more involvement than that."

They don't want it, Marianne wonders, or they're too frightened to ask for it? Her own parents have faded from her life. She's never asked them to visit and they've never asked to come. Every couple of years she flies home, alone, with a shopping bag full of extravagant presents, to stay for a week. They've met Chase a few times, when his team was in Portland playing the Trail Blazers. They thought he was very nice, but she knows they find him intimidating. They never phone her; when they have something special to tell her about, like a sister's engagement or the death of her high school boyfriend, her mother writes a letter, and Marianne calls them.

"She's the best thing that ever happened to Zip," Chase says.

"Mmm," says Marianne.

"Don't you think he seems calmer than you've ever seen him? And happier?"

He does, but Marianne finds Chase's enthusiasm irritating. Since when is he so promarriage?

"Now that he has Flora, and the baby, he's got a reason to be responsible. Don't you think?"

Marianne doesn't answer. She is remembering what a psychiatrist told her and Chase once. It was the time Zip OD'd, and they hadn't known whether it was accidental or on purpose. The shrink watched them sympathetically but, she thought, judgmentally, and talked about how Zip was convinced that nothing he did would ever be good enough.

We know that, Chase said impatiently.

Knowing it is one thing. Navigating it is something else. You have to make it possible for Zip to come to you with problems before they blow up like this.

He can come to me if he wants.

Well, let him know that. But don't give him all the answers. What I would do, if I were you, is just open the door and play dumb.

"I think you're right," Marianne tells Chase now, slinging an arm around his waist, which is level with her shoulders. "He really has pulled himself together."

She comes upon Mimi and Flora on the lawn.

"I thought the altar there," she hears Mimi say. "Not a real altar, of course, just that narrow table from my library, with a cloth over it. A white cloth, do you think, or should we go for a spot of color?"

Then Mimi sees her coming and stops talking. They actually jump apart a little, guiltily, so that Marianne feels she's stumbled upon a tryst.

"I think a colored cloth would be nicer," Marianne offers. "I have some fabrics Chase and I bought in Provence last year that I've never done anything with. Would you like to look at those?"

Sure, they say, exchanging glances, as though they've just unexpectedly gotten away with something.

That's when Marianne decides to go, just for a few days. She worries, because of the way they've begun tiptoeing around her, that everyone will think she's fleeing in a huff, but she can't help that. And as it turns out, Chase doesn't even seem to notice that she's going. "Boston?" he says. "Are you sure you don't want to wait till after the wedding? I'd come down with you, then, for a few days."

"No, there are some things I'd like to take care of this week. Get my hair done, buy a dress for the wedding. And you and Mimi seem to have the planning pretty much under control."

"Well, let's go away together after this whole thing is over." He kisses the top of her head. "We'll do one of those fjord cruises, or that bird-watching thing in Alaska. Think about it."

"I will," she promises.

She stays in Cambridge, at a plain-looking, expensive hotel in Harvard

Square. She constructs for herself the kind of cultivated, sanitized life she imagines she might have now without Chase—museums, bookstores, modest restaurants. Her tastes, after more than a decade with Chase, have inevitably been shaped by him: she spurns Newbury Street and the department stores that would have so attracted her during her beauty contest days and takes instead the ferry that runs out to the harbor islands, where she spends an afternoon wandering around a deserted Civil War fort. The fort is supposed to be haunted, according to the guidebook, by a woman who was executed for trying to help her imprisoned husband escape.

She does go to Filene's basement one afternoon, where she has a momentary flirtation over a table of men's shirts. "What size are you looking for?" asks a man in a tweed jacket standing next to her.

"I couldn't begin to tell you," she says, smiling back at him. She heads down to the dress racks, where she finds a turquoise silk from a fancy store, one she often shops in, reduced to a quarter of its original price. Marianne buys it, feeling it proves somehow that she could survive without Chase. She could get a job, find a little apartment, and shop in Filene's basement. It would take a little extra cunning, but she could do it.

The rehearsal dinner, at Mimi's, is big, warm, and jolly: the nicest event Marianne has ever seen in the Savoie family. A strange collection of people: friends of Zip's in thrift-shop funk, hair bleached and spiky. Flora's sisters and their husbands, the sisters with blue eyeliner and charm bracelets and frosted, blow-dried Princess Di hair, the husbands bricklayers and electricians with careful table manners. Some of Chase's teammates, at a different level from the rest of the guests, like mountaintops poking through the clouds, heartily egalitarian, gods leaning down to converse with mortals. Chase, beaming. Mimi, flitting through, murmuring nervously, "I think we should start getting people into the dining room, don't you?" And Zip, calm and happy, in a navy blazer and the new mustache he's grown over the past two weeks, hovering around Flora, refilling her orange juice, bringing her crackers and cheese.

Flora, to Marianne's surprise, hasn't dressed up at all; she's wearing the olive green dirndl skirt with a man's shirt tucked into it, and she looks uncomfortably bunchy around the waist. She has on knee socks and a scuffed pair of clogs. Her face is so grim and miserable-looking that Marianne feels sorry for her and strolls over to talk. "How are you doing? Are you going nuts with all this wedding stuff?"

"Not really," Flora says, not smiling. "I have been. But now I feel like the whole thing's finally in motion, so all we can do is just relax and go with it."

Mimi puts a light hand on each of their backs. "I think we'd better get people into the dining room."

In Mimi's dining room, with its wide windows overlooking the lake, six tables for eight have been beautifully set. But it doesn't feel at all formal. Loud talk, and every few minutes ping-ping-ping: a knife tapped on a water glass, someone giving a toast. People tell stories about Zip as a child, as a teenager. To Zip and Flora, they end, and everyone drinks. Chase tells about Zip and the skunk. Someone tells about the basketball clinic, and how Zip paid for real hoops when he found some kids in a playground using a garbage can to shoot baskets. Chase gets up again and talks about how in the fifteen years since the family started summering in this place there have been some wonderful parties here, like the one the first year the team won the championship (applause), and the one the second year they won (applause), and especially the one the third year (applause and cheers), but that this is the best party of them all. Dougie gets up unsteadily and says how happy he is to have a new sister-in-law and a new niece or nephew. Embarrassed laughter, and everybody drinks. Zip stands up and thanks everyone for being there and proposes a toast to Flora's parents. Then Flora's father stands up, short and dark and pale, and he holds up his glass and looks straight at Zip and says, "Take care of my girl." A momentary silence.

Danny gets up, the court jester, and defuses things by telling a long unintelligible joke which has "Shit" in the punchline. People laugh uncertainly when it's over, and Danny raises his glass silently and then sits down. Chase stands up again and talks about how happy he is.

After the dinner, Chase takes a couple of his teammates down to the lake for a swim and Marianne stays to help Mimi oversee the cleanup. Mimi says, "Well, I hope we have a groom tomorrow."

"What do you mean?"

Mimi shakes her head. "There's been a psychiatrist in and out of here all week. Let's just pray he knows what he's doing."

Marianne presses, but all Mimi will say is that Zip has been having some problems.

Marianne walks slowly back to the main house. All the lights are on tonight in the tourist camp, in all the cabins that are usually empty: the

Whippoorwill, the Cathy-O, Faraway, Gone. This is how the camp must have been in long-ago summers: lamplight reaching out to meet other lamplight, radios playing softly, muffled voices from behind the cabin walls, distant shouts and splashing from the lake. Climbing the last stretch of path up from the lake, she smells the sweet, unmistakable scent of marijuana. For some reason she doesn't just ignore it and keep walking.

"Who is it?" she asks.

After a moment, Zip's voice. "Me."

"Oh, Zip, don't." For Zip, a joint is never just a joint.

He doesn't say anything.

She takes a few blind steps off the path and makes out his tall silhouette in the darkness, standing still among the trees. "Come on. Put it out."

"I should have let her have the abortion," he says. "She was all set to do it, but I talked her out of it. I was the one who wanted to get married."

"Well, so what's wrong with that?"

"I shouldn't have made her believe she could depend on me."

"Why not?"

Zip starts to cry. He cries for a while, and Marianne holds him. Then he says, "Maybe I could stay with you and Chase tonight?"

She tightens her arms around him and then pulls away. "Go stay with Flora," she tells him.

She won't tell Chase, she decides, getting undressed. If things have been this bad all week, then Chase already knows what's going on. She wonders why they haven't canceled.

Chase and Marianne are still in bed when the door of their room opens and Flora walks in. "Zip's gone," she announces.

They sit up. "What?"

"He kept me up all night saying 'Tell me again why you want to marry me? Tell me again?' and finally I said, 'I'll tell you once more: I love you and I want to marry you. And that's it. No more.' He looked at me and walked out."

Chase throws back the covers. "I'll go find him."

"No," says Flora.

"No," says Marianne.

They both look at her. "He has to come back because he wants to, not because you drag him."

"The hell with that," Chase says, getting out of bed and walking naked over to his bureau. "There are going to be two hundred people standing on our lawn in a couple of hours, and he damn well better be here to face them." He pulls on his clothes and goes out.

"I'm going back to Zip's cabin," Flora says grimly. "And I'm going to stay there until he comes and tells me he loves me."

Marianne pulls on jeans and a shirt and heads over to Mimi's house. Mimi is already dressed for the wedding, in bright blue linen. "I know," she says. "Chase stopped by. What should we do, do you think?"

"Well, it's too late to cancel. People are already on their way."

"Oh, well, canceling. I don't think it's a question of that," Mimi says, frowning. "I'm sure Zip will come around."

Marianne nods.

"But it's so hard on Flora. I'll go to her now, I think, don't you?" Mimi strides off toward Zip's cabin.

Danny and Doug are sitting on Mimi's front porch, tipping their chairs back, smoking. They're both wearing green sport coats and RayBans; they look like employees of some hip, slightly sinister airline. Dougie has his arm in a sling.

"What happened to you?" Marianne asks.

"Fight," he says.

Last night at the party he was fine. She opens her mouth to ask, then closes it.

"Anything we can do?" Danny asks.

She looks at her watch. "Show the guests into the garden, I guess. And act like nothing's wrong."

"Sure thing," says Doug.

In the garden, two hundred people mill around. Zip's old green rowboat is up on pilings, filled with ice and liquor. A yellow tent, its poles wrapped with vines, is filled with flowers and balloons. Danny and Doug, lily-of-the-valley in their lapels, stand on either side of an archway made of two blossoming cherry trees in pots, bent toward each other so that their branches intertwine. "Come on through," they say jauntily to Marianne, and she wonders for a moment if they know who she is.

"Is Zip back?" she whispers to Doug.

"Nope."

"Marianne, how are you?" someone asks, and she is sucked into the party. People say things to her.

"You look wonderful."

"Isn't this the perfect spot for a wedding?"

"Chase must be so thrilled."

She looks at her watch: just after ten-thirty. The wedding is scheduled for eleven.

"Such a beautiful dress. I love the color."

"So Chase is planning to retire after next season? Can't you talk him out of it?"

"What about the bride? What's she like?"

"Where is Chase, anyway?"

"And Zip—where's Zip?" It's ten past when someone finally asks this: Gloria Rangeley, married to Carl Rangeley from the team. Marianne has always liked Gloria, who has her own line of mail-order cosmetics for black women. Mail-order so I don't get totally killed if he gets traded, Gloria says. I move, but the fulfillment house stays in the same place. It's just good business. When are you going to line something up for yourself, to make sure you don't get totally killed? "Is anything wrong?" Gloria asks now, in a lower voice.

Marianne peers back into her kind face, glowing beneath a fuchsia straw hat. "Oh, no, no, just a little delay."

"I heard a rumor that the groom hasn't showed up," another voice at her elbow.

"Oh, I'm sure that's not true," Marianne says.

A quarter of twelve. Chase comes out onto the lawn in a checked shirt and jeans. Holds up his hands. "Thank you all for coming, but I'm afraid there isn't going to be a wedding here today. Please stay, and eat and drink. Thank you again." He puts his head down and ducks back into the house before anyone can talk to him. Murmur, murmur, murmur. A fat lady in a monogrammed sweater is crying. A huge hand wraps around Marianne's upper arm. "Hey, man, tell Chase I'm really sorry, okay?" She hears from someone that the minister is angry: he drove all the way up from Long Island and he's damned if he's going to drive all the way home without his lunch. She hears screaming from the living room, a man's voice, furious. Zip must be in there, and some man is giving him hell. But no, Danny reports, when she sends him in to check, it's a retired stockbroker, an old friend of Mimi's, telling a Wall Street joke. People cut into the Brie, rummage around in the rowboat for beer.

"It was the minister's fault," Marianne overhears someone saying. "He said something to Flora right before the ceremony was supposed to start, and she took off."

"No, it was Zip who took off," someone else says.

Marianne looks up at the shaded windows of her bedroom, wondering if Chase is up there. How can he stand it, listening to this party going on? She wants to go up to him, comfort him, ask about Zip—does anyone know where he is? but she's become, in the absence of Chase and Mimi, the host of the party, and she keeps saying thank you to people who tell her how sorry they are.

Finally Chase comes back out and holds up his hands. "Thank you very much for coming. I've closed the bar now. Thank you for coming." The guests begin to move at once, seven-footers ducking under the cherry-tree archway. "Please take your presents back with you," Chase says, his eyes full of water. It's the kind of crying no one acknowledges and neither does he; people are having quiet farewell conversations with him as though it's not happening.

Mimi is out on the lawn too, now, an old Shetland sweater thrown over the shoulders of her party dress. She is crying in a sniffly, brittle way that makes people not dare to approach her. She flutters around looking very busy, doing nothing, talking to no one. Every now and then as people pass by her, discreetly looking away, she recognizes friends and she snatches at them, crying, "You're not *leaving*?" Yes, yes, we have to get back, work, traffic, they mumble, and she lets go of them.

"Where's Flora?" Marianne murmurs to Doug, not wanting to intrude on Mimi; but he, oblivious, calls out, "Hey, Mom, do you know where Flora is?"

"Her father's with her," Mimi says, coming over to them. "They're taking her home with them." She catches sight of the rowboat, still half full of bottles. "Oh, no," she cries, her voice carrying over the lawn. "Oh, Chase, Chase! What are we going to do about the liquor?"

He sprints over to her, not wanting to conduct this conversation in shouts. "The Ritchies paid for it, so we can't exactly keep it."

"Is Zip back?" Marianne asks him. It's the first chance she's had to ask.

"He's in the woods," Chase says flatly. "He's sitting on the rocks down by that little waterfall. He wouldn't come."

"What about a charity ball?" Mimi asks, sniffing. "Could we donate it, do you think?"

"I don't know of any," Chase says.

She takes out a handkerchief and wipes her eyes. "Well, then maybe the best course is to return it to a liquor store and send Flora's family a check."

"But most of it's been opened," Chase points out. "All the foil is off the champagne."

Marianne walks away from them. Danny is folding up the wooden chairs that were set up under the trees for older people who might not be able to stand through the whole ceremony. Dougie watches him, grinning; he can't help because of his hurt arm. "How did you hurt it, anyway?" Marianne asks, standing right in front of him.

"In a bar. This guy said I was sitting too close to him, and I said it was public property, and he hit me."

"Like this?" she asks, punching his hurt arm. "Or was it more like this?" Punching harder.

He stares at her, not even moving to protect himself.

"I don't know what goes on in this family," says a voice behind them, and Marianne turns to face Flora's mother, pale and red-eyed in her shiny gray mother-of-the-bride dress. "But it's sick. And it's got to stop."

She waits for someone to answer her. Over her spangled shoulder Marianne sees Chase trying to catch her eye, shifting from foot to foot. "Excuse me," Marianne says and goes over to him.

He puts an arm around her and bends his head to speak into her ear. "Zip's back. He's upstairs, waiting. I'm going to take him to the hospital."

She nods.

"Will you be here when I get back?" The anxiety in his voice is new.

"Sure," she tells him, and then she goes back to help Danny finish folding the chairs. Doug is trying to help too, now, using his good arm to stack the chairs on the grass. He makes the stacks too high; at one point the top chairs start to slide off, but Marianne catches them and settles them uneasily back into place.

Exchange

■■■■■■■■■

It has rained for nineteen days, long gray rain that sounds on the metal railing of the balcony like tap water filling up a pot. The old woman who lives in the window opposite appears periodically like a figure in a German clock, checking the sky, checking the time, checking the American across the street who lets men stay the night.

Astrid has changed her name here, temporarily, posing as Richard's sister—Mlle Bialowski—to get cheap rent since subletting is *interdit*. The name is just a convenience for both of them, something to throw the concierge off the track while she cooks stale leeks and listens through the wall.

Richard is in the States now, trying to get together a show in New York. Although he has proved a useful contact, Astrid is beginning to feel that taking his apartment was a mistake; his life keeps intruding, filling up the space. When she thinks she is alone, one of his lovers comes to the door or the telephone rings. It is his one great luxury, the phone—he has to clump down a flight of stairs in the hall to pee, but he can call all over the world from his bed. These days it is the creditors who appear, demanding the money he owes around the city to galleries and art stores. Angry men curse at her in French, glare at her suspiciously, their eyes darting around the room. She tells them he is gone for the summer, she does not know where; she makes up lies for him even though he left the apartment filthy and is overcharging her on the rent.

She is sweeping up one day, the incense burning on the orange-crate table, George Harrison singing "All Things Must Pass" in the corner, when a knock comes at the door. She turns down the volume on the old Bell and Howell cassette recorder, anticipating the concierge with some complaint, but standing there instead is a boy who does not look like a creditor, at least not one from the shops, another lover perhaps, with another kind of debt.

"Richard n'est plus là," she says.

"Je sais," the boy answers in halting French. Strangers always believe she is a native speaker, not Parisian necessarily—she is too heavy, too tall—but Belgian maybe, or Swiss. "Je viens"—he pauses—"obtenir la clef."

"Oh, right," she says, switching to English, sparing him, although she is tempted to let him strangle himself in the pluperfect. "Come in. I forget your name. Richard wrote it down somewhere."

"Leland. Leland Pratt."

He closes the door behind him and squats up against the wall. Astrid motions toward the big cushions under the window, but he shakes his head. "I'm fine," he says, perched like a large, frail bird.

"Are you a student?" she says, making small talk, fumbling around in the cupboard for the key. "How do you know Richard?"

"I've actually never met him. I study in the States with someone he knows."

"I hope he prepared you for the studio. It's just a big empty space with a little room partitioned off in the back. Not nearly as livable as the apartment," she says dryly, gesturing at the floor to ceiling plank and cinder block bookshelves, the frameless bed covered with a heavy, dusty pelt, the taxidermed llama in the corner wearing a bashed felt hat.

"I know. I know." Leland seems impatient. He stands up and stretches his arms behind his back. Suddenly he goes gray and heads for the door, asking for the WC. He is gone a long time, too long, and while Astrid is standing there trying to decide whether to go after him, he reappears on the landing looking sheepish and very ill.

She moves toward him as he starts to pass out in the hall, pulling him inside before the concierge comes out. He is very light and his hair smells like some kind of tree. She gets a towel and runs it under cold water, wrings it out, moves it around his face and the back of his neck. He opens his eyes, disoriented and embarrassed, then jerks away from her.

"Please don't touch me."

"I'm sorry," she says, handing him the key, but as he starts to gather up his things, it becomes clear that he is in no shape to go anywhere.

"Look, it's all right," Astrid says, helping him to the cushions while he protests. "It's probably the water. Why don't you rest a while?" She lights a fire because the room is cold, and when she notices that he has fallen asleep, she slips out for something to eat.

Around the corner at Le Boulot, the black and white cat wanders in through the curtained doorway, checking under each table for scraps. As usual, Astrid orders a glass of burgundy and a plate of couscous; it is cheap and good although the age of the meat is questionable, disguised in Algerian spice. The same people come night after night—old men with bad teeth who order the custard; a middle-aged woman who sits alone and reads; groups of young Moroccans in tight black pants who flash gold molars at Astrid with blatant desire. After weeks of just glaring, Madame speaks to her occasionally, won over, despite the concierge's gossip, by Astrid's flawless French.

When Astrid returns to the apartment, Leland still hasn't stirred. She is tired and can't work anymore, but she's not ready to sleep. She opens a cheap bottle of Côtes du Rhône and curls up on the mattress, listening to Leland's breathing in the dark. A siren whines in the distance as she tries to empty her mind of the manuscript she is translating, free-lance—a dry Marxist discussion of the dialectic between socialism and the market economy. She agreed to do this piece precisely because it is outside her field; she has no feelings whatsoever about the content, no interest, besides the game of shifting words around. She especially likes idioms, expressions which have no syntactic equivalent; she keeps a running list in a small notebook of phrases she overhears on the street or in cafes: croquer le marmot, casser la croûte. She pours another glass of wine and unclips her hair from the big barrette, which is pinching her head.

Astrid is somewhat startled by her own hospitality. In her more objective moments she would admit to a kind of suspiciousness, a paranoia even, which makes it hard for her to understand her willingness to take Leland in. She can't tell what she is feeling—annoyed partly, worried about the manuscript deadline, eager in some strange way, maternal (he is very young), slightly aroused. She pushes her hand between her legs and closes her eyes, thinking about no one in particular; a shadowy figure appears, then suddenly the smell of some unidentifiable flower—a flash of purple— which makes her come violently.

In the morning, Leland seems to have recovered. Astrid goes out for baguettes; when she comes back, he has made tea and picked up the room. He talks only about her—he asks question after question but evades answering any. He wants to know what she is writing. How old she is. How many brothers and sisters she has. Whether her parents are still living. She feels as if she is filling out a family history on a questionnaire.

His portfolio is propped up against the wall alongside his backpack, but when she asks to see some of his work, he refuses, quite frantically, to open it. Astrid tries to turn the conversation to Richard, but Leland becomes agitated, inattentive. After a while he gets up and goes over to the corner.

236

She thinks at first he has changed his mind about showing her his sketches, but he feels around in the flapped pocket of his pack, bringing out a pipe and a little square wrapped in foil. He gets very serious as he pushes the hash into the bowl, making such a ceremony of it that Astrid can't refuse. She feels like a diplomat in a foreign land, served brains or monkey paw, but she draws on the pipe until she is drifting, Leland's voice swirling like tea leaves in a cup.

They are in rooms somewhere, an old house; he describes them one by one. He takes her through mirrors and closets and attics and drawers, up stairs, along the border of Oriental rugs, but there is no one there, no people, the house is empty, echoes, and they keep circling back and back in ever diminishing circles toward one room the door of which is closed, the door of which he will not open, the room which is, after all, where the secret lies.

Astrid is pulled into the rhythm of his voice, but suddenly it stops; his head drops to his knees and he begins emitting noises like some keen raptor circling around and around something so far below that she cannot see or imagine it. She says the only word she knows to say to him, his name, she says it over and over until it is a chant, a song.

Astrid doesn't see Leland again for a couple of weeks. He is presumably installed on the Rue des Rosiers, surrounded by Richard's life-size statues that glow in the dark, translucent, lit from inside, milky-colored, as if they were covered with some kind of membrane or caul. Whatever Leland does there he keeps to himself; she has no idea whether he knows anyone at all in Paris, whether he has friends, how he spends his day.

She has been tutoring an actor named Vincent from Le Théâtre Liquide, a kind of group grope, she gathers, playing in a space somewhere near the Louvre. He says he needs to learn English to go to New York. Like Richard, he imagines New York to be a place to undo the past or find the artistic or sexual passion which eludes him. Vincent plies her for stories—he wants conversation, not grammar—and she makes up what he wants to hear. For this he pays.

Her real work is stalled. She came to Paris ostensibly to audit courses in literary theory at the Sorbonne and Vincennes, but the critical fluency she achieved seems to work against her, undercutting her thinking instead of shoring it up. She thought at first she was going to work within the context of expatriate women—Sylvia Beach or Gertrude Stein—but slowly she has become preoccupied with a semantic analysis of footnotes, not page numbers and ibids, but the significance of the margin, the little texts outside of but generated by and dependent on the larger ones. She is at this point trying to both categorize footnotes—those that are asides, those that are annotations, those that are critically cannibalistic—and explore them as markers for something else, but she never gets that far. All biography has fallen out of her work, all plots and people. She knows she has no clear sense of purpose, but the work of plucking at little numbered notes has become seductive, compulsive. She keeps quoting and cross-referencing with fine-point black pens, filling up box after box of three-by-five cards.

Astrid climbs the four flights to Vincent's apartment, stopping at the second landing to pee, almost suffocated by the smell of waste in the small closet where she squats in the dark. Outside Vincent's door, quatrième à gauche, she leans against the wall to catch her breath; the smell of urine rises up the stairwell from the floor below. She knows why she has come. She feels as if her body is disappearing. She wants something warm and wordless, something which cannot be translated or revised.

"Qui est là?" Vincent asks when she knocks.

"C'est moi. Astrid," she says, accenting the last syllable so that her name sounds like someone else's.

"J'arrive," he says, and then opens the door, pulling her inside, closing his arms around her, his chin on her head.

The room, although small and shabby, is carefully arranged. There are pears in a wire basket on the sink. The bed is in an alcove beside the door; a large print of Gustav Klimt's "Le Baiser" is taped to the wall.

"I am so content to see you. Vraiment." He moves slowly, like a dancer, but he is not wasting any time. "J'aime ça," he says, following Astrid's eyes to the Klimt. Then he reaches for the buttons of her shirt, undoing them with one hand while he strokes her with the other.

"Speak English," she says, because in English his sounds are unhinged and mean nothing.

Vincent is perfectly focused, incapable of being distracted: reality does not distract him from his plans for New York; the closeness of Astrid's body does not distract him during his English lessons; the sounds she makes do not distract him as he pushes inside her, his long hair falling into her face. His own pleasure, however, seems irrelevant; he comes quickly, soundlessly, then without missing a beat moves his mouth between Astrid's legs, where he brings her over and over again to the edge of a dizzying blackness which she both resists and waits for, disappearing into a space that is dark and fetal.

She knows less about Vincent than she does about Leland, but the relationship, which would have once seemed to Astrid empty or shallow, seems merely elliptical, an intense, pulsating encounter, as if she were communicating with a distant but compassionate dolphin or whale. She knows that someday he will suddenly disappear, sounding, called back by some migratory rhythm or ancient song or current of the human heart. She likes the elusiveness of their meetings, the immediacy; when she gives over her body to him, it is like drowning, slightly suicidal, enough to take the edge off.

At Filles du Calvaire, Astrid gets off the metro—the station smells like steam and nougat; the same woman she has seen at other stops around the city sits against the wall, begging, a baby asleep in her lap, covered with coins. Astrid walks home along Rue Vieille du Temple, which will lead her past Richard's studio. An old woman with a harelip stands in a doorway selling brown eggs, cartons piled on a wooden table in front of her. She says something to Astrid which Astrid doesn't understand; her hands, covered with scabs, flutter around her face like injured birds.

Astrid stops outside the green metal warehouse door to Richard's studio, looking for the bell. She needs a shower; her thighs are sticky and the smell of Vincent's patchouly is in her hair and on her skin, a scent which both attracts and disturbs her. The door slides open; a woman Astrid does not recognize is standing there, a sketchbook and pencil in her hand. Over her shoulder, Astrid can see what appears to be a figure-drawing class, a nude woman seated on a chair, a circle of people on the floor around her.

"Je cherche Leland," Astrid says.

"Connais pas," the woman says, shaking her head.

"Il y habite," Astrid says; the woman disappears inside and after a few minutes returns.

"Oui," she says. "La chambre au fond."

Leland is painting; he looks up, frightened, trying to block the six or seven canvases propped against the wall.

"What are you doing?" he asks.

"Nothing. I was coming back this way, so I stopped. Who are those people?"

"Some class. I don't know," says Leland, turning the pictures to the wall. "Richard arranged it. I assumed he would have mentioned it. They come here on Wednesdays."

Astrid is trying to take in what she sees. On each canvas is a child, the same child—sometimes nude, sometimes clothed in the same flowered dress. Leland has painted her as if through water—reflected, distorted. Astrid is taken aback by the look in the child's dark, fixed eyes.

The train to Prague is almost empty. Outside the window, Astrid sees a tunnel looming as they round a curve; suddenly she is plunged into blindness, her eyes wide open, the smell of the diesel abruptly overpowering the other senses. She panics for a minute, cannot breathe. Her knees bump into Leland's in the darkness.

Leland is still unable to explain the necessity for this trip. The day after Astrid saw the paintings, he appeared at her door, paced around the apartment, agitated, dispensing information about visas and couchettes. It was obvious that there was some disturbance at work behind his itinerary, and he frightened Astrid a little—his distraction, his energy—but Prague was intriguing. Besides, her work was not going well, the rain never stopped, Vincent had left her for an actor named Jean-Michel. She let Leland convince her to come, drawn out of her boredom into his neediness, his strangeness, his danger.

He has packed a lunch for them to eat on the train—cheese and wine and sandwiches and fruit. Eating takes up a good part of the afternoon; they discuss the pears and oranges in adolescent detail, and Astrid invents stories about Richard and the men who keep showing up at the door.

Just before the border a stern official appears, asking to see documents and bags. He wants to know about cash and cameras; he is very specific. He questions Astrid about the color of her eyes, insisting, despite the information on her passport, that they are not green. She is frightened at first, but afterward Leland says she was being stupid, that he was playing with her, that it was a game. He looks annoyed.

Prague is gray and bleak with empty streets. Astrid is still shaken by the guard and the barbed wire and the towers with guns positioned toward the tracks. No one speaks English and they have no idea where to go or where to stay. Leland no longer seems in charge; he is vague, disoriented. They change a little money at the station, and as they are getting ready to leave, a middle-aged woman who has overheard them in line approaches, offering to take them to a hotel. Leland thanks her and before Astrid can think, they are getting into the woman's car. Films flash through Astrid's head— they are being kidnapped, set up, robbed, they will end up at the bottom of the Vltava, never to be heard of again. But they end up instead in the lobby of a respectable hotel, where they find vacancy and cheap, hot food. The woman disappears.

Downstairs, the man at the desk wants payment in advance, but they have only changed enough money at the station for one room. This concerns Astrid slightly, not in principle but in terms of Leland's increasingly erratic mood. He shifts like quicksilver, relaxed then angry. She leaves him to settle in, and when she comes back from the bathroom, he is talking to himself, drinking wine from one of the two bottles he brought with him on the train. His hands are shaking.

Astrid asks him if he is alright, and he looks at her, startled. It is his work, he says, lucidly at first; it is not coming the way he had hoped. There is a chasm between the vision and the brush. Actually, he says the "victim" and the brush and then corrects himself, pushing his hair back from his face.

"The woman in the car said we must see the Hradčanské Náměstí," Astrid says. "And the Malá Strana."

These foreign words seem to calm him, but only momentarily. Astrid senses him sliding into the pit, the gap. He points out the window, where the moon is a thin, pale line, full of itself, like a scar. "If only I had words," he says. "In a box. I would keep the lid on and take them out at night. Night is the worst. I see everything at night." He puts down the wine bottle and holds his hands out toward her, palm side up, revealing the scars across his wrists. "Words have edges," he says. "Do you understand?"

Astrid wakes up on the window seat, the sun streaming in on her face. Leland is asleep in a chair. It is late in the morning and she is hung over. Down the hall in the bathroom, she leans over the toilet and throws up.

She leaves a note for Leland and goes downstairs, where she orders coffee in the empty dining room and traces the pattern of the fine, white cloth with her spoon. She is in over her head; this she knows not only through common sense but experience. Astrid has a kind of radar for damage; she senses it before it shows on the screen, is drawn to it before she reads the warning. Once again she has let madness win, no questions asked; she is pulled to it like dancer to dance, repeating over and over again the long, frantic waltz of her childhood.

Leland comes down very cheery like a child fresh from a nap. He orders a big breakfast with the last of the money and wolfs it down. He is chatty and sweet, checking out baroque cathedrals and castles in the guidebook he picked up in Paris in the gare.

They start out walking toward Lesser Town, Astrid's heels blistering painfully in her shoes. Leland reads aloud touristy tidbits as they cross the river over a bridge flanked by barbed wire and icons painted on wood, a strange combination of fervor and fear.

They change money in a hotel across from a small restaurant where they decide to eat. As they are waiting in line, an old man comes out from behind the desk and asks whether they are exchanging travelers' checks or cash. When Astrid tells him she has francs and dollars, he ushers her into a small office behind a curtain. "This will speed things along," he says in very good English, taking the money and handing her an envelope filled with korunas. She waits for Leland to exchange his American Express checks, and they cross the street for lunch.

They ask the waiter who brings the menus to translate, but they don't understand a word he says. They finally point to a plate at a nearby table loaded with some kind of meat and dumplings, and Leland performs an elaborate charade of pulling a cork out of a bottle and filling two glasses; the waiter nods and comes back smiling with the wine.

"Very good," Astrid says.

Leland smacks his lips, rotating his glass in his hand. "Na zdravi."

"What's that?"

"To your health."

"How do you know that?"

"Guidebook. Very helpful. You can't get far without a guidebook, Astrid."

The fresh air has sobered Astrid up, and she takes a sip of the wine; it is thick and sharp, like some kind of cheese.

"I was thinking," he says, "of finding the office to extend the visas. I like it here. I might paint."

Astrid pokes at the salad, which has just arrived. "I can't," she says. "Stay if you want. I've got work to do."

"You can't go," he says, very quietly. "You brought me here. You have to stay."

"Leland."

He has grown dark again, eclipsed. "Why do you all do this?" he asks. "Go away." His hands are fumbling with the salt shaker, pouring little piles, which he picks apart, grain by grain. Astrid moves her chair around the table to the corner next to his, touches his arm.

242

The woman at the next table is watching. A small dog with a ribbon in its hair sits on her lap, licking the edge of the plate.

"Leland. Let's go outside."

He knocks over the chair getting up, and Astrid leaves money on the table. They walk for blocks, Leland striding ahead and Astrid following, slowed by the blister on her heel which gives her a jolt of pain every time she steps down. He walks with a kind of desperate purpose, stopping abruptly at the entrance to a large garden from which rises a battlement or castle wall.

Thick flowers with a sweet, heavy smell lead to bushes, then hedges cut with paths, until they are deep within a labyrinth where the leaves reach taller than their heads, where the spaces get smaller and smaller as they go. Astrid is overcome with the feeling of being suspended in time, sure that if they go far enough, answer the riddles, they will end up in a temple or shrine.

She rounds a corner and finds Leland sitting cross-legged in the middle of the path. "I didn't mean it," he says. "Someone left the water. It wasn't me." He seems to be having trouble breathing, and Astrid kneels next to him. "Give me some words," he says. "You have so many words. All I have is paint and water. Blood."

This is the moment of exchange, the one lurking ever since Leland climbed up Richard's stairs, the price Astrid pays for giving him the key. She feels herself shutting off. She doesn't want to hear, but the story crouches like a minotaur behind the hedge.

"I was supposed to be watching. I thought I could hear. When I went to look, she was—floating. There really wasn't enough water to float. Just lying there in the water in a little dress. She looked so—surprised."

Astrid is overcome by the smell of the plants. It is hot. She cannot breathe. The strong smell of flowers always makes her feel nauseous, faint.

Leland says, "She was only three. My sister." He sighs. "Do you see?"

Astrid feels like she is going to scream; she will not be able to stop. Leland begins to hum. She has a strange feeling in her head as if someone has pushed the button on a slide carousel; the picture shifts. She is not sure which way to go to get out of the maze. There must be signs. Tourists could not just disappear here on summer afternoons. "Let's go home," she says, hoping Leland can hear her, extending her hand. She feels suddenly very old, so old. "Come on. We'll see about the trains."

Leland stands up slowly. He is very pale, like a medium coming out of a trance; he runs one hand over his eyes, erasing the images stored there.

At the station they find a train that will leave that night. When they buy the tickets, Astrid looks at the envelope full of korunas and realizes that there are too many, five or six times what there ought to be. She asks Leland to check his wallet. Minus the lunch, he is just about right. It takes her a minute to realize what has happened. Leland, in fact, is the one who points it out; hers is black market money, a reward for Western currency.

"We have to spend this," Astrid says, watching a group of guards circulate through the station, remembering the inspection on the train. "They count the cash. They know how much we came in with. If they check, they'll see that this is too much."

Leland doesn't take any of this seriously. "What do they care? Hide it. Put it somewhere."

Astrid is suddenly scared, more cautious than she remembers becoming. Borders are to be taken seriously; crossing over has implications, a certain price. "Besides," she says, "when are we coming back to Prague? What good are korunas if we don't spend them here?"

They start down a street lined with shops, but as it is Saturday afternoon, they are all closed. They see cameras and watches, but these are all things they have been asked about on the train, officials keep count, they will know. Possessions, unlike feelings, cannot appear without explanation out of thin air.

"We'll have to eat it," Leland says as they pass a window full of fruits and breads and salads and pastry and pâté. They buy as much as they can possibly eat before the Austrian border, more, but it's not enough; they have at least seventy-five dollars left over.

The day has turned warm and they cross over into a large park where there are families and lovers, children with boats. Watching them, Astrid gets the idea to hide the money where someone will find it; just before they leave for the station they wad up the bills and tuck them into bushes and benches and niches in the stone wall.

Leland sleeps most of the way back to Paris. He is exhausted, his story finally translated, the words trapped now, sacrificed, inside the maze. As the train rushes by fields of sunflowers and small Austrian villages, the summer stretches out unbearably long ahead of them until Leland returns to the States and Richard comes to reclaim his bed, and Astrid can take her real name back.

Terry Tempest Williams & Leslie Ryan

In the Thoreau Tradition

Leslie Ryan possesses raw, sensuous, tactile power in her prose. Her stories expose what society has chosen to hide. We begin to recognize the abuse of children as an extension of our abuse of the Earth. We painfully witness how the cultural image of women has not only betrayed us but muted our voices, given us a false image of ourselves in the mirror.

Leslie Ryan's voice shatters the mirror. Because she faces herself with searing honesty, she allows us to do the same. Her courage becomes our own. We are moved, altered.

I first met Leslie in Missoula, Montana. It was a February afternoon in 1993, along the banks of the Clark Fork River. I saw in her eyes the beauty and wildness of a woman who dares to touch fire, who recognizes wind as spirit, and who is not afraid to be in the service of her imagination. She moves me deeply. She is my mentor, a critical voice for our time. I find her fearless, wise, and acutely moral.—**Terry Tempest Williams**

Terry Tempest Williams's first book, *Pieces of White Shell: A Journey to Navajoland,* won the 1984 Southwest Book Award. Other books include *Refuge: An Unnatural History of Family and Place, Coyote's Canyon,* and *An Unspoken Hunger: Stories from the Field.* She is the naturalist-in-residence at the Utah Museum of Natural History in Salt Lake City.

Leslie Ryan is a graduate student in environmental studies at the University of Montana, where she also teaches in the Wilderness and Civilization Program.

The Erotics of Place

■■■■■■■■■■■■■■■

A woman stands on her tiptoes, naked, holding draped fabric close to her body as it cascades over her breasts, down her belly and legs, like water. A strand of pearls hangs down her back; her eyes are closed. She is at peace within her own erotic landscape.

This photograph, taken at Studio d'Ora in Vienna in 1934, is the first image I see in Det Erotiske Museum in Copenhagen, Denmark. I take another step into the foyer and find myself confronted with a six-foot golden phallus mounted on a pedestal. I am tempted to touch it, as I recall the bronze statues of women in museums around the world whose breasts and buttocks have been polished perfectly by the hands of men, but I refrain.

A visitor to this museum in Copenhagen can wander through floors of exhibits ranging from a solitary Greek vase, circa 530 B.C., depicting Pan chasing Echo, to a wax tableau of Fanny Hill, 1749, to a prostitute's room reconstructed from an 1839 Danish police report.

Spiraling up to the fourth floor (you may choose to descend at this point to the Aphrodite Cafe for coffee and pastries), the visitor arrives at the Erotic Tabernacle, the climax of this museum experience. Here, you are assaulted with twelve television screens, four across and three down, which together create a montage of pornography from 1929 through 1990, complete with the music of Pink Floyd's *The Wall*.

As I watch these images of men and women simultaneously moving from one position to the next, I wonder about our notion of the erotic—why it is so often aligned with the pornographic, the limited view of the voyeur watching the act of intercourse without any interest in the relationship itself?

I wonder what walls we have constructed to keep our true erotic nature tamed. And I am curious why we continue to distance ourselves from natural sources.

What are we afraid of?

There is an image of a woman in the desert, her back arched as her hands lift her body up from black rocks. Naked. She spreads her legs over a boulder etched by the Ancient Ones; a line of white lightning zigzags from her mons pubis. She is perfectly in place, engaged, ecstatic, and wild. This is Judy Dater's photograph *Self-Portrait with Petroglyph.*

To be in relation to everything around us, above us, below us, earth, sky, bones, blood, flesh, is to see the world whole, even holy. But the world we frequently surrender to defies our participation and seduces us into believing that our only place in nature is as spectator, onlooker. A society of individuals who only observe a landscape from behind the lens of a camera or the window of an automobile without entering in is perhaps no different from the person who obtains sexual gratification from looking at the sexual actions or organs of others.

The golden phallus I did not touch, in the end, did not touch me. It became a stump, a severance of the body I could not feel.

Eroticism, being in relation, calls the inner life into play. No longer numb, we feel the magnetic pull of our bodies toward something stronger, more vital than simply ourselves. Arousal becomes a dance with longing. We form a secret partnership with possibility.

I recall a day in the slickrock country of southern Utah where I was camped inside a small canyon. Before dawn, coyotes yipped, yapped, and sang. It was a chorus of young desert dogs.

The sun rose as I did. There is a silence to creation. I stood and faced east, stretched upward, stretched down, pressed my hands together.

I knelt on the sand still marked by the patter of rain and lit my stove, which purred like my cat at home. I boiled water for tea, slowly poured it into my earthen cup, then dipped the rose-hip tea bag in and out until the water turned pink. My morning ritual was complete as I wrapped my hands around the warmth of my cup and drank.

Not far, an old juniper stood in the clearing, deeply rooted and gnarled. I had never seen such a knowledgeable tree. Perhaps it was the silver sheen of its shredded bark that reminded me of my grandmother, her windblown hair in the desert, her weathered face, the way she held me as a child. I wanted to climb into the arms of this tree.

With both hands on one of its strongest boughs, I pulled myself up and lifted my right leg over the branch so I was straddling it. I then leaned back into the body of the juniper and brought my knees up to my chest. I nestled in. I was hidden, perfectly shaded from the heat. I had forgotten what it felt like to really be held.

Hours passed, who knows how long; the angle of the sunlight shifted. I

realized something had passed between us by the change in my counte-
nance, the slowing of my pulse, and the softness of my eyes as though I
were awakening from a desert trance. The lacelike evergreen canopy
brushed my hair.

I finally inched my way down, wrapping my hands around the trunk.
Feet on earth. I took out my water bottle and saturated the roots. I left the
desert in a state of wetness.

The Erotic Museum in Copenhagen opened July 26, 1992. It closed on
August 31, 1993, because of financial difficulties. More than 100,000 visi-
tors from around the world had paid to see erotica on display.

"The erotic has often been misnamed by men and used against women,"
says Audre Lorde in *Uses of the Erotic*. "It has been made into the con-
fused, the trivial, the psychotic, and plasticized sensation. For this reason,
we have turned away from exploration and consideration of the erotic as a
source of power and information, confusing it with the pornographic. But
pornography is a direct denial of the power of the erotic, for it represents
the suppression of true feeling. Pornography emphasizes sensation with-
out feeling."

Without Feeling. Perhaps these two words are the key, the only way we
can begin to understand our abuse of each other and our abuse of the land.
Could it be that what we fear most is our capacity to feel, and so we anni-
hilate symbolically and physically that which is beautiful and tender, any-
thing that dares us to consider our creative selves? The erotic world is si-
lenced, reduced to a collection of objects we can curate and control, be it a
vase, a woman, or wilderness. Our lives become a piece in the puzzle of
pornography as we go through the motions of daily intercourse without
any engagement of the soul.

A group of friends gather in the desert—call it a pilgrimage—at the con-
fluence of the Little Colorado and the Colorado Rivers in the Grand Can-
yon. It is high noon in June, hot, very hot. They walk upstream, men and
women, moving against the current of the turquoise water. Nothing but
deep joy can be imagined. Their arms fan the air as they teeter on unstable
stones, white stones in the river. They are searching for mud with the con-
sistency of chocolate mousse and find it, delicious pale mud, perfect for
bathing. They take off their clothes and sink to their waists, turn, roll over,
and wallow in pleasure. Their skins are slippery with clay. They rub each
other's bodies—arms, shoulders, backs, torsos, even their faces are painted
in mud, and they become the animals they are. Blue eyes. Green eyes.

Brown eyes behind masks. In the heat, lying on ledges, they bake until they crack like terracotta. For hours they dream the life of lizards.

In time they submerge themselves into Little Colorado, diving deep and surfacing freshly human, skins sparkling, glistening, cold and refreshed. Nothing can contain their exuberance but the river. They allow themselves to be swept away—floating on bellies, headfirst or backs, feetfirst—laughing, contemplating, an unspoken hunger quelled.

D. H. Lawrence writes, "There exist two great modes of life—the religious and the sexual." Eroticism is their bridge.

Ole Ege is the man behind the Erotic Museum in Denmark. It was his vision of eroticism that he wanted to institutionalize. It is his collection that now resides in storage somewhere in Copenhagen.

Standing on the sidewalk next to the red banners that advertise the museum, I watched each object, each exhibit, each wax figure being carried out of the white building and loaded into two Volvo moving vans on Vesterbrogade 31, minutes away from Tivoli Gardens, where the harlequins danced.

That was Labor Day weekend 1993. Seven months later, the museum opened once again. Ole Ege's vision of the erotic life is being celebrated, this time in a new location and with a more solid base of support.

"Denmark has been liberated sexually for twenty-five years," he says, "but we are not yet liberated in our minds. It is a matter of individual morality how one conceives this subject. For me, eroticism relates to all the highest and finest things of life. Every couple on earth participates in this confirmation of the creation, the urge we have to share ourselves, to make each other whole."

The idea that governs an erotic museum and the ideal behind an erotic life may never find a perfect resolution. Here lies our dilemma as human beings: nothing exists in isolation. We need a context for eros, not a pedestal, not a video screen. The lightning we witness crack and charge a night sky in the desert is the same electricity we feel in ourselves whenever we dare to touch flesh, rock, body, and earth. We must take our love outdoors, where reciprocity replaces voyeurism. We can choose to photograph a tree or we can sit in its arms, where we are participating in wild nature, even our own.

The woman in the desert stands and extends her arms. Rumi speaks, "Let the beauty of what we love be what we do. There are hundreds of ways to kneel and kiss the ground."

The Other Side of Fire

■■■■■■■■■■■■■■■■■■■

I have heard that storytelling starts with the body and ends with the body. That's what gives stories the ability to snag the mind by its ankles from behind and land it face down in something: life if the story's good, blandness if it's not. But as a woman I worry about this. For most women, the body, like the story, is not a simple thing. It's a battlefield where lies and truths and power go at it. A woman's mind might wander from skirt to skirt in that smoky place like a dislocated child, looking for some grounded legs to stand by, or on, for years. The woman might end up knowing herself only as a casualty, or recognizing herself only by her scars. While there may be some truth in such an identity, it is only a partial truth, and a potentially destructive one. I want a different story.

I never thought much about fire until a few years ago, when I began teaching survival in the Great Basin desert of southern Idaho. I worked in a wilderness therapy program for troubled youth. The idea was that direct contact with the natural world could help these kids gain a more healthy sense of identity and empowerment.

Some of the teenagers who ended up walking around the desert like hunter-gatherers had been court-ordered to do so. A few of the boys arrived in cuffs, with their hair shaved down to the rind on one side and left to seed on the other. On their forearms they displayed homemade logos of heavy metal rock bands, scratched in with sewing needles and flooded with blue fountain pen ink. They wore the tale of their crimes like dog tags, and we call these narratives war stories.

But most of the boys didn't come that way. In spite of a few shocking tales, the boys' toughness hung on them uncomfortably. The manic energy they used in comparing transgressions made me smile, because beneath it they seemed to writhe like grubs set down in unfamiliar terrain, glistening and blinded by their recent emergence from childhood but as yet unsure of how to burrow into the next phase.

The girls came to the desert differently. Their fear wasn't just a thing to guess at beneath layers of toughness and tattoos; it was as evident as the black lace panties and see-through underwire brassieres they wore for twenty-one days of rigorous hiking. Their stories, shared in secret with the other girls, were less war stories than love stories—or, more specifically, sex stories—but they were stories of power and identity just the same.

We instructors taught our students how to make backpacks from their blankets and string, how to construct debris huts and other shelters, how to identify and gather wild edibles, and basically how to keep themselves alive in difficult terrain. But the hardest thing we learned out there—the thing that made the students cry in frustration—was how to make fire with sticks.

I have been questioned about the relevance of bow and drill firemaking to everyday life and I have been challenged on the social structuring of wilderness therapy programs, which mostly benefit rich, white children. Wouldn't these kids feel a lot different about survival if they really had to do it—if they had to make fires on the floors of their freezing city apartments, rather than on this fabricated desert game?

I can only answer that question from my own experience, with a story that also takes place somewhere between war and love.

When I was twelve, my younger brothers and I were abandoned for a year or so in an apartment on the south side of Richmond, Virginia. Mom was wherever Dad had left her, probably back in the old house where she had been struggling with mental illness for years. After repeated complaints from our neighbors, who thought we children were being hurt and neglected, the court had ordered our father to remove us from the old house. We relocated on the other side of town, where no nosy neighbors knew us. At first I thought we would all live in the apartment together— four children and our father—and start a new life. But it didn't work out that way.

We still don't know where Dad lived during that time. At first it was every few days that he came back, bringing what we needed to survive. Some groceries: Spam, milk, and a case of Bisquick boxes. Then every week he would come. Then there was no pattern, and we couldn't tell when we would see him again.

Before long the phone got disconnected. The power got shut off. We were living in a husk of a house with no resources. The dishes in the sink had been crusted for so long they began to flake clean. The toilet hadn't been flushed in what seemed like months. We just kept using it until it began to overflow, and after that we shut the bathroom door and went in the new construction site under a pile of boards. Some of the windows in the apartment were broken out—one from my head, one from my brother's fist, others from things we threw. My brothers were age ten, eight, and four. We fought.

We also made a pact. If anyone found out we lived alone, Dad had said, they'd break us apart. Mom was too sick to take care of us, so we'd all have to go live with different families, and we'd never see each other again. The four of us had gathered in the kitchen one day by the dry sink, and I scraped the crud from a sharp knife with my teeth. We sliced a bloodpact into our hands: never tell.

The neighbors on the left had evidently abandoned their apartment in a hurry. We went in there a lot at first, eating the food they had left and looking at the bloated fish floating in the tank. There were parts of a broken waterbed, some lava lamps, clothing, and a bunch of empty boxes. All their wallpaper was swirled with bright metallic patterns, like our kitchen paper, but patches of it were torn down and left hanging. No one ever came in or out there, and after the food was gone we stopped going there too, because it was a creepy place.

The neighbors on the right acted like we didn't exist. I think they knew we had gone into their apartment and stolen food, because they got double bolt locks and began to talk loudly about calling the police if they saw any delinquents around. We saw that we could get caught and separated, so we stopped taking from them.

My brothers learned from an older boy how to steal from stores. They could walk to the 7-11 in about half an hour. They stole ready-made food from there, since we had no electricity to cook the Bisquick and everything else was gone. The boys refused to eat Bisquick raw. Mostly they stole small food, for safety. Candy bars were usually the biggest they got from the 7-11, because the clerks could see down the aisle pretty easily. From Safeway, though, they could get more, like peanut butter; it was easier, because the clerks changed more often and didn't expect kids to be stealing. Sometimes they'd get extra for the baby, who couldn't come. I don't know how long this went on. Nine months, maybe a year.

Then one day I found myself standing in the kitchen. It was coming on winter, dusky in the house. A wet wind blew through the broken windows. I lifted my bare feet up and down on the cold kitchen floor. I was staring at the stove, scooping dry Bisquick from the box with crooked fingers. I wanted to turn on the stove. I wanted to wave my hands over the fiery concentric circles of the working heating element. I wanted there to be power in the house.

"I am twelve years old," I said out loud.

Bisquick floated out into the air as I spoke. In summer I had mixed the Bisquick in a bowl with sprinkler water and eaten it wet like that. Now the sprinkler faucets were off. The boys had shown me where they drank from the creek; the water was oily and bright orange-brown. I wouldn't do it.

"Bisquick should be cooked," I said.

When was the last time he came? I couldn't remember. He might never come back. Could we actually freeze here?

Something about the stove started to infuriate me. It was supposed to give us something.

"Damn thing," I said.

Big and useless. How it made these promises and never kept them. I spit chunks of Bisquick at it, but they were too dry to stick. They fell all over my arms and chest, making a pattern of white, dusty splats.

I pulled the burner control knobs from their sticky prongs and hurled them one by one across the kitchen at the orange metallic wallpaper peeling from the wall. They left the paper dented like bent foil.

I grabbed a big metal spoon from the dish pile and banged it on the steel edge of the stove. I wanted sparks. I wanted gouges. It was the cheap kind of spoon and its bowl just bent back perpendicular.

"Damn you," I said, with the Bisquick on my teeth like plaque.

The baby was four and he still couldn't talk. He did know how to poop in the lumber. I was still getting good grades at school, because I had learned to read at a young age and I was placed in the gifted classes, but my brothers were not doing so well: they had missed over 100 days of school each. We received a letter about it, addressed to Dad. I had to do something. I surveyed my options.

The only reading we had were old *Scientific American*s and the other magazines under the mattress where Dad used to sleep. *Scientific Americans* were all men. The mattress ones were all women: *Penthouse* and *Playboy*. Dad liked their articles best. All of us had read them.

I read them again. There were women who had sex with all their best friends, their bosses, delivery people, and pets, with everyone watching everyone else, and it seemed to make things better. "Dear Xavier," they wrote to their friend Xavier, a woman who was pictured only as a pair of red lips with a penis-shaped lipstick going in. They told her all about it.

I read about special techniques women could learn to please men, like mouthing unwaxed cucumbers. Men took women to cooked dinner for this, and gave them promotions. They'd provide apartments, heated, for the whole family.

I walked to the bathroom doorway and stood outside. No one ever went in there. Stuff had actually flowed onto the floor. We could smell it all over the house. But the bathroom had the only mirror. I stripped off my pants, shirt, and underwear. I held my breath, opened the door, and climbed onto the sink counter.

In the murky light seeping in from the hall, I looked at my legs in the bathroom mirror. There were three triangles where the light came through, just like Xavier said men liked: one between the ankles, one between the knees, one between the thighs.

A stiffened orange towel lay on the small bathroom counter. I wrapped it around my mouth and nose like a gag so I could breathe. I turned around on the bathroom sink to look at the backs of my legs and butt.

If I swayed my back I looked curvier. I bent down with my butt stuck out and my hands on my knees to get the sideways picture, checking the curve of dim light along my spine and the flatness of my stomach. I was still holding my breath for as long as I could because the towel smelled almost as bad as the bathroom.

I squatted above the sink and looked into my pupils, wide and black above the bristling cloth. I said aloud through the mask, "You have one thing."

I remember a time not long after that stove day when I was being hit by a jealous man. He was nineteen years old; I was twelve. He had six motorcycles, a punching bag, and a seemingly unlimited supply of drugs. I couldn't leave; he was giving me the drugs I sold for money. I wish I could say I sold them for food money, for food I would share with my brothers. This did happen sometimes. But not often. I wasn't a good mother.

What I really wanted was to be someone. What I really wanted was power, and the only way I could get it was to take it from someone who had more than enough. Drugs were the currency that allowed my body to be exchanged for money, and money is a poor person's idea of strength and possibility. So I just clamped my teeth, stood there, and let my friend hit me.

As he got madder, one zigzagged vein began standing and pulsing in his forehead like lightning. He was hot, coiled up red with his fury.

I, on the other hand, felt like a block of ice. Each blow to my head seemed to break off little pieces of my mind; they would go floating up into the corner of the room and stick there like ice chips behind a river rock.

Soon my body was standing alone in the bedroom, being hit.

But not me. He couldn't get at me. I was hovering alongside the brown ceiling stain from the upstairs toilet. I could watch my head lolling around as he cuffed me.

Do whatever you want to my body, you jerk, I said to myself. That's not *me*.

It was the same way having sex with him, and with the other men who, as I see in retrospect, had no business being sexually involved with a twelve-year-old girl. When I was with them, my mind would slip out the back of my head and go look out the window, if there was one.

My mind became more and more a body unto itself—in time, when it left me on the bed, I could feel its dry, bare feet shuffling across the floor. One time it made it all the way to the door and paused there with its delicate spirit fingers on the knob. When it looked back to say good-bye to my body on the bed, something—compassion, necessity?—made it pop back inside.

After this went on for what seemed to be a long time, I began to worry about my brothers. One night the eleven year old and I sat in the living room watching TV (the power was on at the time). We were both stoned, and the vertical hold on the TV didn't work, so we were watching Captain Kirk's head and torso being severed and lifted by a constantly rising black line. My brother told me that some of the men I'd been sleeping with had given the baby pot to smoke while they were smoking, and maybe other drugs, too.

This, I said to myself, is not what I want our lives to be. I quit doing drugs and didn't allow any of those men in our apartment again. All my friends disappeared.

I made another plan. My body had gotten me into this trouble; my mind would get me out. I had good grades, but they weren't useful yet. In order to be a good mother to these boys I'd need a job.

But I knew that a girl of my social class couldn't get a job; my clothes were embarrassing, my hair greasy, my shoes fake leather with unglued soles that slapped the ground as I walked. I was thirteen. I couldn't work for three years. I did look sixteen already, though; someone might be fooled into hiring me if I had the proper attire. Even if I couldn't get work yet, I reasoned, it was best to steal my wardrobe now, because as long as I was under sixteen, nothing would go on my permanent record and expose us if I did get caught.

I hitchhiked downtown to a fancy department store called Miller and Rhodes. This was before the days of electronic theft devices. I told the salesladies my father had asked me to come look for something nice for my mother—she was about my size, I said—and he'd be back later with me to see what I'd found. In the dressing room, I opened my big Nauga-hyde purse and stuffed in a gray wool business suit: tailored skirt, vest, and jacket, completely lined. I broke the hanger in half and stuffed it in too and left the rest of the clothes there.

From that department I went to lingerie. I picked out a peach-colored Christian Dior teddy, pure silk. It snapped discreetly at the crotch; one hip was cut out and flounced with pleated gauze. I stole that too.

I see now that my faith in my mind was skimpy. My body was still the bottom line for power. I resented the fact, but I was a practical girl. Even if I was lucky enough to get a job with my suit and my grades, I'd need to be high class underneath, too—for my boss, and for the real work that women do.

When I got home, I went up to my room and found my suitcase full of Barbies, which I was ashamed about still having anyway. I had written my name in pen all over the plastic luggage a long time before, in big curly handwriting with exclamation points and flowers. I took it in my father's closet and dumped the Barbies on the floor so no boss would see Barbies in my room. I cleaned the little Barbie shoes out of the side pockets, folded the gray suit and the silk teddy into separate piles in the suitcase, and hid the suitcase under my bed.

As time went on, I added to the suitcase with a tan pantsuit, some oxford shirts, a pair of leather sling pumps stolen right off the rack, red lace bikini panties with bows on them and a matching bra, and the sexy kind of ny-lons that need a garter belt.

Before the suitcase was full, though, my father had come back, appar-ently to stay. When he came, it was late at night. He had a woman with him.

He called us downstairs one by one to where she sat at the three-legged kitchen table. Most of the lightbulbs were blown out, so only half her face was visible in the dim light from the hall fixture.

The woman was young, twenty-seven or so. She was twenty years younger than my father, but she had three children of her own. By the time I came downstairs to stand rigidly beside the boys, the woman was crying. We were embarrassed by her emotion, and by the way she said she would marry my father and save us.

She did marry him, but she couldn't save us. She could make sure we had shoes and meals and schooling, for which I am grateful. But she couldn't protect us from our father, who was violent and owned her love. She couldn't even protect herself.

The skirts she wore, and the power they signified, offered no refuge to a child. They were too much like the ones I had stolen. All the pretty garments underneath which were supposed to lead my stepmother somewhere better actually only dragged her farther into my father's control, like bridles and bits. In a landscape of boys and men and lies about power, though, they were the only skirts she and I knew. A year later, when the nine of us lived in a three-bedroom apartment, my own suits and panties were tucked in the suitcase under my bed, waiting there like passwords.

There are other lies about power and identity, more subtle than the ones told by pornography. When I first learned, not long ago, that being abandoned in a house without utilities or food is called "child abuse," I smiled. When I learned that a twelve-year-old girl is a child, and a child being molested by anyone—an adult or another child—is called "sexual abuse," I grinned. Suddenly I had a strange, different kind of power over the men who had hurt me, and it lay in my scars: if I had been wronged, then I was on the side of the good, and the men were on the side of the evil. Although I might not be stronger, or richer, or better in any other way, I was morally superior to them. And the moral superiority of the victim brings her power.

Like the virtue of victimization, the promise of pornography—that a woman's body is her identity and her source of strength—wasn't entirely wrong. But the way in which both of them *were* wrong, no person could ever teach me. The desert had to do that.

In my midtwenties, I was led to the desert less by a decision of intellect than by a response to blood urgency. Going there was like picking up a baby who's face down in a puddle.

Through all those years after middle school, my mind and body had stayed as distinct from one another as the wool suits and the garter belts. My mind had helped me get a job and go through college on scholarships. But as time went on it grew more and more controlling, until it became tyrannically disdainful of my body. By the time college ended I was living almost completely in my head: the intellectual jargon of modern philosophy rang in my brain all night like an alarm, and I hardly knew if or why I was alive.

Fortunately, my body had better sense. She spoke up from under the bed, where I'd kept her locked up like a caged animal and had fed her only scraps for years. She said, "Get outside."

I went west, to the desert, to a state where I knew no one and took a job for which I had little preparation other than backpacking.

I've heard the Great Basin described by one survival student as "Nature's Worst." It's sage and basalt country: gray and brown and fairly nondescript at first. The hunting and gathering Paiutes who lived there in early times were disparagingly labeled "Diggers," because they ate roots and grubs rather than something charismatic like buffalo.

In the rain, the Great Basin ground, where it's not rock, turns to slimy mud. If you have to walk when it's wet, mud will grow on your bootsoles in bricklike platforms, your quads will cramp with the weight of them, and your ankles will roll above the bootlocks like they're broken. When the sun sucks the moisture out of the mud again, the ground will crack into miles of dusty pieces.

In some places, a six-foot-tall person can lie in the dirt and make dust angels without knocking into anything but basalt gravel and stickers, so people call the desert barren. But the desert isn't barren. It's alive and tells the body stories that are true.

When I began teaching survival, wandering for several months through the basalt-pillared canyons and the expansive plateaus of the Great Basin with some blankets, knives, cooking cans, and personal items, I underwent a transformation.

My hands twisted wet bark into cordage, carved firesticks, and dug holes for coalbeds; my fingers and palms hardened into dark, basaltlike chunks of flesh. Wind and sun made my hair spiny as the wild wheat we'd gather near old homesteads; the nomadic days chiseled a landscape of calluses and cracks into my feet. My dung shrank like a coyote's, and my breath came slow and reptilian.

I came to know a little about the creatures who passed their lives out there. Snipes would swoon above us at dawn like bats. Grouse would do the unthinkable—eat sagebrush, puke most of it back up in pellets, pass the rest through in slimy wads like black slugs—and live normal, healthy lives in the process. Golden eagles would fly over with their writhing meals—rabbits or snakes—in tow. Overnight, badgers would excavate holes big enough for a twenty-gallon drum; with their bare hands, they'd

258

put a shovel to shame, plowing through cementlike earth in the dark. And the sun ignited both ends of day with what looked like fire; morning and evening never tired of being burned that way.

My mind and body began separating less and less often, mostly because I was learning to survive out there, and doing so did not require that my mind float up in the air and watch bad things happen to my body.

In fact, the desert required just the opposite; in order to survive there, I had to be fully present. When the summer heat seemed intent on vaporizing my scalp as I walked, my senses would tell me where to locate shade. They'd show me which cranny was safe to crouch in during a rainstorm. They'd let me know which plant was wild carrot and which hemlock.

In the desert, a mind that wanders far from the body can land a person in strange territory, far from water or cover. If at any time I stopped listening to my body and to my lived experience, I might get lost. I found myself realizing that power does come from the body after all, but in a very different way.

On the first winter survival trip I led, I met a student who brought some things together for me. Dawn was fourteen years old. Her face was tinged with a solemn and unnerving coldness, like the blush on frost-nipped fruit. On that trip, she was the only other female. For some reason, I wanted her to be the first to make bowdrill fire.

On the trail, Dawn was a quiet girl, and distant. Like so many other students, she triggered in me the sense that something had been lost. I didn't know why she was there.

On day ten of the trip, we awakened to a low dawn in the mouth of a wide canyon. We'd each built a fire the night before in a rock-lined pit and then buried the coals. Eight hours later, the earth beneath me was still as warm as hands. Four teenagers and another instructor lay around me in their snowy pods, each tight in a sheet of plastic and two blankets. Three boys snored out of time with each other, one had come unhatted. His hair stuck out in a unicorn spike.

Later that day, I was working with Dawn on her bowdrill fire. I had already let the boys quit trying; they were cooking lentils a short distance away. Big sagebrush, seven feet tall, stood around us on an unlikely patch of fertile riparian soil. Twenty degrees, platy sky, preweather stillness. Serviceberries were shriveled on the bush; the wild onions, yampah, and nettles we'd gathered all year had dried to bony stalks and blown away. Loose strands of gray-brown bark ribboned the tall sage; they scraped in a brief breeze.

Dawn knelt on a thin layer of granular snow. Her left hand, blistered and ruddy from carving, cupped a bone handsocket that served as a pivot point for a sage spindle. Dawn worked wood considerately, and her spindle was just right: like a stout pencil, it was a little longer than her hand and thick as her index finger. She'd sharpened the upper end of the spindle to fit into the handsocket. The lower, blunt end was black from friction.

When the blunt end was newly carved, before it had begun to burn, it had shown the sage's concentric growth rings. The wood grain moved out from them like the linking strands in a spiderweb. I told Dawn I hadn't seen many things prettier than that pattern. She gave me a sideways, suspicious look.

The thong of a halfmoon bow girdled Dawn's spindle, and by stroking the bow back and forth with her right hand, Dawn could drill the spindle down into a plank of sage. The friction between this fireboard and the spindle would rub off clouds of smoke and charred wood fibers called punk.

The punk would drop down through a pie-shaped notch in the fireboard. Hotter and hotter punk would accumulate there, and it would eventually weld itself into a small coal. Then the firemaker would gently lift the coal into a nest of well-rubbed sagebrush bark, and her long, steady breaths would turn it into flame.

Theoretically. But Dawn still stared at her bowdrill set as if she were illiterate in fire, even though she had cut the set herself. Technically, she was fine. Perfect form. I stayed after her about it, keeping her up later than the boys almost every night, trying to figure out what was wrong. Her light hair whipped back and forth above the fireboard, her bowing arm cramped tight, and her breath came hard, but each day ended the same: no punk, no fire.

She'd say quietly, "I'll never do it."

None of the other students had made this type of fire yet either. Everyone could make sparks by striking a quartz or flint rock against their carbon steel knife blades, and they got fires at night this way, even Dawn.

But something about bowdrill spooked them. It seemed so old, like magic. There was nothing but their own bodies and the body of the sagebrush twirling together, and the result was fire.

The boys had a bowdrill-related superstition. The one with the unicorn spike, George, would shake a crusty ash cake at Dawn and say, "Dude. You gotta believe."

On day eleven, the group had hiked the usual distance of about seven miles. We'd made camp near a shallow basalt cave. It was "don't get your hair wet" weather, but Dawn and I wanted to wash up. We heated two billycans of water on a small fire, grabbed our bandannas, and retreated to the shadowy cave, where we could undress away from the boys.

White owl splats looked like paint along the head-high inner edges of the cave. Dawn and I shifted our cold barefoot weight on the basalt gravel and tried to give each other as much bathing privacy as possible, but then an echoing crack and rush snapped along the walls and we both jerked to the sound. Rock and ice fell from a ledge outside.

I saw then in the half-light that the girl had a secret. Low on her breast-bone, where no one could see, a lattice of rippling white scars ran over Dawn, like someone had thrown a net on her. Unlike the superficial heavy metal logos the boys flaunted, her grid was a private and permanent state-ment from herself to her self; white and geometric as a chain-link fence, the pattern was more certainly the sign of her own neat hand than the cramped signature she made on paper.

Later, when I talked to a supervisor on the radio, she said Dawn was cruel at home. She was cruelest to what was most vulnerable: her younger sisters and the pets. Helpless animals called forth a meanness in her, and trapped creatures flipped something inside—she became vicious.

The supervisor also told me a story about Dawn. She had been seeing a bad therapist not long ago.

He had told her this: "Listen. If you can't get along at home, you'll end up on the streets. You'll need food. You'll need shelter. You'll need warmth. And to get those things, you'll need money. You're a fourteen-year-old girl. You have no marketable skill. You have nothing."

I imagined him pausing and scanning her.

"Well," he'd continued, "you do have a nice body. You could use that."

He showed her magazines, how the girls—eleven, twelve, sixteen—had found their pimps and set up their survival strategies.

He was trying to scare her into behaving at home, but when I asked her about it Dawn said, "He didn't tell me anything I didn't already know."

On day twelve, I was leading, so I called a silent hike. I'd woken up in a funk; I wanted some time to think. We had a five-mile jaunt up and down scree slopes, through icy sage, and over frozen coyote turds. I kept turning to find the group shrinking on the near horizon. Dawn was farthest back, straggling forlornly.

I realized I was stalking the desert like a madwoman, clamping my teeth and pounding my digging stick on rhyolite blocks without noticing, every time I had to wait.

I thought of the untold stories that had caused Dawn to carve a grid on her chest and to torment helpless things. I imagined what had compelled her to shut her body in a cage of scars. I read once that two-thirds of all people jailed for abuse have been victims themselves.

There is something pathological about inhabiting victimhood, and about living off its skewed sense of power and identity. It's like being in a high basalt tunnel. It's all right to hang out there for a while, while the actual storm of abuse is occurring; the true victim doesn't have much of a choice. The high walls are protective, and "moral superiority" offers an overhang of some dignity. But moral superiority itself can become an abusive trap, and there's not much to sustain a person in that place, where the floor is a sharp cushion of dark gravel. Like anger, victimization is a place to move through. The next step is survival.

I don't know what comes after that.

Dawn wasn't moving; she was fenced into one of those partial truths that quickly become lies. The pornographic therapist told her to separate her mind and body and peddle the body part; her role as a victim told her that power lay as much in being scarred as in scarring. Both lies make battle-fields of women's bodies; they require that we keep hurting our bodies somehow, because our power and identities depend on it. But these lies are based on an incomplete assumption: that strength lies only in our having power *over* ourselves or others.

Day thirteen marked Dawn's turn to lead the hike. Overnight the temperature had dropped from 20 to 0, and the wind shot up over the mesa rims in a wall of velocity. We began walking over a major plateau at sunup, and by midday it was − 15 in the wind.

At one point we set our eyes on a big chunk of basalt three miles away which appeared periodically through the whipping, granular snow. We planned on crouching there for a minute of rest, but when we arrived, the wind crashed around the rock like icy surf. It knifed through the blankets we had wrapped around our sweaters, and when George stopped there to pee, his zipper froze open.

By dusk we had reached a system of shallow caves and overhangs in a sheltered basalt canyon. We made camp there.

Squatting on the ground, chipping away pieces of frozen earth with my digging stick to make a coalbed pit, I realized why I had been so anxious for Dawn to be the first to make bowdrill fire. I'd wanted her to have power over the boys, so she'd believe in herself. But the desert doesn't teach power over. It teaches something else.

Mastery of fire has long symbolized humankind's power over nature, and it's hard to interpret the forms of fire we usually encounter—electric stoves, internal combustion engines, or nuclear warheads—otherwise. It's true that bowdrill fire can be used to teach us power over the land and over each other. But it can also be used to teach us power through, and within.

Standing in front of a dead electric stove is nothing like kneeling beside a smokeless fireboard. Regardless of her race or social class, unless the stove girl is a master electrician who can illegally tap into power from a faraway source, she is bodily helpless before the cold metal cube. All she can do is break it apart and throw it around. The stove teaches her that her body can't bring her power, unless she uses it to take power from someone or somewhere else, at the expense of her spirit.

When she's kneeling by her fireboard, though, the cold girl is free to choose another identity. In fact, she can identify with the world through the bowdrill set. After all, she chose the tall, dead sage plant, cut the branches from it, and shaped the parts herself. In choosing and shaping her tools, she has created a sense of autonomy. If the tools don't work, there are things she can do about it, with her mind and body together: push down harder, go faster, examine the set, smooth out the parts, try again.

Fire by friction requires something more than turning a knob on a stove. It requires spirit, or at least, in Dawn's case, the belief that mind and body can go safely together in the world. It requires the faith that a woman's power does come from within her body, but not separately from her mind.

Even though a girl feels individually empowered by making friction fire, she never does it entirely alone. As anyone who has tried to make fire from sappy or sodden wood will tell, she makes flame only through her surroundings, by the grace of the fire which exists already in the sage and in the natural world at large.

In some spots in the Great Basin, basalt towers spewed as fire from the recesses of the earth just 3,000 years ago. In these spots, firemaking seems less individual than collective: it's an invocation of an ever-present, hidden power.

The attentive student comes to tell which plants—like sage, clematis, and cottonwood—are full of fire, and which are not. The fire in her own arms shifts with her physical or psychic state. In this sense, friction firemaking enacts mystery and provides a link with a different sense of identity. The woman has power within herself and through her connection with the natural world, not power over them.

This was a sense of identity I could never force Dawn to accept. She'd have to choose it herself or find a different one on her own, probably through a long chain of experiences. Her story might end up sounding nothing like mine, or the other girls' love tales, or the boys' war stories.

Dawn's flint and steel firemaking skills were good enough for safety and she had hiked well in the lead. I wouldn't keep her up bowdrilling any later than the others from now on.

After finishing my firepit, I went and sat beside Dawn under her overhang, out of the wind. She looked small, sitting back on her heels rubbing tinder. I got out the map and measured the day's route with string.

"Fourteen and a half miles, Dawn."

She quit rubbing and looked up. "What?"

"You led fourteen and a half miles without a break."

Dawn stared at me. I heard the irregular sounds of the boys breaking up wood.

After a while she said, "Either it wasn't fourteen and a half miles, or I didn't lead."

We were silent.

"You led fourteen and a half miles without a break," I said again. I cut the string and laid it over the knee of her wool army pants, across the long strands of sagebrush bark tinder, which spread around her like a dress. The Paiute Indians, "Diggers," used to weave their clothes, boots, and blankets from such bark—the same bark they blew into flame.

"You must be tired," I said. "You can skip bowdrill tonight."

Dawn's camp stayed quiet until after dark. I was about to go checking on her when the sound of grinding firesticks echoed out from under her ledge. I sat for a while wondering whether or not she'd want company for this attempt.

After a few minutes the good smell of sage smoke traveled out toward my camp. I was on my feet heading toward Dawn's spot when I heard the bowdrill stop and saw a glowing pile of punk moving slowly through the air on her knifeblade.

The cherry coal disappeared into the dark tinder. She lifted the bundle to blow. The tinder nest began to glow orange, and its dim light revealed Dawn's uptilted face as she sent her breath through the fibers.

I walked up just as the bundle took flame. The fire lit the ceiling of her overhang for the first time, and she still held the bundle aloft. But she wasn't watching the fire; she was looking up. Chiseled into the rock overhead was a petroglyph, left by the Paiutes or the Shoshone: a series of concentric half-circles like a sunset, or like half the pattern of a pebble thrown in water. Dawn didn't smile, but I saw the reflection of fire in her eyes.

Al Young &
Monica Wesolowska

Squaw Valley Community of Writers

t was Mira's tough yet lovably supple voice that caught my ear and imagination while I was reading this chapter, the proposed opening from Monica Wesolowska's novel-in-progress. The voice is pitched in a key that made me forget at once the droning flatness of those all too familiar suburban voices that pop up relentlessly in contemporary workshop stories. This voice, whose natural time signature is the present tense, is routinely as listless in its utterances about deep-seated desires as it seems when describing a cocktail party, a backyard barbecue, the raking and bagging of Connecticut leaves in autumn, or Marin County lawn trimmings year-round. "Hefty Bag stories" are how Gwyneth Cravens characterized these present-tense monologues.

The true source of heft in Monica Wesolowska's writing is life itself and a sensitivity to the way we live and die on Earth at the close of a darkening millennium. Her characters are roundly grounded in the global here and now, in the Neo-Nazi Nineties.—**Al Young**

Al Young has published eighteen books, including *Heaven: Collected Poems 1958–1990, Drowning in the Sea of Love: Musical Memoirs*, and *African American Literature*. He has received NEA and Guggenheim fellowships, among other honors and awards.

Monica Wesolowska lives in Berkeley, California, and has published poems in the *Berkeley Poetry Review* and elsewhere. This excerpt from her novel-in-progress, "Fort Noah," is her first published work of fiction.

Distances

■ ■ ■ ■ ■ ■ ■ ■ ■

To get to Tokyo from Istanbul,
it's fun to travel when the weather's cool.
To reach Madrid by way of Edinburgh,
it might be best to leave from Glockamorra.

The Shangri-La you dream about comes close
to meeting mute desire—an Ivory Coast,
the Gold Coast of the past, fountains of youth.
All colonies project like light from booths
in darkened rooms of mind; a picture forms
and moves and moves again and spills and warms
spaces between the heartbeat and wet breath.

The distance anywhere—from birth to death,
from sit to stand, from heat to snow—
invents itself, unravels as you go.

Airborne

■ ■ ■ ■ ■ ■ ■ ■

Your beauty, soft Seattle, wasn't subtle;
it turned on light, and seemed at times so cracked,
Ranier could hold her head above your rubble
of cloud and sky alike; erased, snowpacked.

To places where the world once disappeared
we fly. Wild water helps; big clearings don't.
The turns your thighs and belly took are smeared
and jammed with journeys you still say you want
to end. But that's the catch: You like it wet.

You like life darkened, muted; islands, space
and breathing room. From up here all I get
is what I see: You've lost your quiet race
to come in last. Your subtleties are growing.
But night light slows, you know. So how's it going?

A Lizard Considers the Season

Upward floating
without
sky 1, sky 2, sky 3,
the open-domed light
of blue & low overhead,
this stillness the color
of late September.

Sadness plays
no place in
such spacious unraveling
of skin dried out as breeze,
as heat.
Hot, surf faces south.

Easy, rock, now,
easy, tree.
Touch me, smooth me,
wrinkle me here,
rough me up there.
Reach me where no blue blaze has
sunned or burned before.

Do I blacken
like old silver, neglected?
Do I shine in my climb the way joy resides
not around the corner but just beneath
the surface of these angles inched in &
out of dartable dots
& morsels of light
that feed the lion of light?

Alone in my aloneness,
I ooze
blue night.

Cool light, fathom me, please,
and fatten the paths that lead away
from crows
on frosty eaves

A Toast to Charles Bukowski

■■■■■■■■■■■■■■■■■■■■■■■■

Clipboard elegance ain't got nothing on you
back fresh from bar room fronts & fights &
the fakery of youth more invented than avoided.
In dauntless nights Longfellow's Evangeline could've even cut,
you would've been Gabriel, her unkeepable old man

No wasteland-blasting trumpeter, either,
but a true accordionist. Kicked out of Acadia,
you'd be just the angry immigrant (a German-
born Pole) to squeeze or be squeezed.
Fuck you, fuck you, fuck you, King George!

We're talking literature here, Prince Charles:
talking walking to New Orleans in your winter underwear.
Troilus & Cressida, Orpheus & Eurydice, Ulysses & Calypso.
Bukowski & Linda? Nah, Bukowski & Nemesis
(Si Semen might be the early to middle bop take).
How's that for running what was underground back into the ground?

But, really, Buk, I got news for you: All those French,
those Dutch, those German, those break-away Muscovite & Tokyo kids
who hit DeLongpre Avenue to re-be Bukowski, to re-play your L.A.,
    alcohol & all,
they now re-claim those colorful alley & gutteresque
frontiers you & Tom Waits so handsomely zapped.

Mira

■ ■ ■ ■ ■ ■

Seen from a hammock, the day was all stripes, blue and white, sky, beach, sea, like the flag of some pacific country, and Mira thought she could lie there forever. The others had peeled down to their swimsuits within seconds of finding this place and run off toward the sea as though each second here were worth one previous hour of hot, miserable transit, and they could balance out the day within ten seconds. Mira didn't think life worked that way.

Sam's gesticulations caught her eye. He was signaling to her. He had stopped with the others around the stench, some dead thing downwind. She sat up in the hammock just as Sam's "come here" arms were turning into "don't bother" and they were all turning for the sea again. She caught up her breath and let it go. "Sighing," Sam called it. She tilted out of the hammock. It was just that it had been many years since she was last at a beach, five, maybe ten years, it was hard to remember how long, only that she had been a child then, and it was eerie to think how much had changed.

She began from the top, undoing each button down the front of her long floral dress. Perhaps it was just this particular beach that was getting to her. It was long, thirty kilometers according to the guidebook, and it seemed to go on forever. She looked up from her buttons—she was belly-height now—and could see the beach way on the other side of the bay, a pale scratch trailing off into blue. It was like the scratch her brother had accused her of making on his car, the scratch that eventually rusted. She was rougher with her buttons now and gaining on her knees.

Why had Sam chosen this beach over all the rest in Mexico? It was like some vast and eerie moon resort. All of the *palapas*, or whatever they called these huts, even this one, the recommendation from the guidebook, were deserted, row after row of listless hammocks and brightly colored empty tables. The owner of this one had appeared only long enough to introduce herself as Ofelia. Mira reached the last of the buttons. The two halves of her dress fell open. She surveyed the mounds of bags and clothing strewn in a circle out from where she stood. Perhaps Ofelia had been distressed at their proprietary sloppiness.

Although she felt an urge to straighten things out, Mira limited herself to taking off her dress and folding it across the back of a chair, slipping out of her shoes and placing them side by side under the chair. At least there was no one around watching her adjust to life in a swimsuit. The curves of her body, which had fit the floral dress so well, now seemed to mock the little bits of cloth that cut her body into segments. Along the elastic edge of each segment, her flesh bulged.

This was Joy's idea: Joy had insisted that bikinis were absolutely necessary for Mexico and she had dragged Mira shopping. She had said a department store sale was an "experience" Mira could not miss—although, for herself, she insisted, she only ever shopped at thrift stores. Remembering that "experience" still made Mira squirm. There had been tons of people and she and Joy had been caught up in the frenzy of trying on more than they could afford (including the floral dress), squeezed together into a single dressing room under fluorescent lights for what seemed like hours, and it had been too much all at once: she had started to cry. She was still mad at herself for letting Joy think it was only flattery she had wanted. "It's so you!" Joy had said about the leopard-spotted bikini: Mira had stopped crying. It was surprise, really, that stopped her. She had never thought of herself before as characterized by leopard spots. But everyone seemed to think so, even Sam, whose first gift to her was the leopard-spotted chiffon scarf she had tied around her head. She pulled a tail out from under her hair. It really was a wonderful scarf. She wished she was as much of a sensualist as she once had been, in her teens, when Sensualism had been her religion, when a pair of Italian leather boots promised to make her happy for life.

On a whim, she pulled the scarf across her face. The chiffon felt good against her skin but even better was how it muted the hard blue and white edges of the day. With the scarf still over her face, she walked to the edge of the *palapa*. She felt safe that way. Perhaps this was what it felt like to be an odalisque. The beach and sea bled into each other, brownish yellow from the scarf. She could understand rationally that this beach her friends had brought her to was beautiful, that it was worth the many bus rides; she could understand it well enough to murmur politely, "So beautiful," and "I am so glad we come here," but she didn't *feel* its beauty. It was as if there were something like this scarf between her senses and her feelings that kept her from feeling anything, good or bad, too keenly.

When the scarf was full of the stale smell of breath, she let it drop. Above the sea, light glanced off the backs of large gliding birds. Birds always seemed so wonderfully free, like kites cut loose, but it hurt to watch them against the late afternoon sun. She wished the others had waited for her. She could understand how they wanted to wash the long day from them as soon as possible, but it made her all the more self-conscious about her own slow seriousness.

That large pale blob rising and falling with each wave must be Joy and Fabian. She could imagine how they were clinging to each other, their long legs tangling like seaweed beneath the water. It wasn't their affection that she minded. She had a lover here, too. In fact, she realized he was waving at her from the water now. How long had he been watching her? She waved back. Sam. Her husband.

She had to keep reminding herself that it was just a legality, that it should not affect the natural progression of their friendship, but it was hard to remember the reasoning behind her marriage when people still treated her as though she were a refugee. People like that woman in pink on the last stretch of road to the beach. The woman was trying to be polite, the way Americans did, catching herself up each time she said Yugoslavia, changing it to the "former Yugoslavia," as though Mira needed to be reminded of the war in her country.

"And what kind of a name is Mira?" the woman had asked, wanting, obviously, for Mira to do the impossible, to put herself on one side or another. She had felt that rebellious side of herself welling up, the side that would say, "I'm Yugoslav, Yugoslav, Y-u-g-o-s-l-a-v. Do you understand?" but no one ever did. Questions about one's nationality were expected to be answered simply, factually, not idealistically. But what was wrong with claiming an ideal for one's nationality? Wouldn't the world be a much better place if we all carried passports to Utopia?

She had wanted to lecture that pathetic pink woman but instead she found the manners of her mother reining her in as though her mother were actually there, answering for her. "It's a . . . pretty name, yes, a pretty name," she had said, sounding almost stupid until she thought to add, "In my country, we choose names that we like. That's all," which shut the woman up. It wasn't that she liked to be cruel and push people from her. It was just that sometimes the distance seemed too great to cross.

Sam was still standing in the surf, facing her way, looking impatient, his arms akimbo. She should at least go join him but instead she pulled the scarf back across her face to look at him. For some reason, this made her

274

laugh. The tickle of it? The game? She wished there were some kind of costume she could wear for a while, a fitting-in costume, the magical equivalent of an all-purpose black dress, so that she wasn't always having to explain who and what she was. It occurred to her suddenly that harem women didn't wear scarves *over* their eyes, as she was doing, but around.

You see! This just proved how stupid it was, the whole war. People like her, who knew as little about Islam as their neighbors, being labeled Turks and shot at. But she supposed it wasn't surprising if you'd ever watched anger erupt before, your own, a stranger's. In fact, she'd experienced something like it on her arrival in New York, when someone had tried to take her wallet. She could not believe how quickly she went from being a sight-seer to being a madwoman, chasing a stranger across a busy street screaming, "Stop, thief," like in the movies. She still could not believe how she tore his coat into little pieces when she caught up—he was old and frail, as was his coat, both all wrinkles—and it broke her heart in retrospect but, at the time, it was all momentum. He was calling her crazy, stomping his feet, and moaning about his tattered coat; she was saying over and over, "My wallet," having lost the rest of her English across the street. There had been that one moment of fear, when she stopped and noticed the multi-racial circle pressing around them and the thought popped into her head, "This is America. This is how race riots start," and then someone managed to persuade the thief to empty his pockets and there was her wallet in her hand and the thief and the crowd were gone. The strange thing was how bad she felt for having torn the coat of an old, poor man. So what had made her chase him down? And what if he had threatened her with something worse than losing her wallet? Was that not how wars began?

But she wasn't going to think about this now. She would turn all the adrenaline of that story into a rush for the sea. She was here, after all, to enjoy her "honeymoon." She unknotted the scarf under her hair slowly and pulled it from her, concentrating on how it slid across her shoulders like a hand. Like Sam's hand. If she just paid enough attention, perhaps things would start to feel good again. She carefully draped her scarf over the folded dress on the back of the chair.

She couldn't decide if they clashed, the flowers and the spots, or went together in a daring way. Anyway, she liked them both and didn't have much else to choose from. She pulled the elastic of her swimsuit down over her buttocks and made the triangles of the bikini top—with their inserts of fake leopard fur—as broad as possible across her breasts before she stepped over the line between shade and sun on the sand.

She broke into a run immediately. Perhaps it was the heat on their feet that had made the others run so frantically. In fact, in the very act of running, she felt for a moment the same childlike glee she thought she had seen in the others, but it didn't last long. Her breasts were bouncing like crazy. She stopped to check the knot in back. Still tied. Since she couldn't stop for long before the soles of her feet demanded she go on, she had to be content with putting a hand across the top of both breasts to minimize the bouncing. What had she been thinking in that dressing room? What was the word Joy had used—voluptuous—and Mira had let herself be convinced by it. Joy did not understand big breasts at all, clearly. The string of the bikini was sawing at Mira's neck. It was as if her breasts were mocking her once they discovered the flimsiness of the cloth meant to hold them.

She was so involved with her breasts that she didn't hear the sound of wings until the last second. A cloud of vultures obscured her view of the ocean and then was gone. She swerved just in time. Belly up on the sand lay a turtle, a well-like hole the size of a vulture's head eaten out of its middle. So this was what the others had stopped to look at. She bet Sam had been calling her to bring his camera. Typical. Looking into the slime of the tattered belly, she had a feeling of revulsion for Sam, the way she'd felt at the movies last week, right at the climax when her throat was constricting against the swell of tears, and Sam had leaned over to say, "Wow. Did you see that camera angle?"

The heat on her soles forced her on until she reached damp sand. She stopped right where the waves seemed to be contradicting each other so that none in all their shallow interlacing could push a frothy edge to her toes. She watched, fascinated, knowing that this feeling of being able to predict the movement of the waves was not the same as controlling them and still she was surprised when one pushed past the rest. Suddenly she was standing in the ocean. The wave rushed almost to the turtle and then it paused. She was ankle deep in warm, clear water. Along the edge of the wave, the froth rolled lazily as though it were the fur trim on a giant regal cape that was being settled on the sand, and then the pause was over, the water was rushing back, still for no apparent reason, obeying weaker waves eager for their turn. The water clouded in the rush, full of air and running sand, and she had to curl her toes against it. The current felt so strong. She had to look away to keep her balance, to keep her heart from rushing, too, to keep fear from pricking at her insides like grains of sand.

She focused on the others. Fabian had Joy on his shoulders and it looked as though Sam were trying to pull her off. Her screams of delight carried the way a teenage girl's do, lightly and too far, working like fine-grain sandpaper on the skin, unexpectedly rubbing raw that place where we are all still insecurely young. Sam let go of her hand. Her scream was cut off with a splash. Sam turned, saw Mira, and started toward her.

Mira watched the spot where Joy had gone down. It made her nervous, watching people disappear. She had to watch until she knew that Joy was safe. There was a flash as Joy emerged. Even without her glasses, Mira imagined she was seeing Joy's smile, which was huge, like the ones in commercials for toothpaste. Sam's hand on her shoulder, although she had been aware of him running from the ocean in a giant loop behind her, startled her.

"A little jumpy?" he teased. "You coming in? We can chicken fight," he made a gesture of putting her on his shoulders, "with the love-birds." He grabbed her wrist and pulled. "We'll win."

She twisted her hand and jerked her wrist from his fingers. She didn't feel like fighting with chickens, whatever that was.

"Slowly," she said. She was glad his grasp was small enough to break that way. The person in her that was always turning away, turned away. Sam was looking at her, first at one eye, then the other, as though they might hold different things. She looked back at him. He probably thought he was looking into her but she knew it was her back he was seeing, her back as the person in her walked away. She broke the gaze. She felt guilty letting him look earnestly into her as she walked away.

She remembered now, understood the nausea. That hole in the turtle's belly reminded her of the hole in the man's head, the man she had dragged dead into her lobby, early on, in one of the first shellings. She hadn't known the man was dead. And Sam had made her wait, had made her *wait*, with her hands all bloody, so he could take a picture of them.

"Do you remember . . ." she began.

"Do you mind if . . ." he had also begun. He stopped talking but finished his sentence with a gesture of his head toward the ocean.

"Go ahead," she said, harshly, flatly, indifferently, depending on how he took it. He asked the way Fabian would ask Joy, all solicitude, but he didn't really pay attention to her answer. He couldn't. He no longer seemed to be the person he had been in Sarajevo. He was like any other American now, sheltered, hoping always for a pleasant answer, not wanting to remember. She wanted him to go away, go away, go away but, in fact, it was she who was going away as she had so many times in the past few years.

There was a duet of cello and flute at the base of it, something she had heard in concert right before the siege began, which had turned on in her head when she saw her first blood. She could hear people screaming, running, and knew she had to help, but she did it all as though in a movie, the music expanding in her so that she seemed to float above the mundane misery of other people. This continued happening, at every crisis, but more fragmented as time passed, and then voices started mingling with it more and more until, after the shelling in the hospital, there was a crowd in her head, like at a party where some people were having fun and others were disagreeing, sharp and low voices against a happy hum, and she couldn't take it, being filled with other people. The fear that pushed her out of Sarajevo was a fear of no longer being afraid, of walking into death because she did not see or hear or feel where she was anymore.

She jumped as he gave her a peck on the cheek. She had managed to imagine him away but was brought back to him by the kiss. He was covered in a blond fuzz that had just started drying and springing up and catching the light so that he glowed from head to foot. He was a small man, smaller than she was, but the hair made him seem bigger. She loved it, liked to twine her fingers in it.

He was hopping the wavelets now, swaying his hips like a girl practicing at being a woman. He turned, flirtatiously, making sure she was watching before he ran toward an oncoming wave, knifed perfectly into its translucence, and reappeared on the other side, swimming strongly, smoothly, in the full force of her lust, away from her, with such strokes it seemed there was a shore opposite that he meant to reach.

It was a relief at least to feel lust, to have that one thing be certain. Her body had been so heavy lately, and sex was the one truly good thing about still being alive. Sex meant lying down, having her limbs manipulated by someone else, having her fat kneaded and loved, being invigorated enough eventually to reach out her own hand, touch flesh that was open, warm, and soft, a man's flesh, a man who was not aiming missiles at her from a distance, a man who was as vulnerable to her as she was to him, a man whom she could turn beneath her and mount. She was walking slowly down the wet slope of the shore.

She hated feeling like a burden to them all. She hated how her existence made people feel guilty. She did not want to be a symbol. And yet that was how Sam had persuaded her to leave. He had persuaded her that she would be more useful outside of Sarajevo, using her skills as a journalist, than she would within, using her skills as a provider for her family. Their joint project at the hospital, interviewing rape camp survivors, had seemed so critical at the time as if just telling those stories would make a difference, but now she was horrified by the voyeurism of it, no matter how Sam theorized with his endearing arrogance about having achieved emotional collusion with his subjects. But could she really say that what she was doing was any better? At least he had developed his photographs, while she had done nothing with the stories. They were all still in her, inert. And her only explanation was that, in leaving, *she* had become Sarajevo under siege, powerless to escape her body, its ache, too overwhelmed with how she looked in a bikini to think of larger issues. A wave hit her at knee height. It jolted her and she backed away to higher ground.

How could he leave her standing like this on the shore? How could he bring her to this place? Cut off from the news, she was nothing. She knew nothing. Her family might be dying right now and she was here, somewhere, on a beach in Mexico. She could feel the panic rolling in her stomach, making its naked expanse all the more vulnerable. How could he have thought standing naked like this in the middle of nowhere would make her feel good?

She hated feeling like this, like a coward. She had never had to think of herself as a coward before. Even under siege, she had been brave. Doing normal things like wearing a skirt and heels and buying a copy of the paper had been acts of bravery, but here she was *expected* to do normal things and it was here that she was terrified. It was as if the war had skewed her emotions. She cried inappropriately. She was tough and indifferent about the wrong things. She would laugh and laugh for no good reason, just because it felt good, just because it was so close to crying, this rocking in her belly, and it felt good to be crying, loudly, publicly, under the cloak of laughter. Did Sam understand? Did he understand this as the result of war or did he think it was just her femaleness? Her female hysteria? It was building, the lump in her throat, the sting in her eyes. What she needed was a cigarette or the tequila they had been promising all day.

She exhaled suddenly. Sam was right about her sighs. They came out like a movie star's. But what did he know? Everything for him was fake, was Hollywood. On the plane from San Francisco he had been reading in the paper about a rescue operation for one soldier, for *one soldier*.

"Why?" she had asked. "What makes him so important?"

"More political value," Sam had said.

But why? Because it was a good story? Was not politics really about people getting along? How could the politicians ignore the effect of this war on everyone, on their own people? Like pollution, a war could not be contained. It was passing, as the radioactive cloud from Chernobyl once had passed, silently overhead, a cloud of hatred that would affect the world for generations. Even here she could feel it, the hatred that had rained down into the oceans, that had been ground into a communal grief and deposited as grains of sand upon the very beach where she was walking.

But why could she not write these things down? Why could she only think them, in the wrong places? An airplane passing overhead caught her eye. She could not stand all day at the edge of the water like this. Passing birds laughed at her, "Ha, ha." There was nowhere else to go, no country to return to: it had been divided up. To return, she would have to divide herself. She would be nothing there. And all that was required of her here was to swim in a tropical ocean. How could she be so stupid, such a baby?

She started walking toward Sam into the ocean, dragging her feet. The water ruffled around her ankles like the fancy edges of girls' Sunday socks. She found herself chanting in her head *stupid, baby, stupid, baby.* That was no good. She struggled to change it. It turned into *nothing, you are nothing, nothing.* A wave came suddenly and now the socks were up to her knees. She stared at the pale lower halves of her legs. Again, the strength of the ocean had startled her but this time she was *angry*, angry at her cowardice, angry at the carefree strength of others, angry at the part of her that was Serbian, that was Croatian, that was Muslim, angry at the world that made such divisions within her. She wanted to be out there, riding a gentle swell like Fabian and Joy. She wanted to wrap her legs around Sam's.

Fuck me, she chanted. Sam loved how she said the word "fuck." It made him laugh but it turned him on too. *Fuck me, fuck me,* she mouthed as she kept on walking deeper, as though the ocean were a man she wanted to seduce. *Fuck me.* The water was up to her thighs now like stockings that you wear with garters. In a moment it would be too late to turn back. She twisted to look back up the beach. The sand was white as icing topped with green palms. It was so exotic, just like a commercial, and here they were, the women in their bikinis. She should not ruin it, not be a "spoilsport," as they said in English.

She turned back toward Sam. She should have worn lipstick: it would have added to this moment. Behind him, a wave was building. She did not fear death, no, she feared helplessness, the sense that she had left Sarajevo only in body, that she was split between two places so that she could do nothing in either place, only watch, bear silent, painful witness, watch, as though gagged and bound, from a distance as each attack happened, as they happened now, at this very moment, people dying, being tortured, raped, now, and now, and now, no, she wouldn't think this way, not here, not now because Sam was riding the wave toward her, smiling as he approached, his arms out in front of him. He could be so sweet: he indulged her, invented silly things to do, like the five minutes a day of "positive energy" they sent to the people back home, and in those moments she thought she loved him. For him she would have fun. The wave had passed him and was cresting before her. Fear constricted her chest like a corset but she had tackled fear before. She jumped with momentary glee into the froth, expecting to ride this wave the way the others had, but the heavy water grabbed her by the feet so fiercely she had to wonder who would come and search for her as the ocean pulled her under.

Acknowledgments

Without the cooperation of fellow directors of the member programs of Writers' Conferences & Festivals, this book would be impossible. I also thank Kurt Brown and Kelleen Zubick for all their efforts and Tim Westmoreland for his editorial assistance.

Some of the work in this book has appeared previously, as follows:

Kelly Cherry: "The Almost-Baby"/*Isthmus*, "Alzheimer's"/*Columbia: A Magazine of Poetry & Prose*, "How We Are Taken"/*Hellas*, "My Mother's Stroke"/*Ms.*

Stephen Dunn: "At the School for the Deaf"/*New England Review*, "Empathy"/*Coastal Forest Review*, "Power"/*Iowa Review*, "Road Stop"/*Southern Review*, "The Sensualist's Fast"/*Painted Bride Quarterly*.

Linda Gregg: "The Center of Intent"/*5 Fingers Review*, "Hephaestus Alone"/*TriQuarterly*, "On the Other Side of Love"/*5 Fingers Review*.

Pam Houston: "Eight Days on the Brooks Range with April and the Boys"/*Vogue*.

Gray Jacobik: "Sandwoman"/*Southern Poetry Review*, "Sappho's Voice"/*Prairie Schooner*, "Skirts"/*Georgia Review*.

Philip Levine: "Good Monday"/*Southern Indiana Review*, "Holy Son and Mother of the Projects"/*Indiana Review*, "The Letters"/*Boulevard*, "My Given Name"/*Field*, "The Seven Doors"/*TriQuarterly*.

Tom Paine: "Will You Say Something, Monsieur Eliot?"/*New Yorker*.

Michael Pettit: "A Dog's in Heat"/*Gettysburg Review*, "Lost Gloves"/*Gettysburg Review*.

Francine Prose: "A Coincidence at the Vet's"/*Paris Review*, copyright © 1995 by Francine Prose.

Leslie Ryan: "The Other Side of Fire"/*Northern Lights*.

Bob Shacochis: "Going Back"/*Outside*.

Charles H. Webb: "Buyer's Remorse"/*Quarterly West*, "The Dead Run"/*Laurel Review*, "Flying Fish in the Jet Stream"/*Chester H. Jones Anthol-*

ogy, "Four-Wheeling"/*Puerto del Sol*, "Health"/*Passages North*, "Marilyn's Machine"/*Paris Review*.

Joan Wickersham: "The Off-Season"/*Ploughshares*.

Terry Tempest Williams: "The Erotics of Place"/*Yellow Silk*.

Writers' Conferences & Festivals Member Programs

Amherst Writers & Artists
Antioch Writers' Workshop
Art of the Wild Conference
Arts and Humanities Council of Tulsa
Asheville Poetry Festival
Aspen Writers' Conference
Bay Area Writers' Workshop
Bennington Writing Workshops
Blooming Grove Writers' Conference
Bread Loaf Writers' Conference
Cape Cod Writers' Center
Catskill Poetry Workshop
Charleston Writers' Conference
Clarion Writers' Workshop
Columbus Writers' Conference
Cuesta College Writers' Conference
Cumberland Valley Writers' Conference
Dorothy Canfield Fisher Writers' Conference
Environmental Writing Institute
Fine Arts Work Center in Provincetown
Fishtrap Writers Gathering
Florida Suncoast Writers' Conference
Frost Place Festival of Poetry
Haystack Program in the Arts & Sciences/Summer Session
Hellgate Writers, Inc.
Hofstra University Writers' Conference
How to Get and Stay Published Writers' Conference
Hurston/Wright Foundation
IMAGINATION Writers' Workshop and Conference
Indiana Writers' Conference
Interactive Fiction Ink
Iowa Summer Writing Festival
Key West Literary Seminar, Inc.
Ladan Reserve, Inc.
Latin America Writers' Workshop

Legal Workshop for Writers
Midwest Writers' Workshop
Mount Holyoke Writers' Conference
Napa Valley Writers' Conference
New England Writers' Conference
Oklahoma Arts Institute
Open Road Writing Workshops
Oregon's Rock Eagle Writing Festival
Palm Springs Writers' Conference
Paris Writers' Workshop
Ploughshares International Fiction Writing Seminar
Poets & Writers Information Center
Pomotawh Naantam Ranch
Port Townsend Writers' Conference
Rhode Island Poetry Workshop
Rogue Valley Writers' Conference
Santa Fe Writers' Conference
Santa Monica College Writers' Conference
Sewanee Writers' Conference
Slip of the Tongue Central Coast Writing Conference
Snake River Institute
Split Rock Arts Program
Squaw Valley Community of Writers
Stonecoast Writers' Conference
Sunken Garden Writers' Conference
Taste of Chicago Writing Workshop
Truckee Meadows Community College Writers' Conference
University of North Alabama Writers' Conference
Vermont Studio Center
Victoria School of Writing
Wesleyan University Writers' Conference
White River Writers' Workshop
Wildacres Writers' Workshop
William Joiner Center for the Study of War and Social Consequences
Writers & Readers Rendezvous
Writers at Work
Writers for Racing Project
Writing Center
Yellow Bay Writers' Workshop